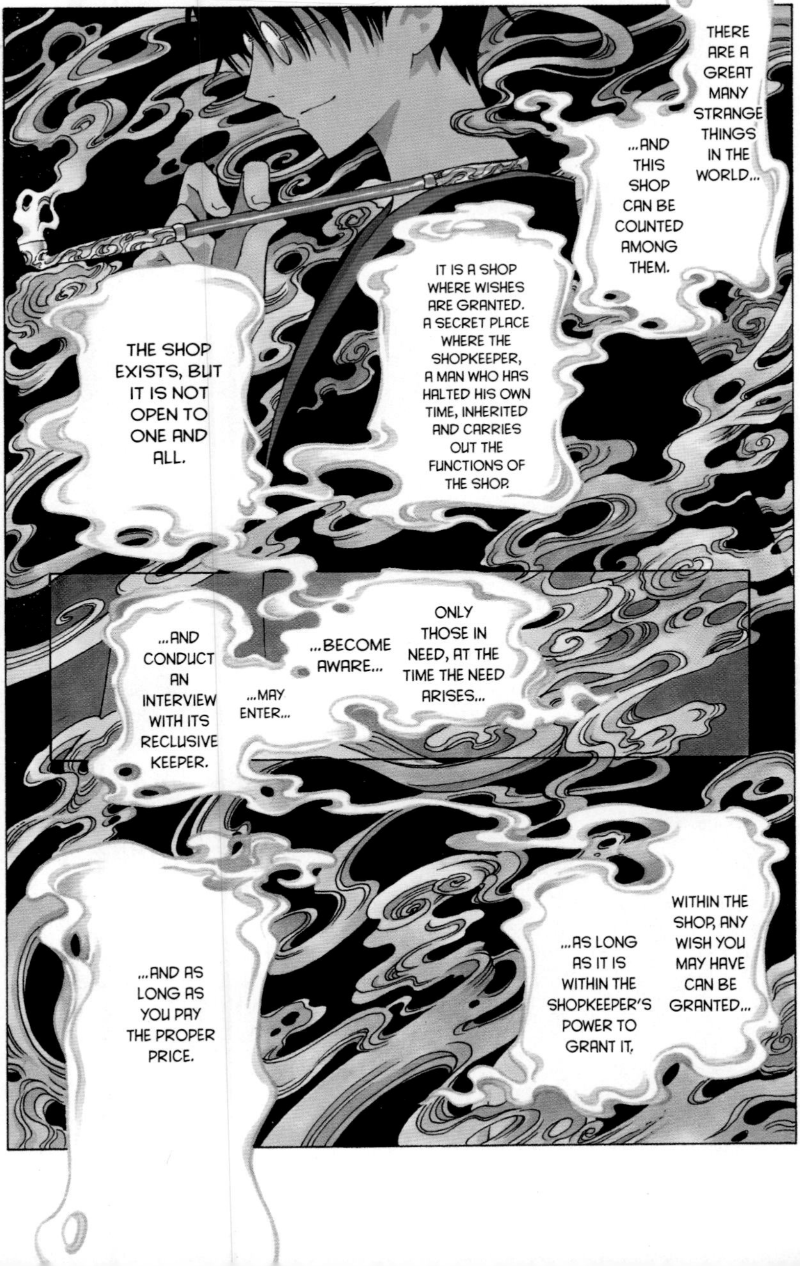
THERE ARE A GREAT MANY STRANGE THINGS IN THE WORLD...
...AND THIS SHOP CAN BE COUNTED AMONG THEM.
IT IS A SHOP WHERE WISHES ARE GRANTED. A SECRET PLACE WHERE THE SHOPKEEPER, A MAN WHO HAS HALTED HIS OWN TIME, INHERITED AND CARRIES OUT THE FUNCTIONS OF THE SHOP.
THE SHOP EXISTS, BUT IT IS NOT OPEN TO ONE AND ALL.
ONLY THOSE IN NEED, AT THE TIME THE NEED ARISES...
...BECOME AWARE...
...MAY ENTER...
...AND CONDUCT AN INTERVIEW WITH ITS RECLUSIVE KEEPER.
WITHIN THE SHOP, ANY WISH YOU MAY HAVE CAN BE GRANTED...
...AS LONG AS IT IS WITHIN THE SHOPKEEPER'S POWER TO GRANT IT,
...AND AS LONG AS YOU PAY THE PROPER PRICE.

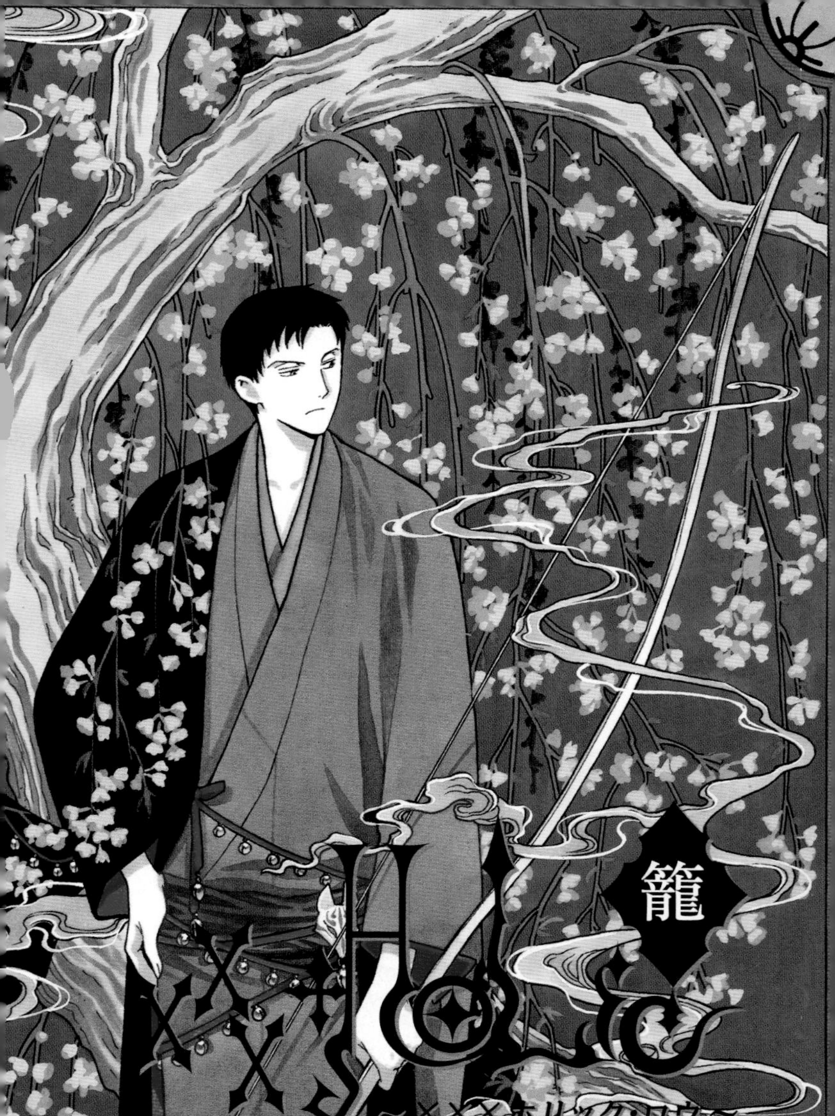
籠
xxxHOLiC
～×××ホリック・ロウ～

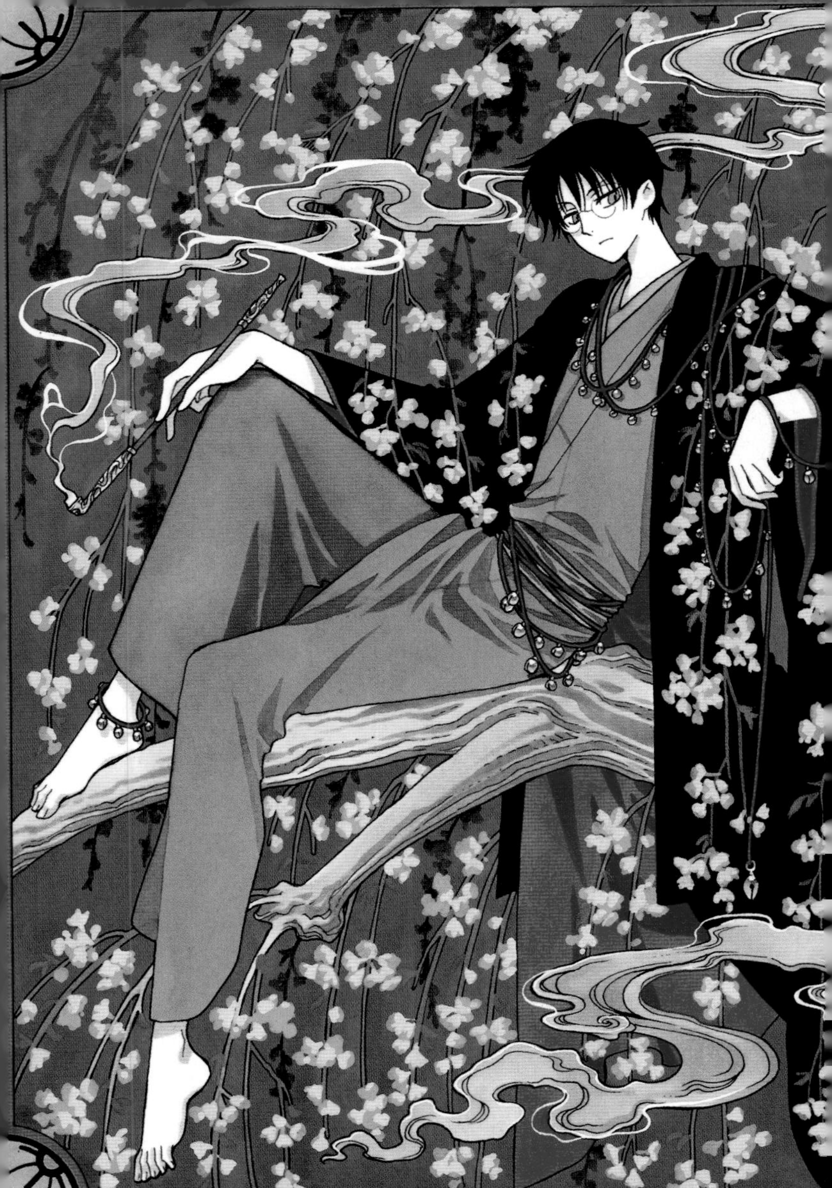

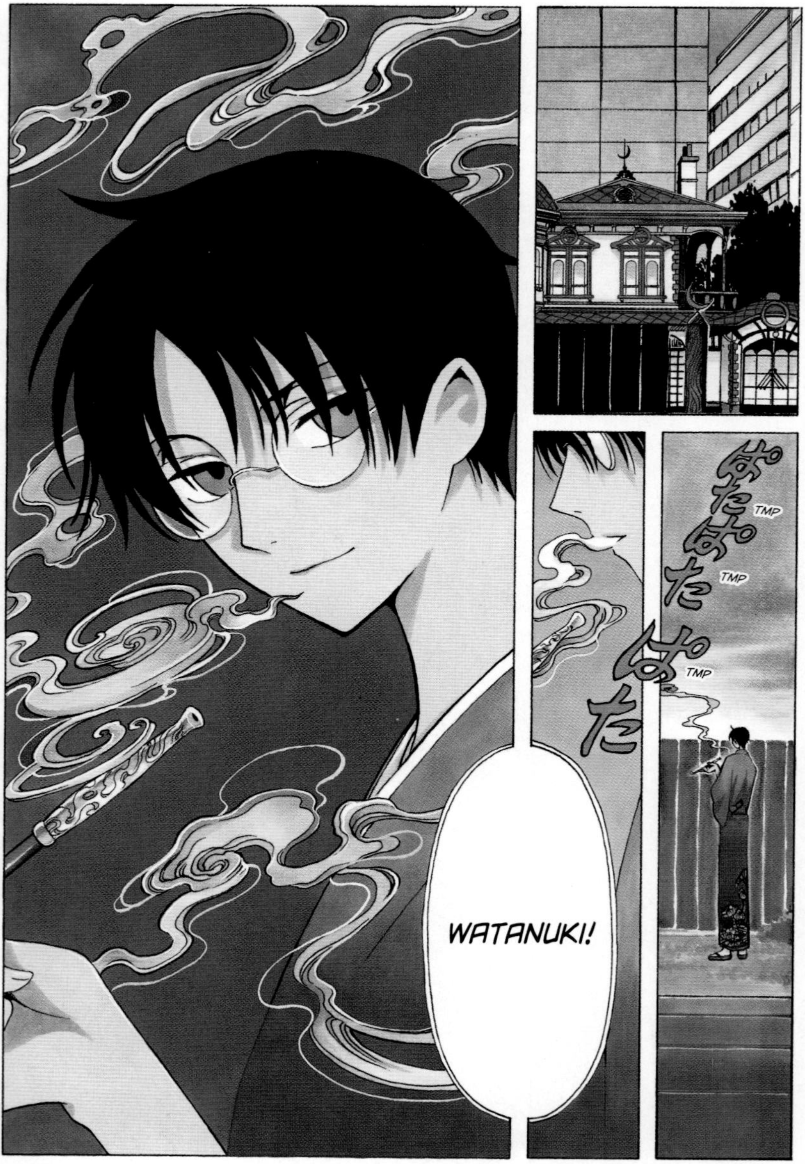
ぱたぱたぱた
TMP
TMP
TMP
WATANUKI!

18

CLAMP

TRANSLATED AND ADAPTED BY
William Flanagan

LETTERED BY
North Market Street Graphics

BALLANTINE BOOKS · NEW YORK

xxxHOLiC, volume 18 is a work of fiction. Names, characters, places, and incidents are the products of the author's imagination or are used fictitiously. Any resemblance to actual events, locales, or persons, living or dead, is entirely coincidental.

A Del Rey Manga/Kodansha Trade Paperback Original

Published in the United States by Del Rey, an imprint of The Random House Publishing Group, a division of Random House, Inc., New York.

DEL REY is a registered trademark and the Del Rey colophon is a trademark of Random House, Inc.

Publication rights arranged through Kodansha Ltd.

First published in Japan in 2010 by Kodansha Ltd., Tokyo

ISBN 978-0-345-53072-1

Printed in the United States of America

www.delreymanga.com

9 8 7 6 5 4 3 2 1

Translator and Adapter—William Flanagan
Lettering—North Market Street Graphics

xxxHOLiC crosses over with *Tsubasa*. Although it isn't necessary to read *Tsubasa* to understand the events in *xxxHOLiC*, you'll get to see the same events from different perspectives if you read both series!

Contents

Honorifics Explained

Throughout the Del Rey Manga books, you will find Japanese honorifics left intact in the translations. For those not familiar with how the Japanese use honorifics and, more important, how they differ from American honorifics, we present this brief overview.

Politeness has always been a critical facet of Japanese culture. Ever since the feudal era, when Japan was a highly stratified society, use of honorifics—which can be defined as polite speech that indicates relationship or status—has played an essential role in the Japanese language. When you address someone in Japanese, an honorific usually takes the form of a suffix attached to one's name (example: "Asuna-san"), is used as a title at the end of one's name, or appears in place of the name itself (example: "Negi-sensei," or simply "Sensei!").

Honorifics can be expressions of respect or endearment. In the context of manga and anime, honorifics give insight into the nature of the relationship between characters. Many English translations leave out these important honorifics and therefore distort the feel of the original Japanese. Because Japanese honorifics contain nuances that English honorifics lack, it is our policy at Del Rey not to translate them. Here, instead, is a guide to some of the honorifics you may encounter in Del Rey Manga.

-san: This is the most common honorific and is equivalent to Mr., Miss, Ms., or Mrs. It is the all-purpose honorific and can be used in any situation where politeness is required.

-sama: This is one level higher than "-san" and is used to confer great respect.

-dono: This comes from the word "tono," which means "lord." It is an even higher level than "-sama" and confers utmost respect.

-kun: This suffix is used at the end of boys' names to express familiarity or endearment. It is also sometimes used by men among friends or when addressing someone younger or of a lower station.

-chan: This is used to express endearment, mostly toward girls. It is also used for little boys, pets, and even among lovers. It gives a sense of childish cuteness.

Bozu: This is an informal way to refer to a boy, similar to the English terms "kid" and "squirt."

Sempai/Senpai: This title suggests that the addressee is one's senior in a group or organization. It is most often used in a school setting, where underclassmen refer to their upperclassmen as "sempai." It can also be used in the workplace, such as when a newer employee addresses an employee who has seniority in the company.

Kohai: This is the opposite of "sempai" and is used toward underclassmen in school or newcomers in the workplace. It connotes that the addressee is of a lower station.

Sensei: Literally meaning "one who has come before," this title is used for teachers, doctors, or masters of any profession or art.

-[blank]: This is usually forgotten in these lists, but it is perhaps the most significant difference between Japanese and English. The lack of honorific means that the speaker has permission to address the person in a very intimate way. Usually, only family, spouses, or very close friends have this kind of permission. Known as *yobisute*, it can be gratifying when someone who has earned the intimacy starts to call one by one's name without an honorific. But when that intimacy hasn't been earned, it can be very insulting.

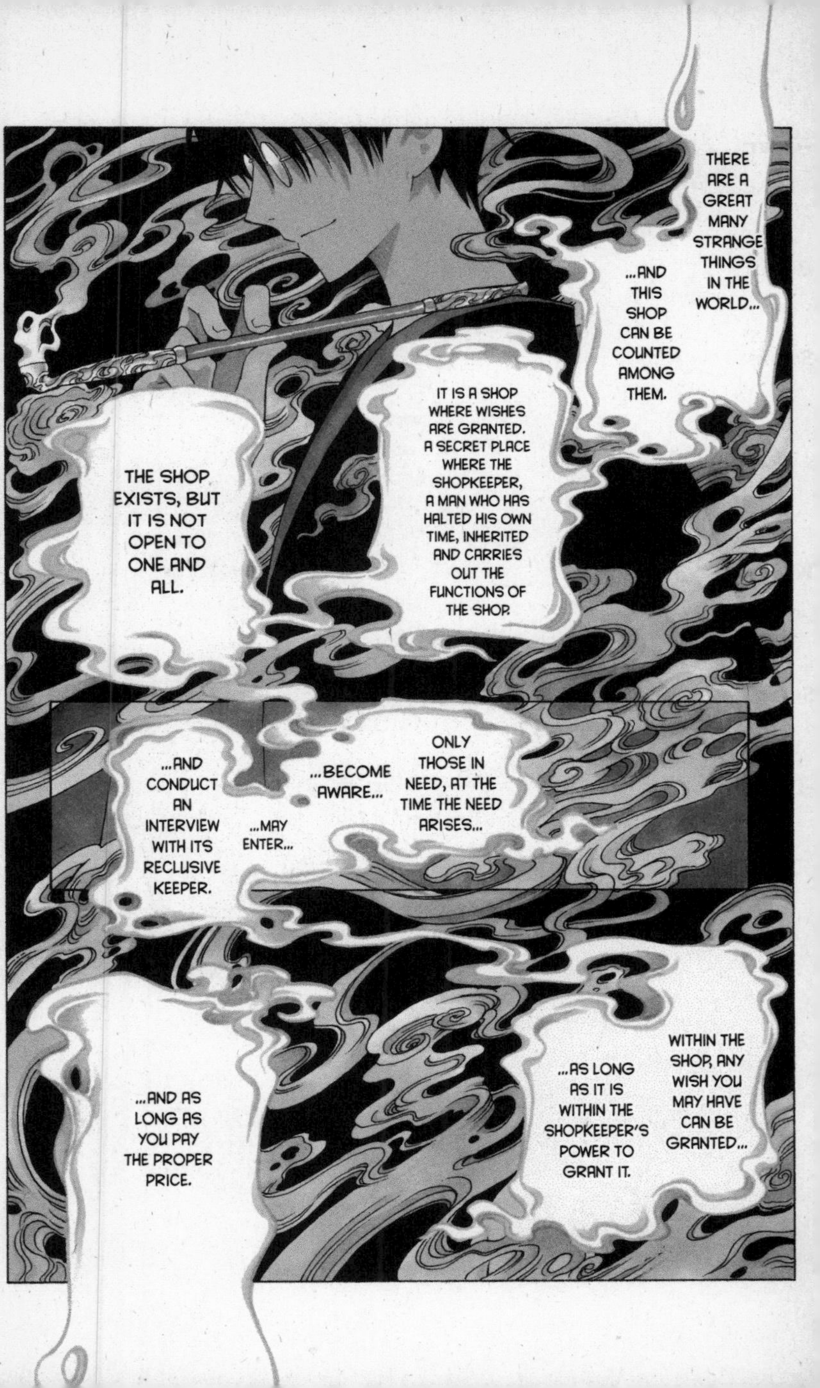
THERE ARE A GREAT MANY STRANGE THINGS IN THE WORLD...
...AND THIS SHOP CAN BE COUNTED AMONG THEM.
IT IS A SHOP WHERE WISHES ARE GRANTED. A SECRET PLACE WHERE THE SHOPKEEPER, A MAN WHO HAS HALTED HIS OWN TIME, INHERITED AND CARRIES OUT THE FUNCTIONS OF THE SHOP.
THE SHOP EXISTS, BUT IT IS NOT OPEN TO ONE AND ALL.
ONLY THOSE IN NEED, AT THE TIME THE NEED ARISES...
...BECOME AWARE...
...MAY ENTER...
...AND CONDUCT AN INTERVIEW WITH ITS RECLUSIVE KEEPER.
WITHIN THE SHOP, ANY WISH YOU MAY HAVE CAN BE GRANTED...
...AS LONG AS IT IS WITHIN THE SHOPKEEPER'S POWER TO GRANT IT.
...AND AS LONG AS YOU PAY THE PROPER PRICE.

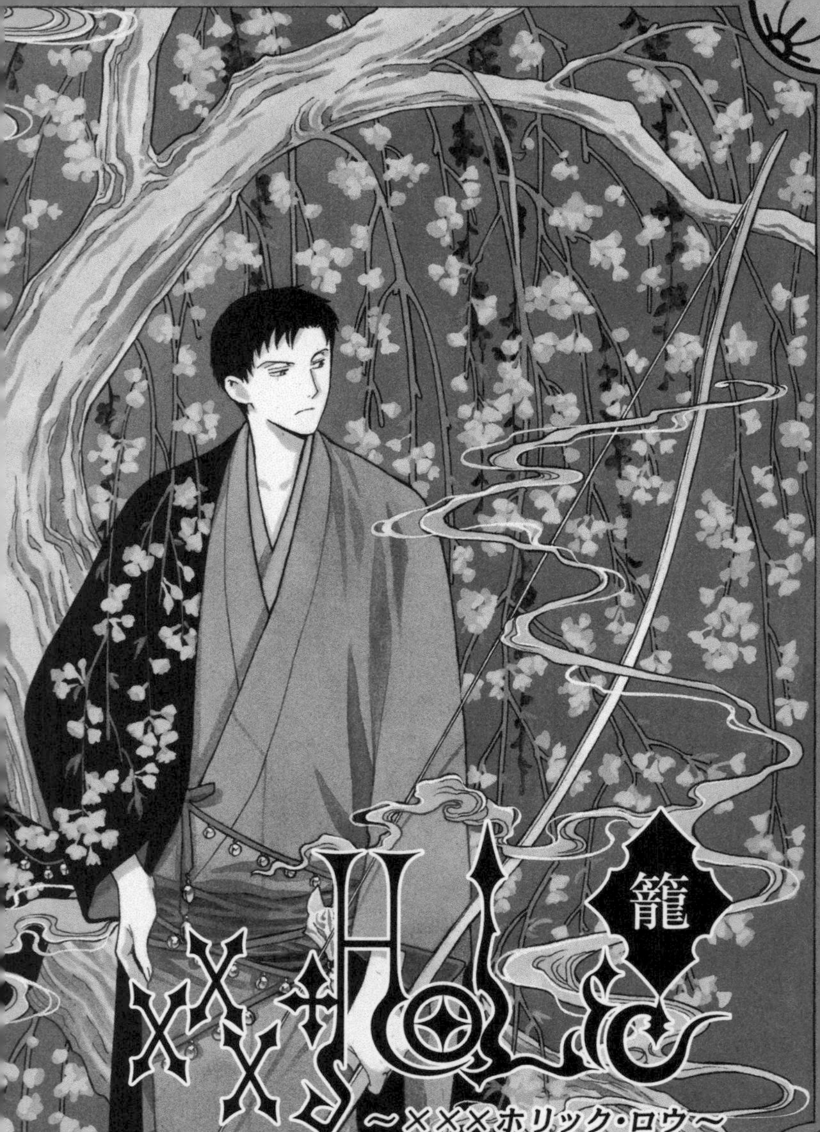
xxxHOLiC
籠
～×××ホリック・ロウ～

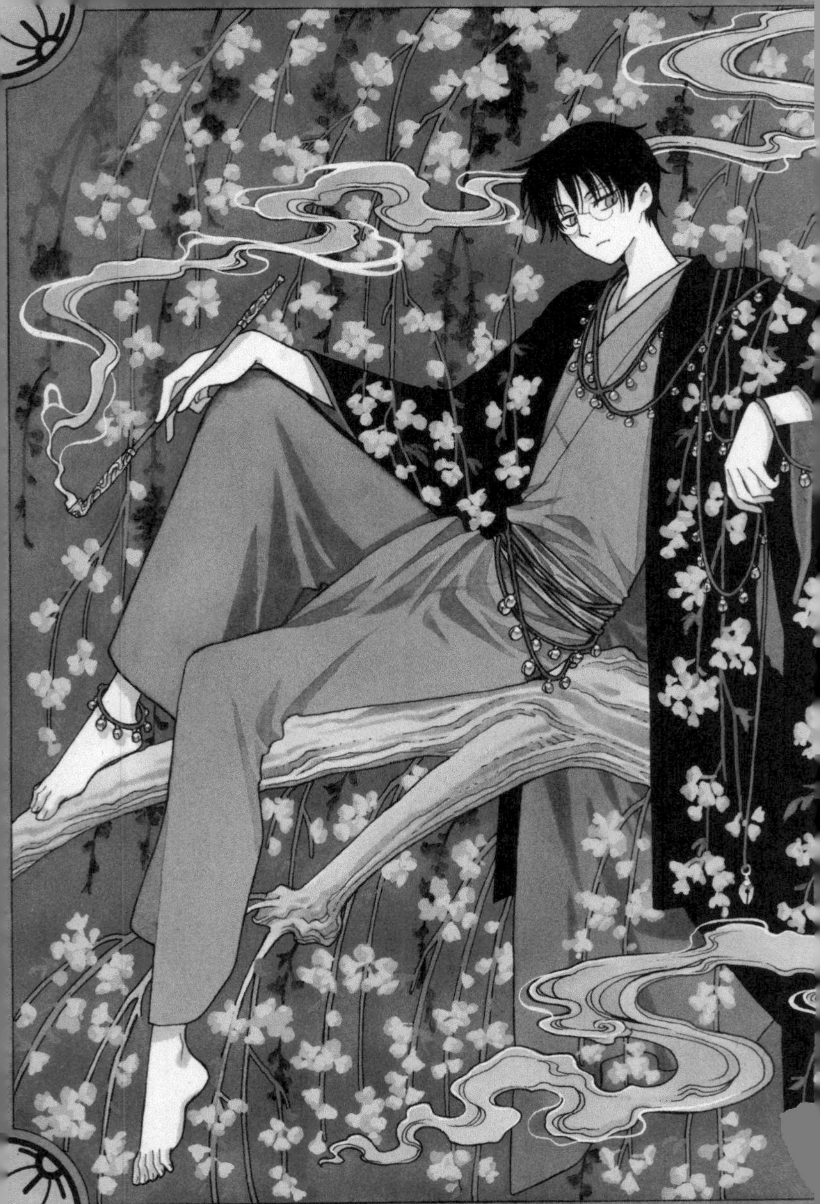

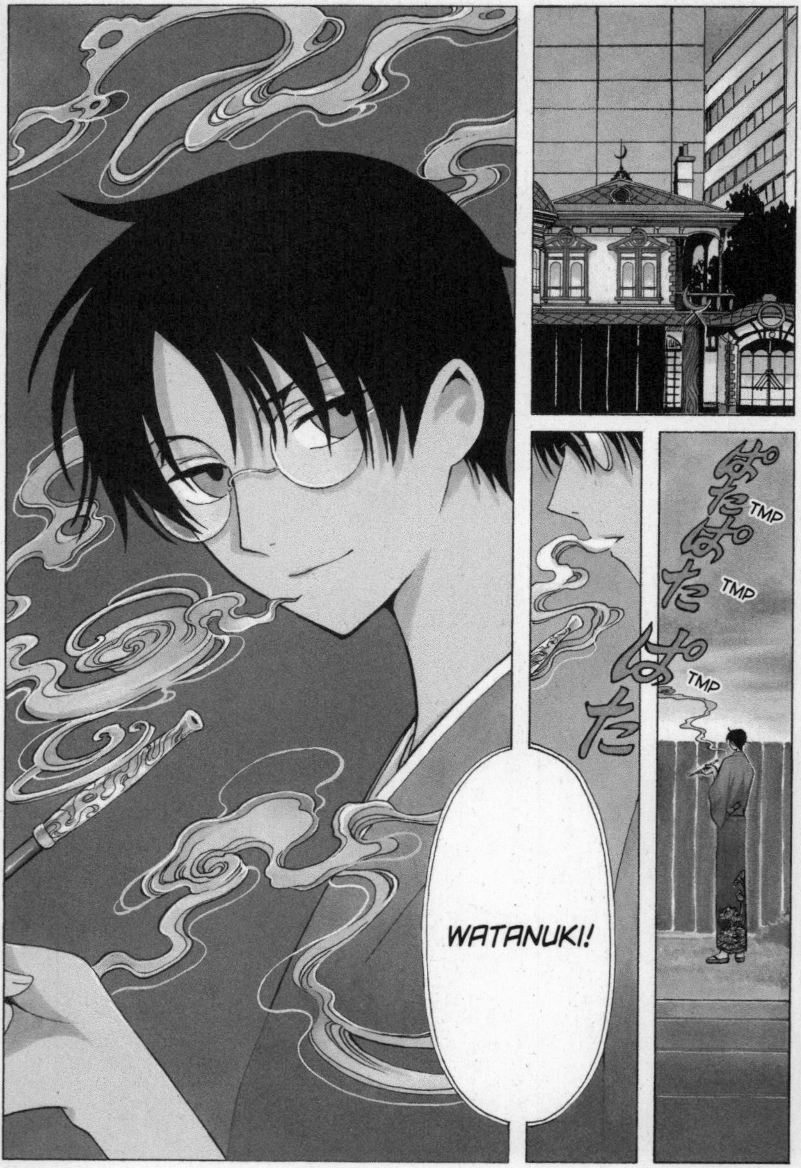
ぱたぱたぱた
TMP
TMP
TMP
WATANUKI!

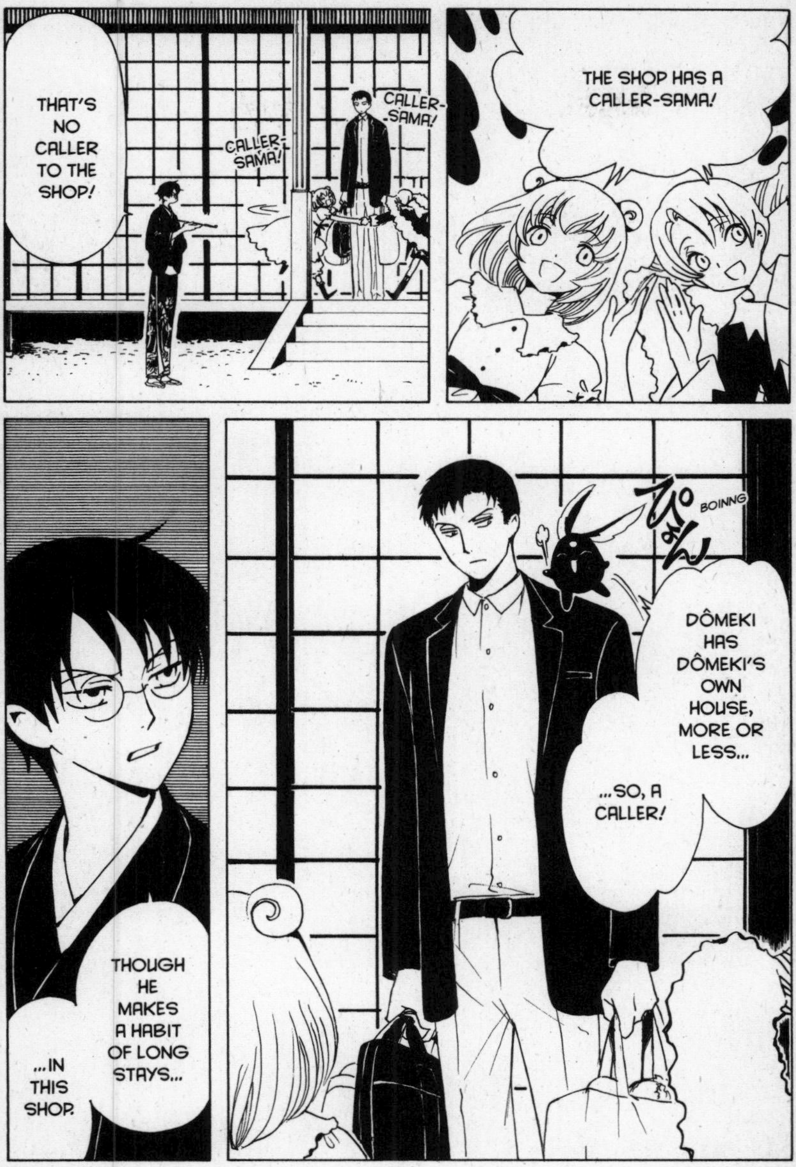
THE SHOP HAS A CALLER-SAMA!
CALLER-SAMA!
CALLER-SAMA!
THAT'S NO CALLER TO THE SHOP!
ぴょん
BOINNG
DÔMEKI HAS DÔMEKI'S OWN HOUSE, MORE OR LESS...
...SO, A CALLER!
THOUGH HE MAKES A HABIT OF LONG STAYS...
...IN THIS SHOP.

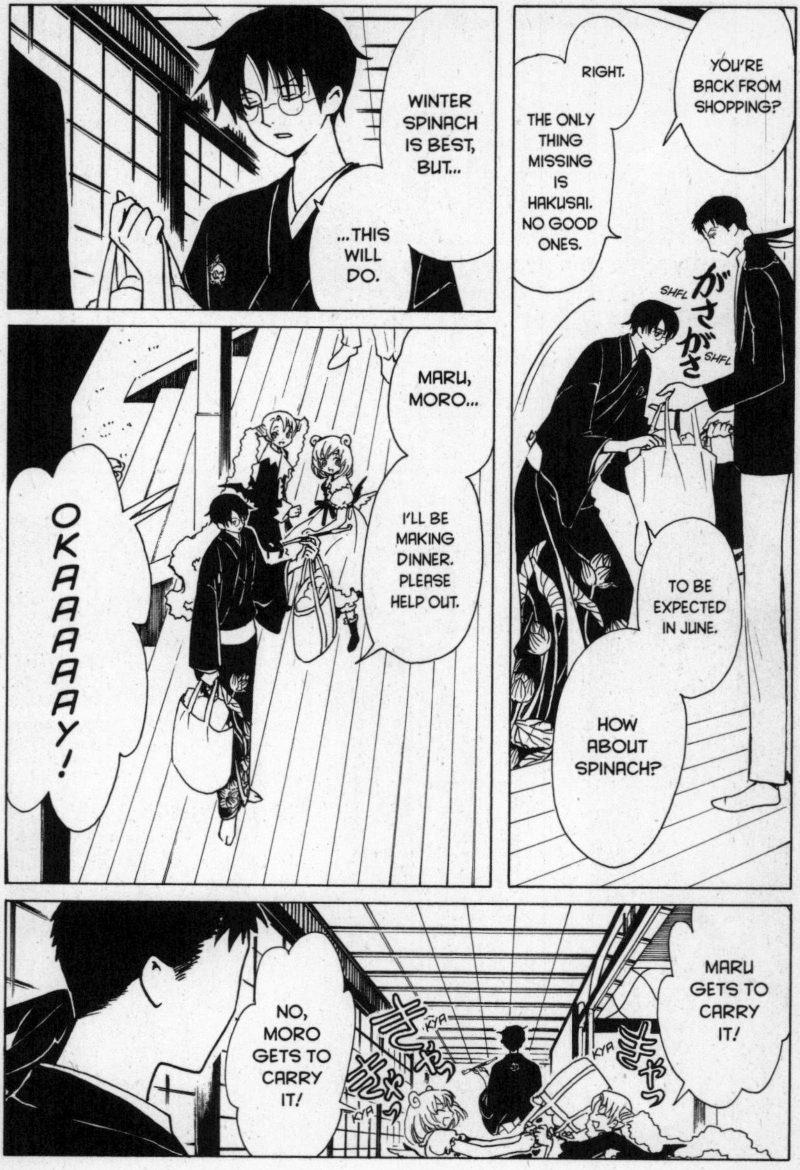
YOU'RE BACK FROM SHOPPING?
RIGHT.
THE ONLY THING MISSING IS HAKUSAI. NO GOOD ONES.
がさがさ
SHFL
SHFL
TO BE EXPECTED IN JUNE.
HOW ABOUT SPINACH?
WINTER SPINACH IS BEST, BUT...
...THIS WILL DO.
MARU, MORO...
I'LL BE MAKING DINNER. PLEASE HELP OUT.
OKAAAAAAAY!
MARU GETS TO CARRY IT!
きゃっ
KYA
きゃっきゃっ
KYA
KYA
NO, MORO GETS TO CARRY IT!

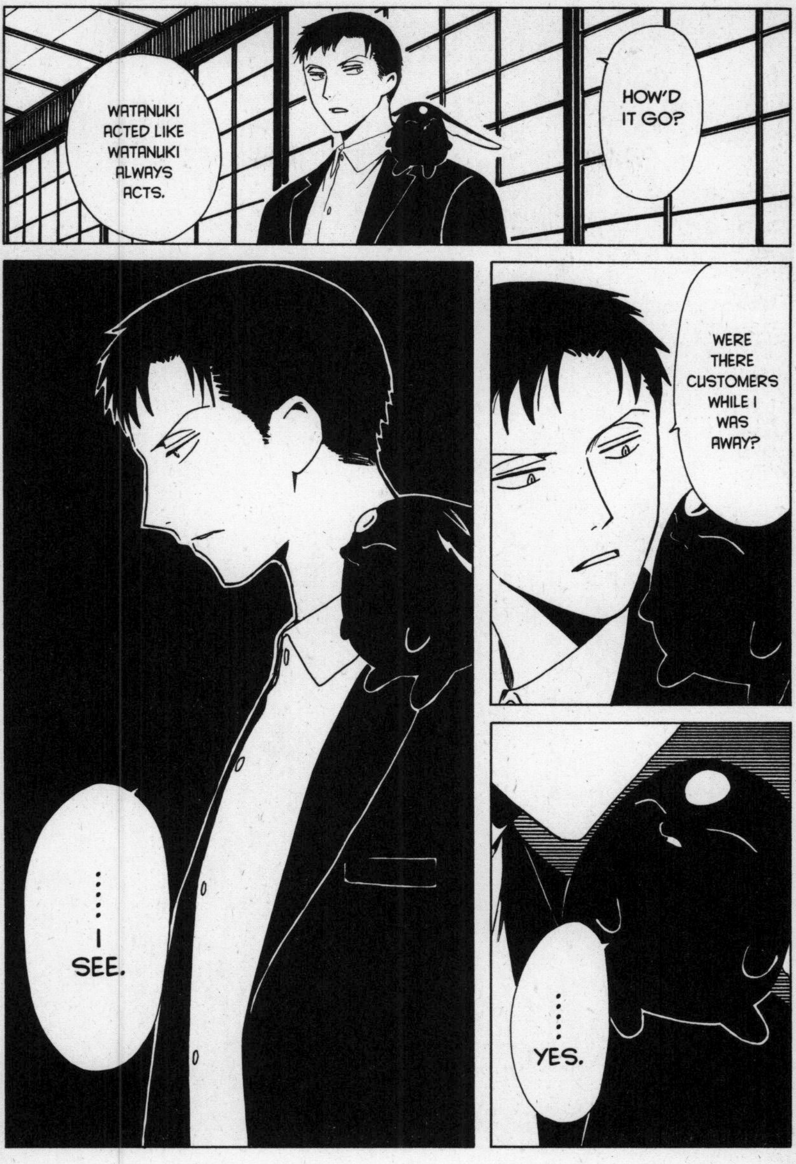
HOW'D IT GO?
WATANUKI ACTED LIKE WATANUKI ALWAYS ACTS.
WERE THERE CUSTOMERS WHILE I WAS AWAY?
....YES.
....I SEE.

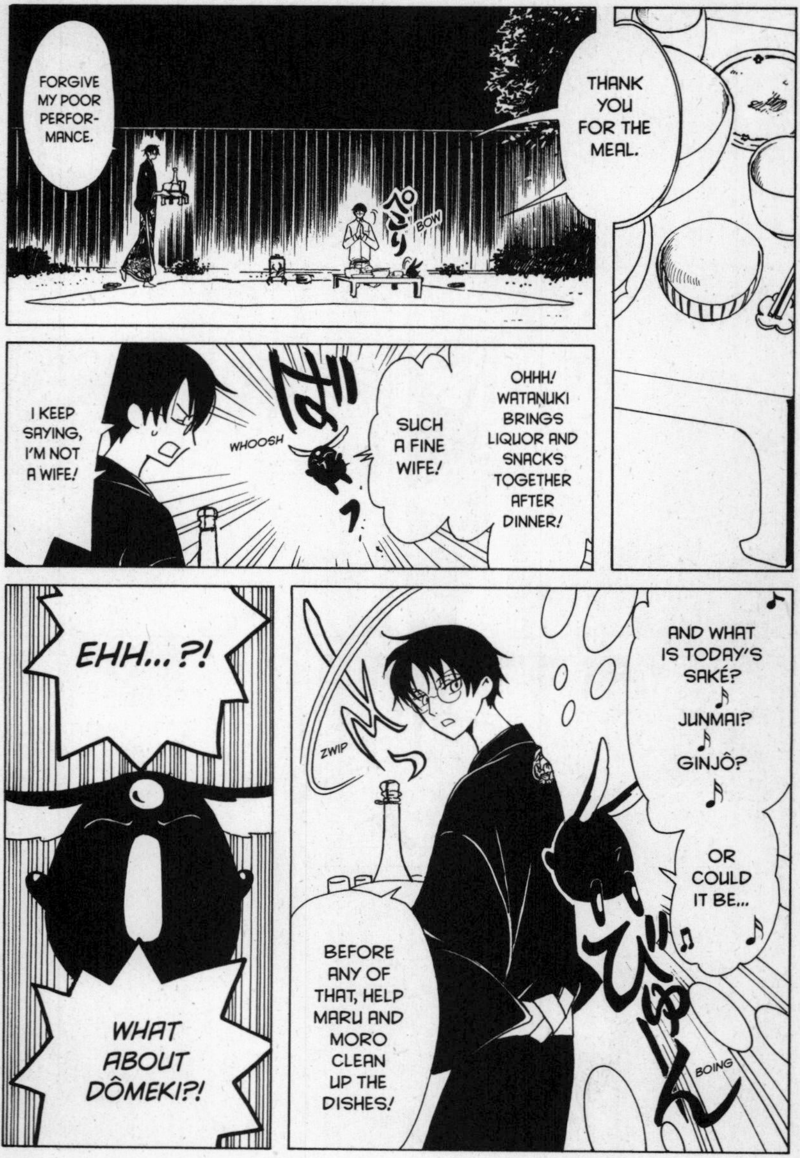
THANK YOU FOR THE MEAL.
ぺこり
BOW
FORGIVE MY POOR PERFORMANCE.
OHHH! WATANUKI BRINGS LIQUOR AND SNACKS TOGETHER AFTER DINNER!
SUCH A FINE WIFE!
WHOOSH
I KEEP SAYING, I'M NOT A WIFE!
AND WHAT IS TODAY'S SAKÉ? ♪ JUNMAI? ♪ GINJÔ? ♪
OR COULD IT BE... ♪
BOING
ZWIP
BEFORE ANY OF THAT, HELP MARU AND MORO CLEAN UP THE DISHES!
EHH...?!
WHAT ABOUT DÔMEKI?!

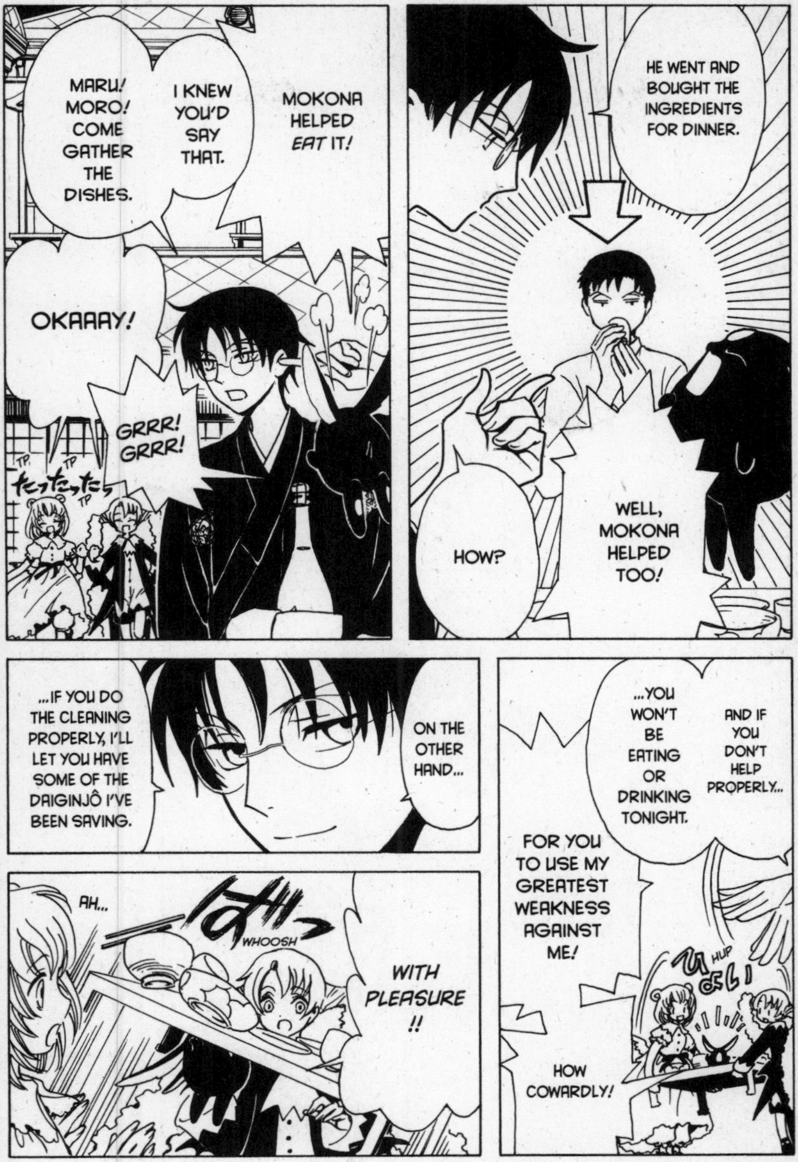
HE WENT AND BOUGHT THE INGREDIENTS FOR DINNER.
WELL, MOKONA HELPED TOO!
HOW?
MOKONA HELPED *EAT* IT!
I KNEW YOU'D SAY THAT.
MARU! MORO! COME GATHER THE DISHES.
OKAAAY!
GRRR! GRRR!
TP TP TP
AND IF YOU DON'T HELP PROPERLY...
...YOU WON'T BE EATING OR DRINKING TONIGHT.
FOR YOU TO USE MY GREATEST WEAKNESS AGAINST ME!
HUP
HOW COWARDLY!
ON THE OTHER HAND...
...IF YOU DO THE CLEANING PROPERLY, I'LL LET YOU HAVE SOME OF THE DAIGINJÔ I'VE BEEN SAVING.
WITH PLEASURE !!
WHOOSH
AH...

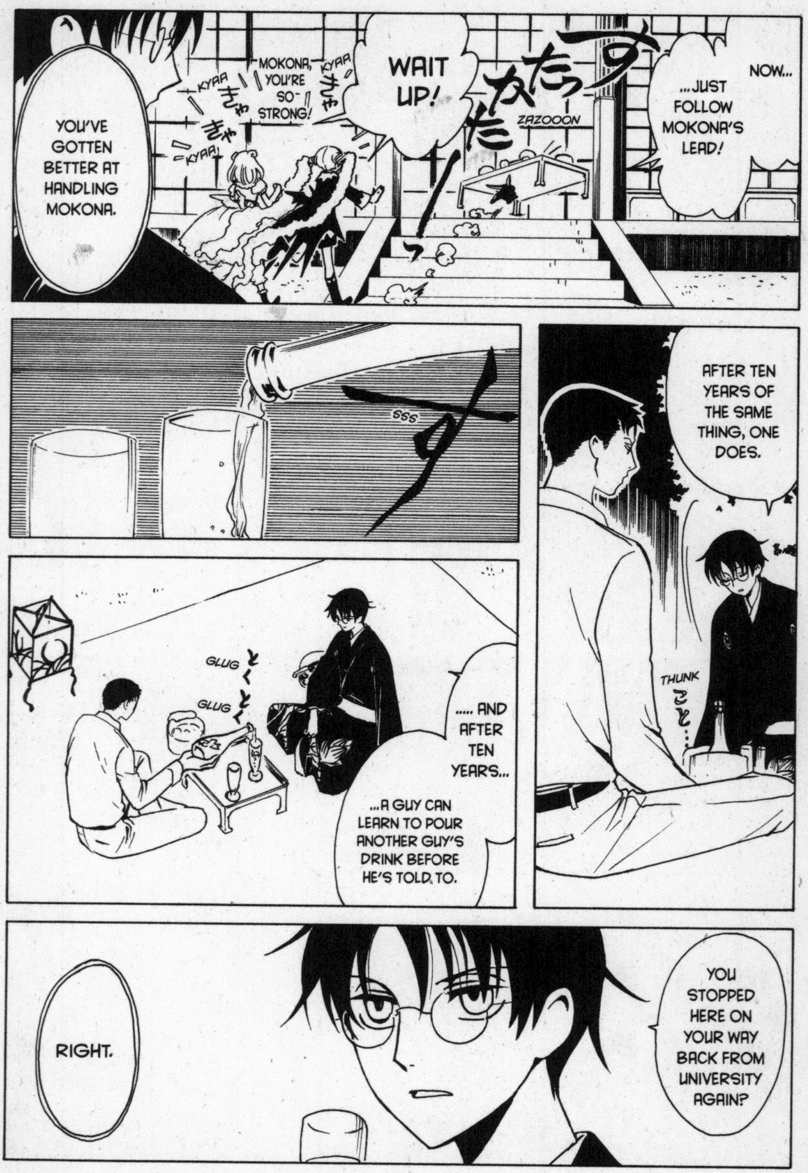
NOW...
...JUST FOLLOW MOKONA'S LEAD!
すたったた
ZAZOOON
WAIT UP!
KYAA きゃ
MOKONA, YOU'RE SO-STRONG!
KYAA きゃ
KYAA きゃ
YOU'VE GOTTEN BETTER AT HANDLING MOKONA.
AFTER TEN YEARS OF THE SAME THING, ONE DOES.
THUNK こと…
す
SSS
..... AND AFTER TEN YEARS...
...A GUY CAN LEARN TO POUR ANOTHER GUY'S DRINK BEFORE HE'S TOLD TO.
GLUG とく
GLUG とく
YOU STOPPED HERE ON YOUR WAY BACK FROM UNIVERSITY AGAIN?
RIGHT.

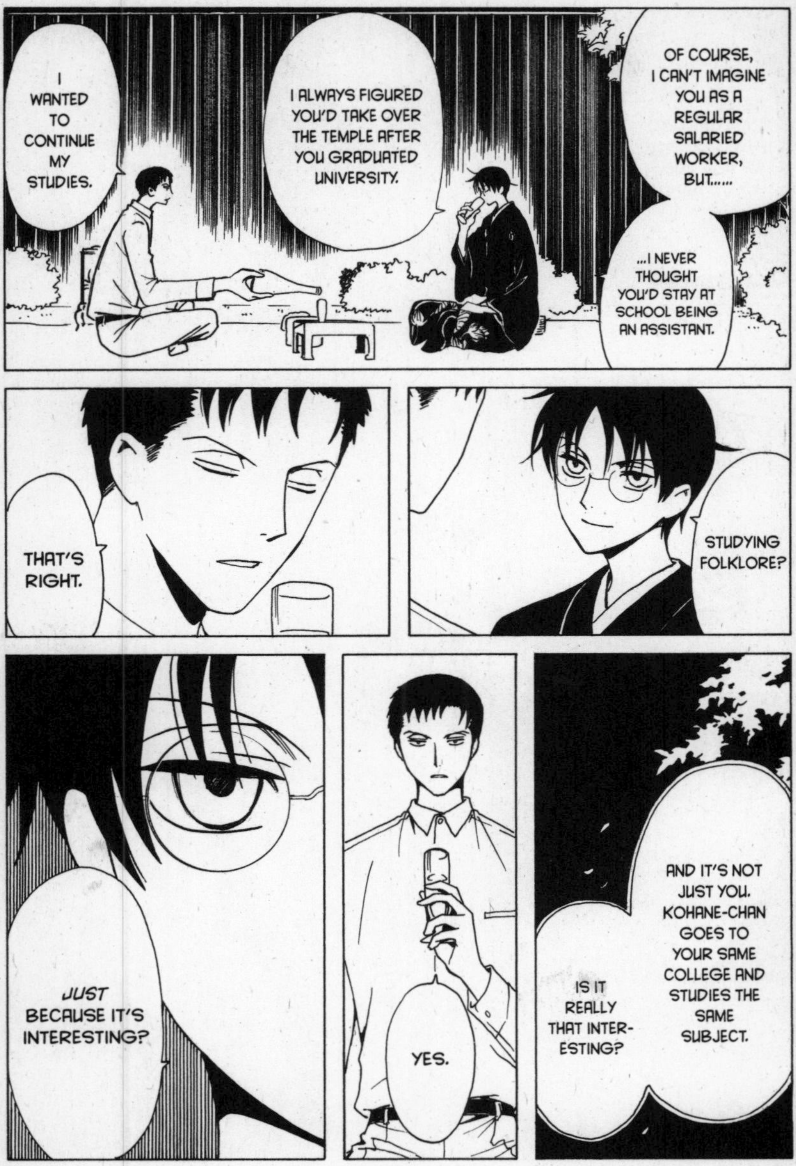
OF COURSE, I CAN'T IMAGINE YOU AS A REGULAR SALARIED WORKER, BUT......
...I NEVER THOUGHT YOU'D STAY AT SCHOOL BEING AN ASSISTANT.
I ALWAYS FIGURED YOU'D TAKE OVER THE TEMPLE AFTER YOU GRADUATED UNIVERSITY.
I WANTED TO CONTINUE MY STUDIES.
STUDYING FOLKLORE?
THAT'S RIGHT.
AND IT'S NOT JUST YOU. KOHANE-CHAN GOES TO YOUR SAME COLLEGE AND STUDIES THE SAME SUBJECT.
IS IT REALLY THAT INTER-ESTING?
YES.
JUST BECAUSE IT'S INTERESTING?

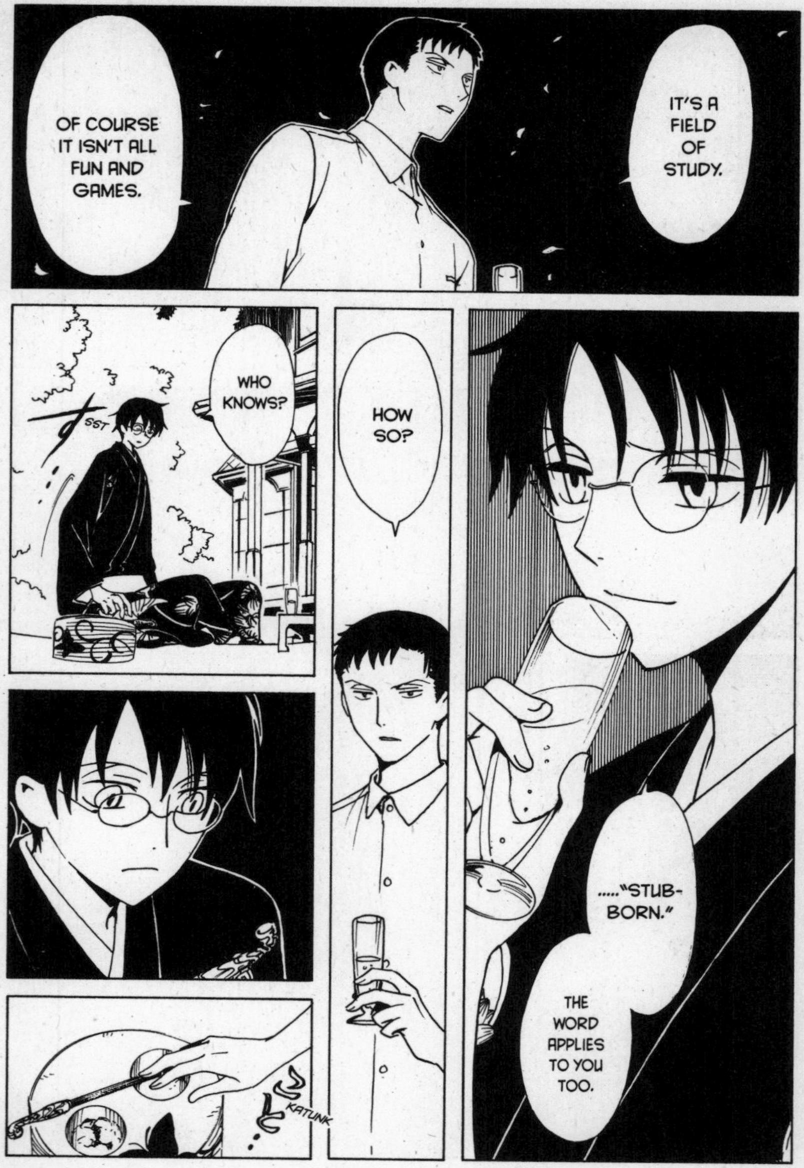
IT'S A FIELD OF STUDY.
OF COURSE IT ISN'T ALL FUN AND GAMES.
....."STUB-BORN."
THE WORD APPLIES TO YOU TOO.
HOW SO?
WHO KNOWS?
SST
KATUNK

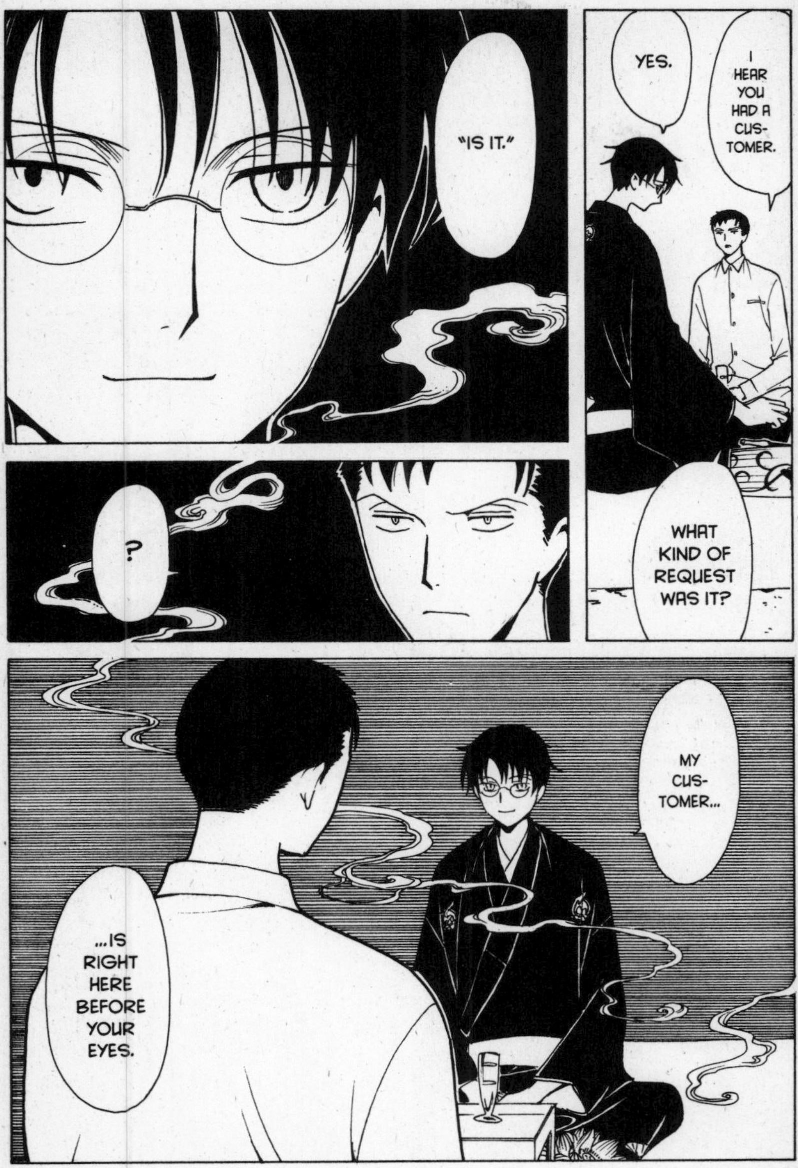
I HEAR YOU HAD A CUSTOMER.
YES.
WHAT KIND OF REQUEST WAS IT?
"IS IT."
?
MY CUSTOMER...
...IS RIGHT HERE BEFORE YOUR EYES.

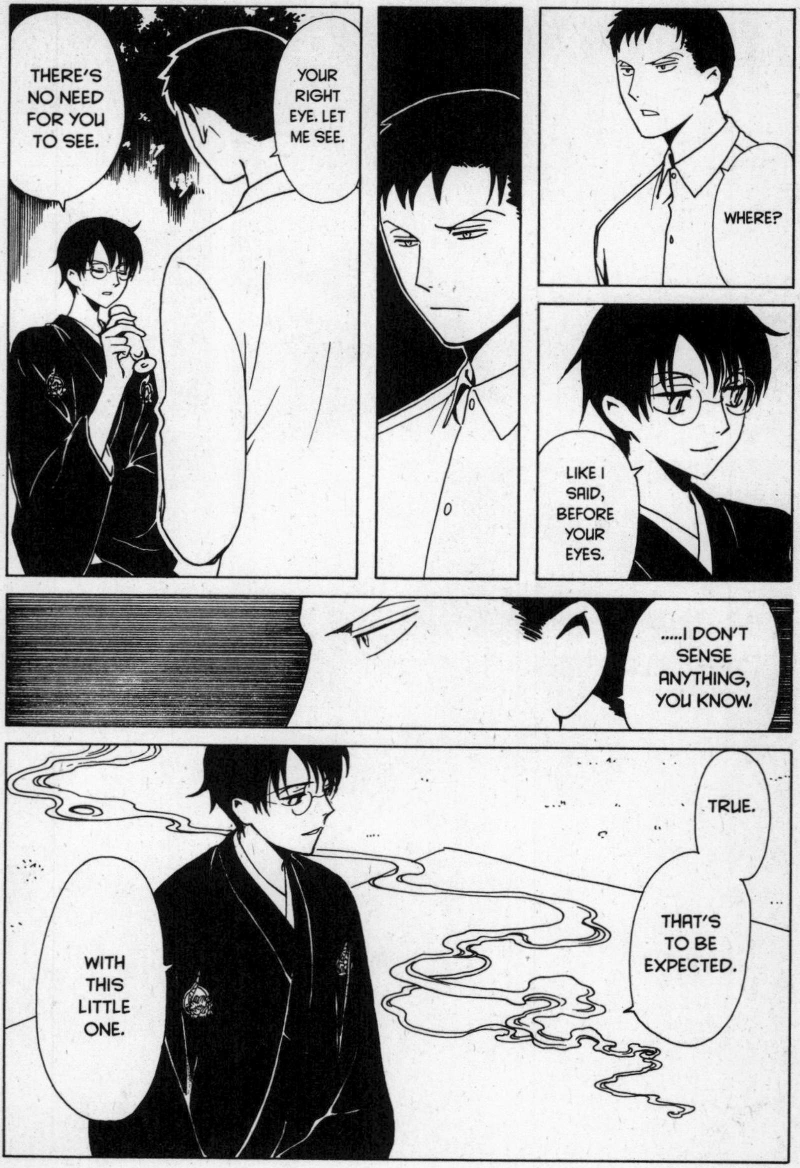
WHERE?
LIKE I SAID, BEFORE YOUR EYES.
YOUR RIGHT EYE. LET ME SEE.
THERE'S NO NEED FOR YOU TO SEE.
.....I DON'T SENSE ANYTHING, YOU KNOW.
TRUE.
THAT'S TO BE EXPECTED.
WITH THIS LITTLE ONE.

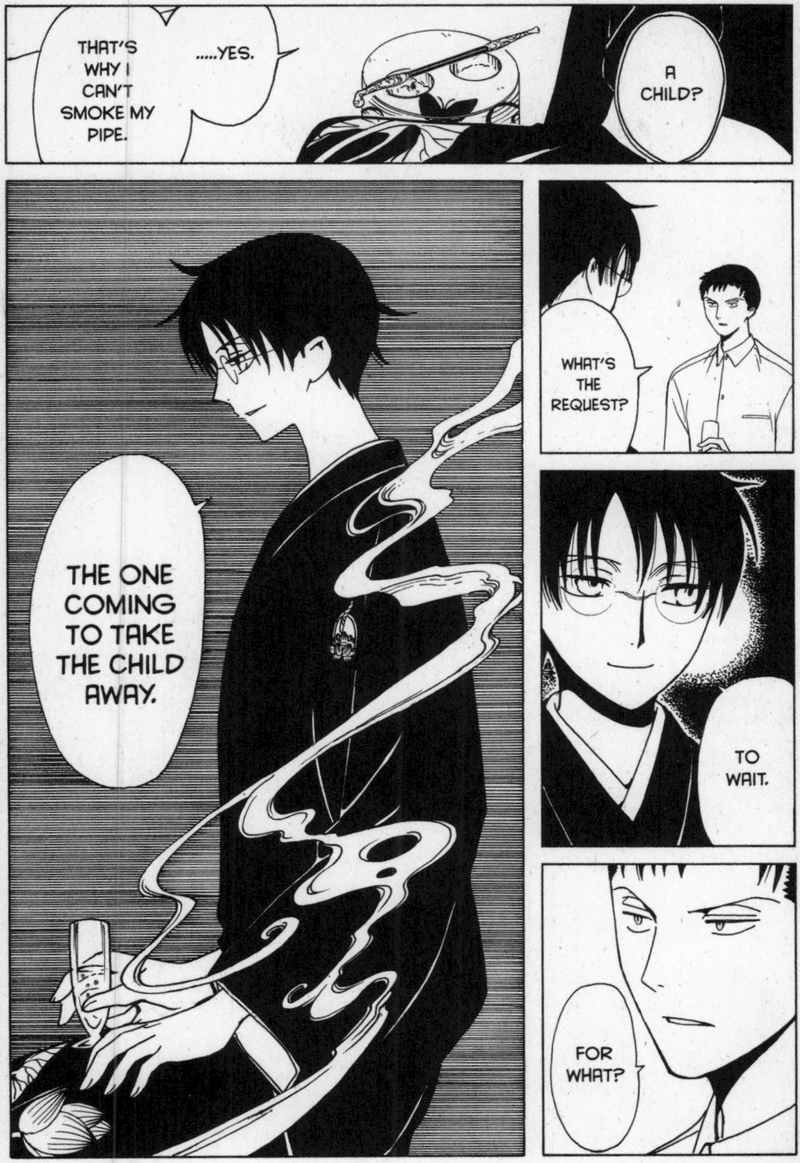
A CHILD?
.....YES.
THAT'S WHY I CAN'T SMOKE MY PIPE.
WHAT'S THE REQUEST?
TO WAIT.
FOR WHAT?
THE ONE COMING TO TAKE THE CHILD AWAY.

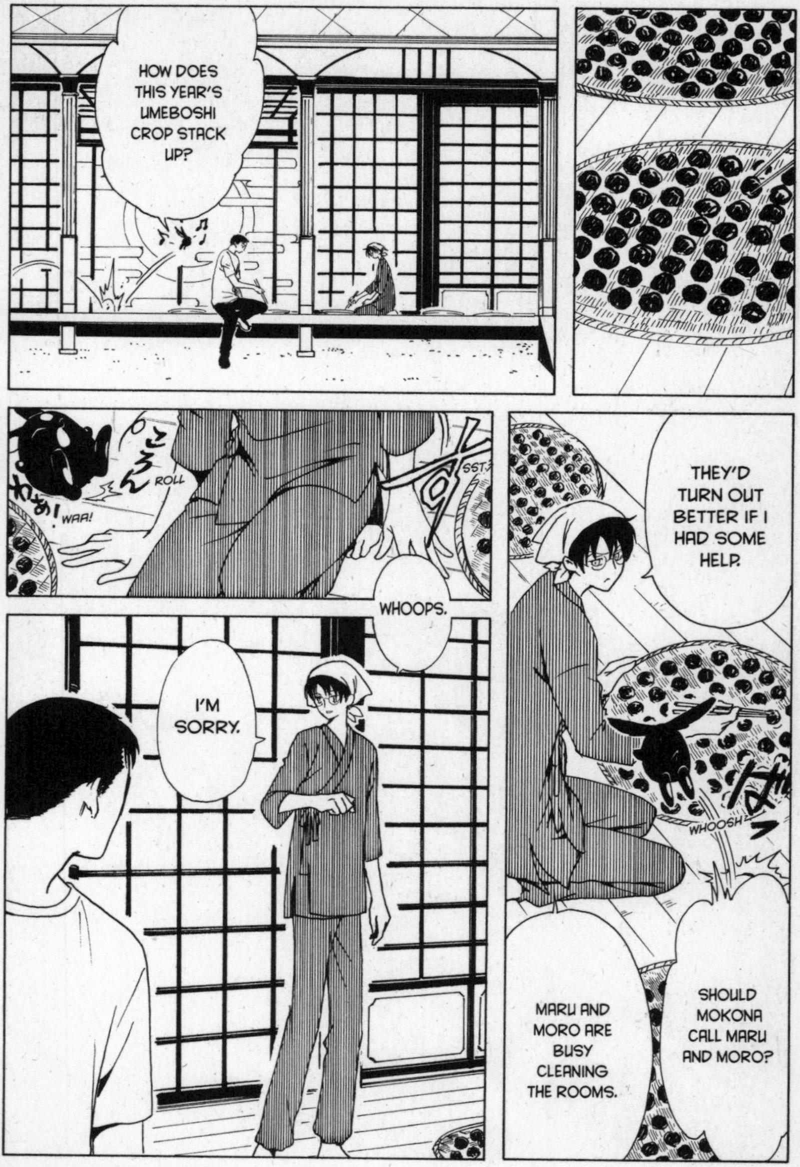
HOW DOES THIS YEAR'S UMEBOSHI CROP STACK UP?
THEY'D TURN OUT BETTER IF I HAD SOME HELP.
WHOOSH
SHOULD MOKONA CALL MARU AND MORO?
MARU AND MORO ARE BUSY CLEANING THE ROOMS.
SST
ころん ROLL
わあ! WAA!
WHOOPS.
I'M SORRY.

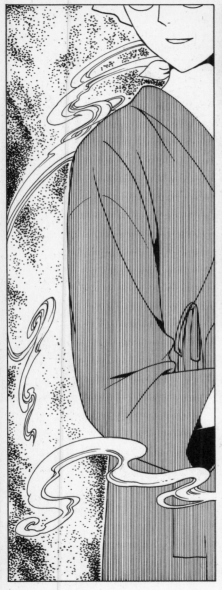

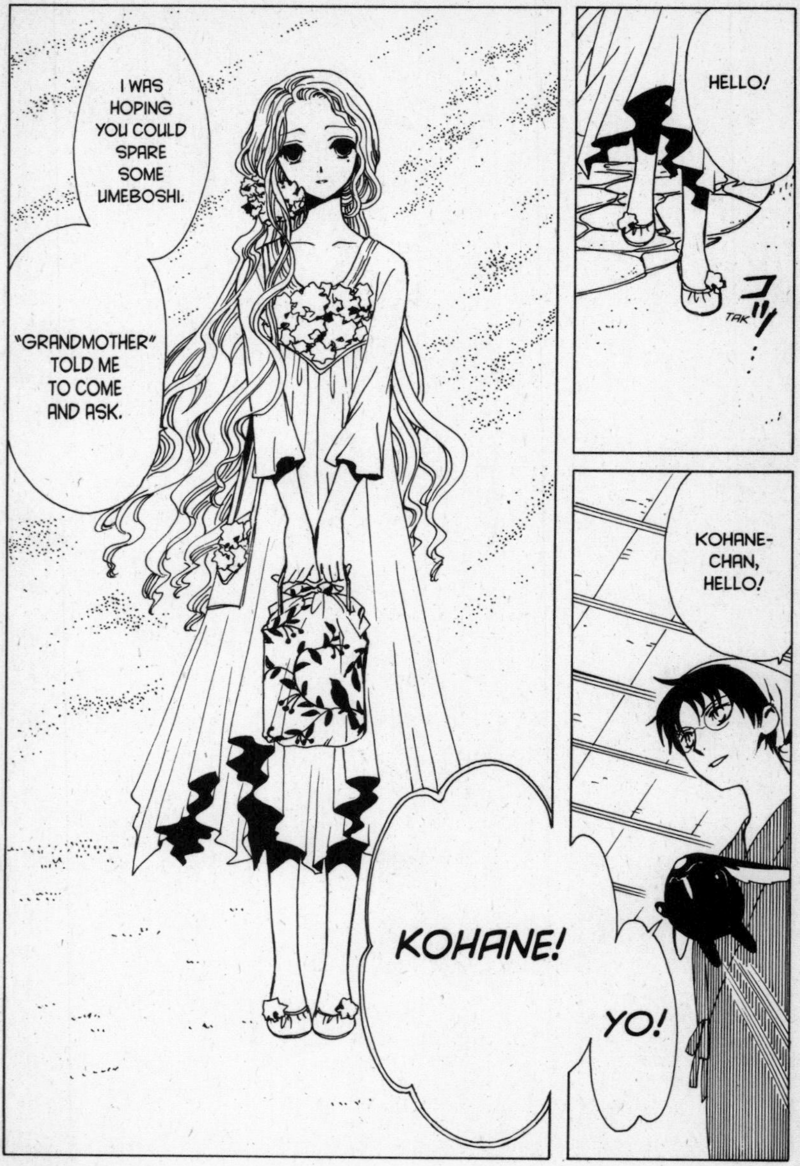
HELLO!
コツ
TAK
KOHANE-CHAN, HELLO!
KOHANE!
YO!
I WAS HOPING YOU COULD SPARE SOME UMEBOSHI.
"GRANDMOTHER" TOLD ME TO COME AND ASK.

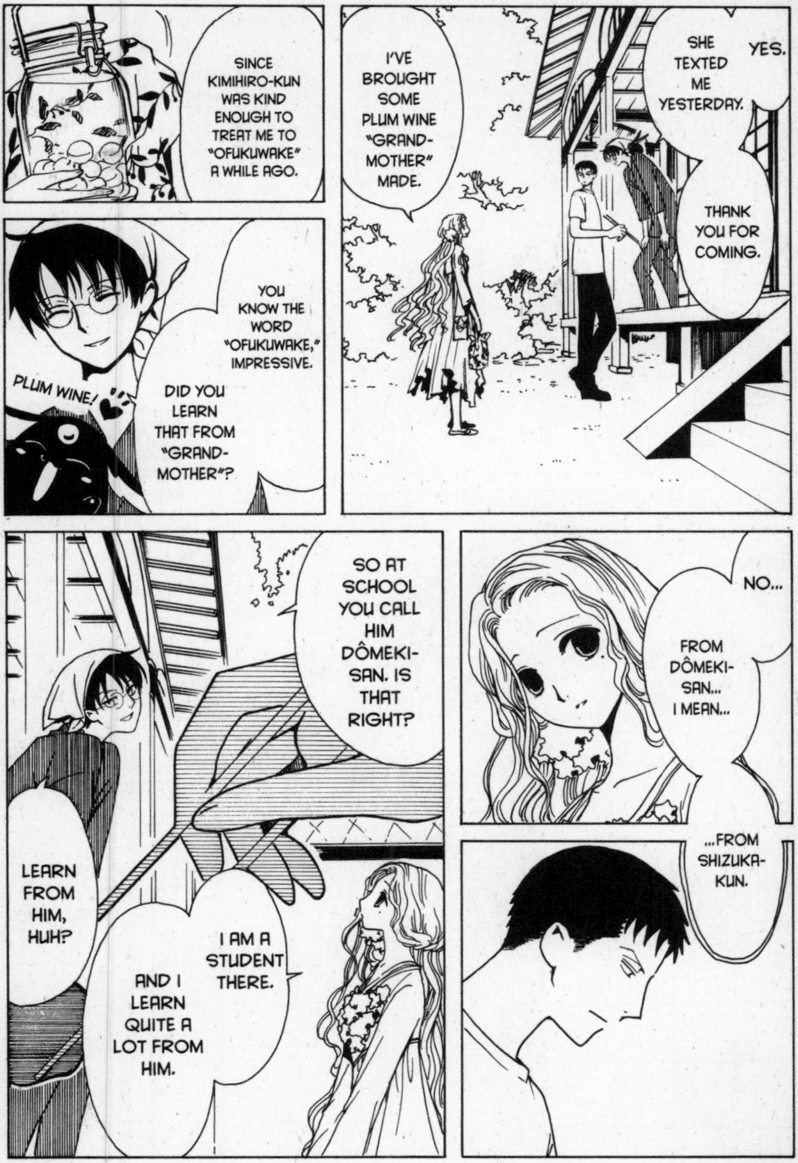
YES.
SHE TEXTED ME YESTERDAY.
THANK YOU FOR COMING.
I'VE BROUGHT SOME PLUM WINE "GRAND-MOTHER" MADE.
SINCE KIMIHIRO-KUN WAS KIND ENOUGH TO TREAT ME TO "OFUKUWAKE" A WHILE AGO.
YOU KNOW THE WORD "OFUKUWAKE," IMPRESSIVE.
DID YOU LEARN THAT FROM "GRAND-MOTHER"?
PLUM WINE!
NO...
FROM DÔMEKI-SAN... I MEAN...
...FROM SHIZUKA-KUN.
SO AT SCHOOL YOU CALL HIM DÔMEKI-SAN. IS THAT RIGHT?
I AM A STUDENT THERE.
AND I LEARN QUITE A LOT FROM HIM.
LEARN FROM HIM, HUH?

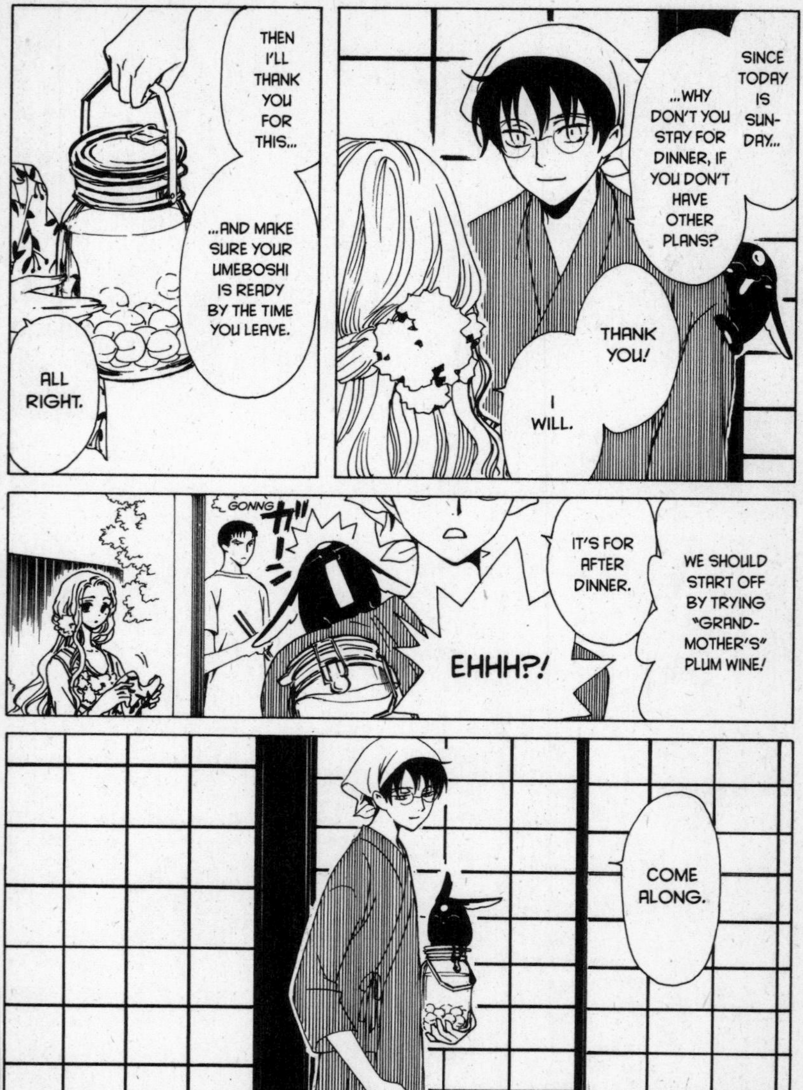
SINCE TODAY IS SUNDAY...
...WHY DON'T YOU STAY FOR DINNER, IF YOU DON'T HAVE OTHER PLANS?
THANK YOU!
I WILL.
THEN I'LL THANK YOU FOR THIS...
...AND MAKE SURE YOUR UMEBOSHI IS READY BY THE TIME YOU LEAVE.
ALL RIGHT.
WE SHOULD START OFF BY TRYING "GRANDMOTHER'S" PLUM WINE!
IT'S FOR AFTER DINNER.
EHHH?!
GONNG
COME ALONG.

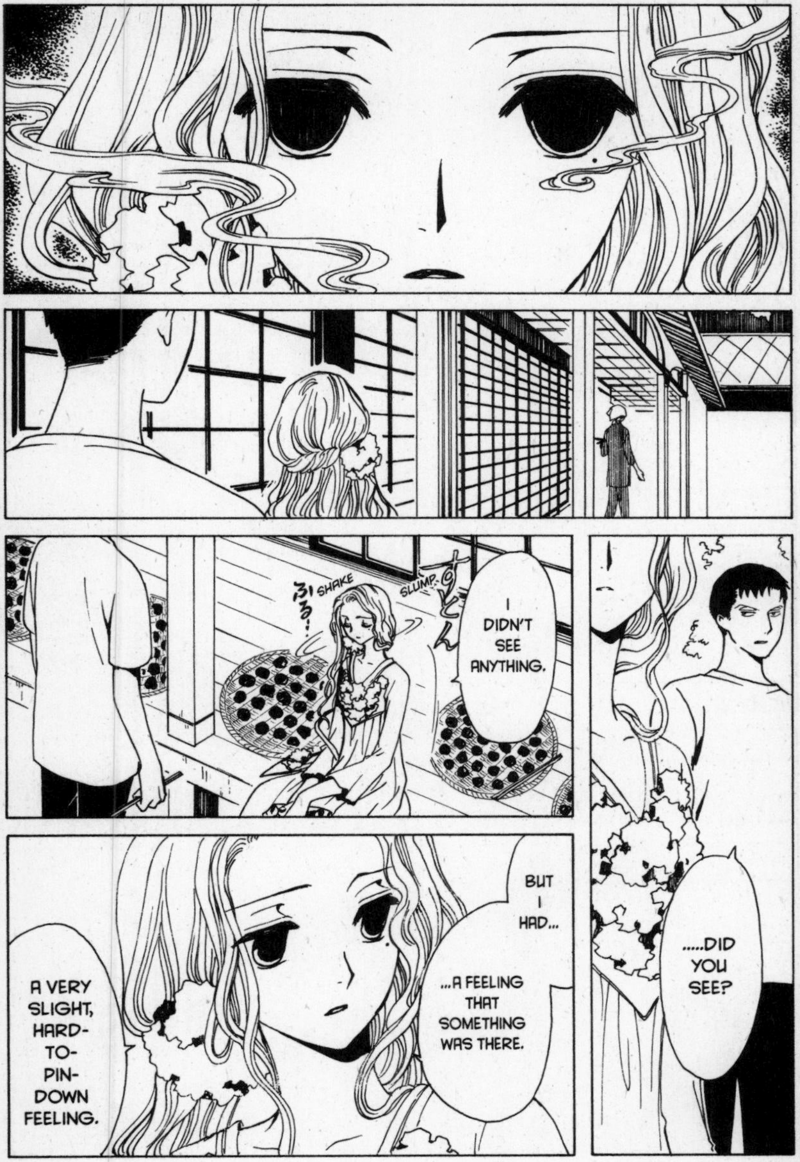

.....DID YOU SEE?
I DIDN'T SEE ANYTHING.
すとん
SLUMP
ふる!!
SHAKE
BUT I HAD...
...A FEELING THAT SOMETHING WAS THERE.
A VERY SLIGHT, HARD-TO-PIN-DOWN FEELING.

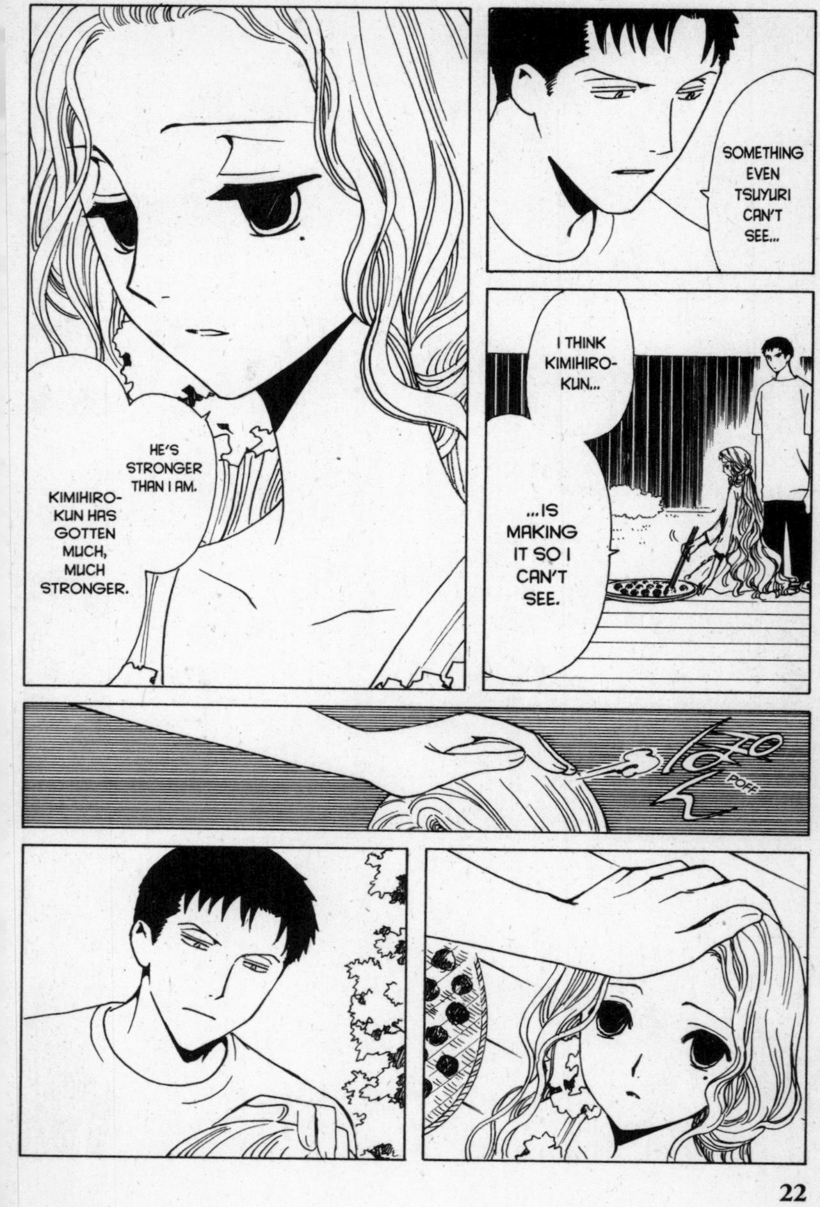
SOMETHING EVEN TSUYURI CAN'T SEE...
I THINK KIMIHIRO-KUN...
...IS MAKING IT SO I CAN'T SEE.
HE'S STRONGER THAN I AM.
KIMIHIRO-KUN HAS GOTTEN MUCH, MUCH STRONGER.
POFF

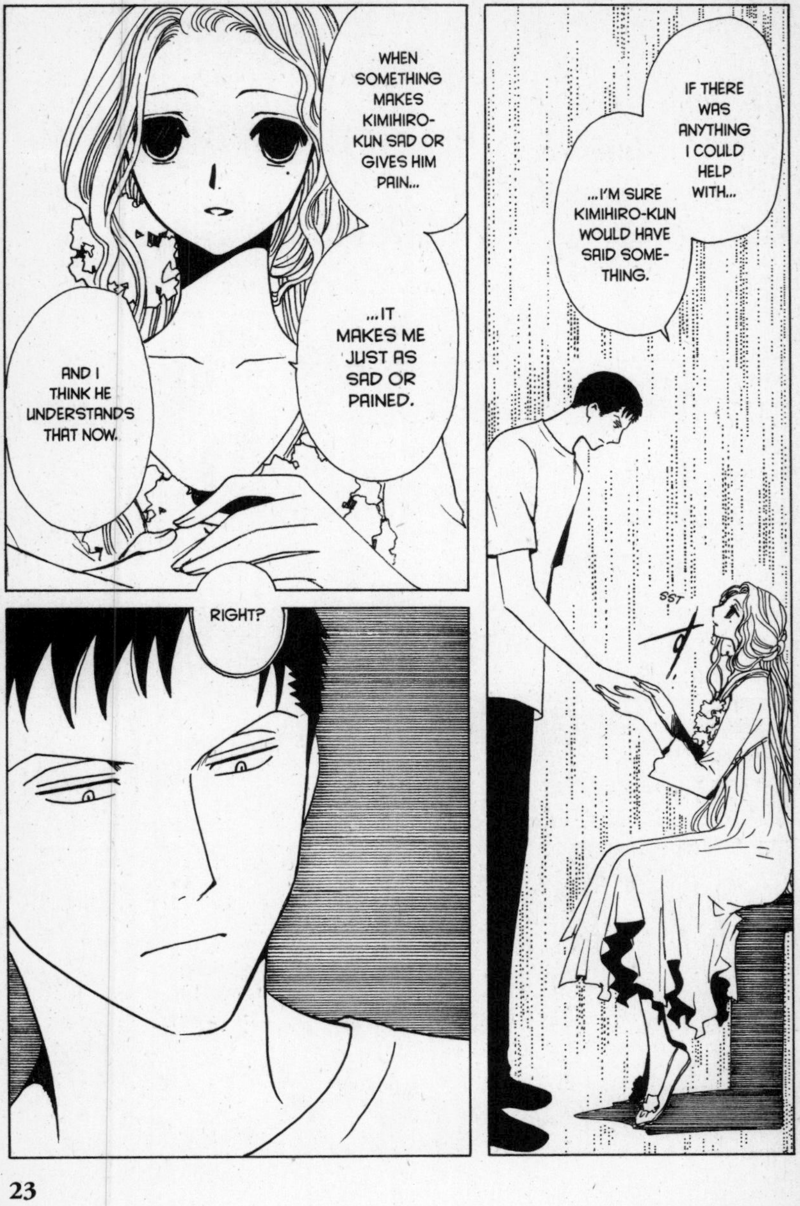
IF THERE WAS ANYTHING I COULD HELP WITH...
...I'M SURE KIMIHIRO-KUN WOULD HAVE SAID SOME-THING.
SST
WHEN SOMETHING MAKES KIMIHIRO-KUN SAD OR GIVES HIM PAIN...
...IT MAKES ME JUST AS SAD OR PAINED.
AND I THINK HE UNDERSTANDS THAT NOW.
RIGHT?

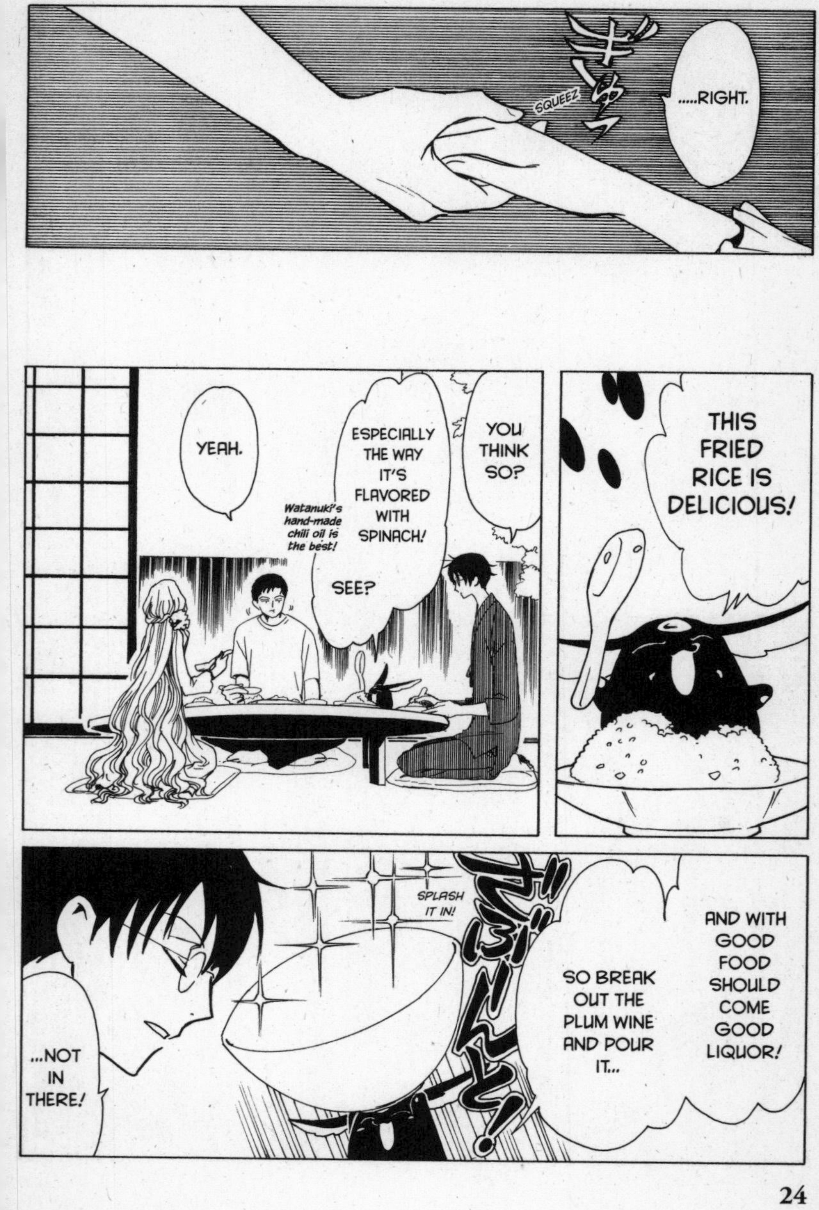
.....RIGHT.
SQUEEZ
THIS FRIED RICE IS DELICIOUS!
YOU THINK SO?
ESPECIALLY THE WAY IT'S FLAVORED WITH SPINACH!
Watanuki's hand-made chili oil is the best!
YEAH.
SEE?
AND WITH GOOD FOOD SHOULD COME GOOD LIQUOR!
SO BREAK OUT THE PLUM WINE AND POUR IT...
SPLASH IT IN!
...NOT IN THERE!

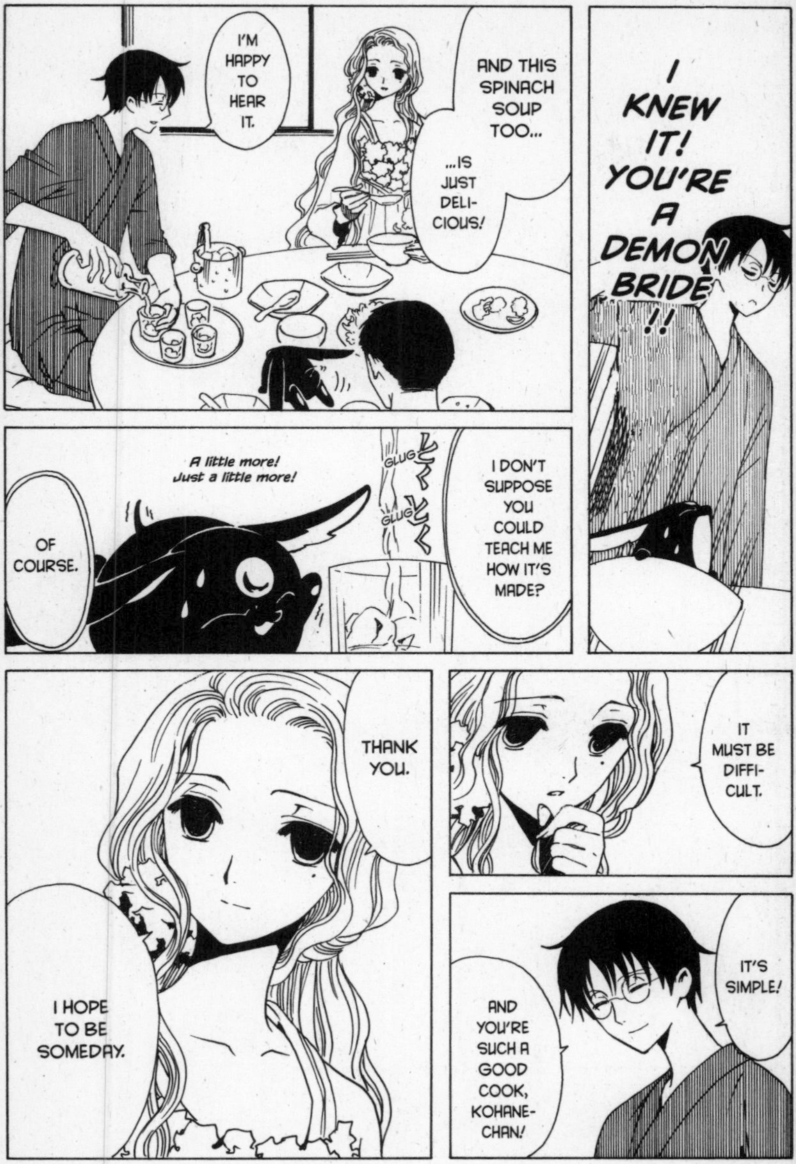
I KNEW IT! YOU'RE A DEMON BRIDE!!
AND THIS SPINACH SOUP TOO...
...IS JUST DELICIOUS!
I'M HAPPY TO HEAR IT.
I DON'T SUPPOSE YOU COULD TEACH ME HOW IT'S MADE?
GLUG
GLUG
A little more! Just a little more!
OF COURSE.
IT MUST BE DIFFI-CULT.
IT'S SIMPLE!
AND YOU'RE SUCH A GOOD COOK, KOHANE-CHAN!
THANK YOU.
I HOPE TO BE SOMEDAY.

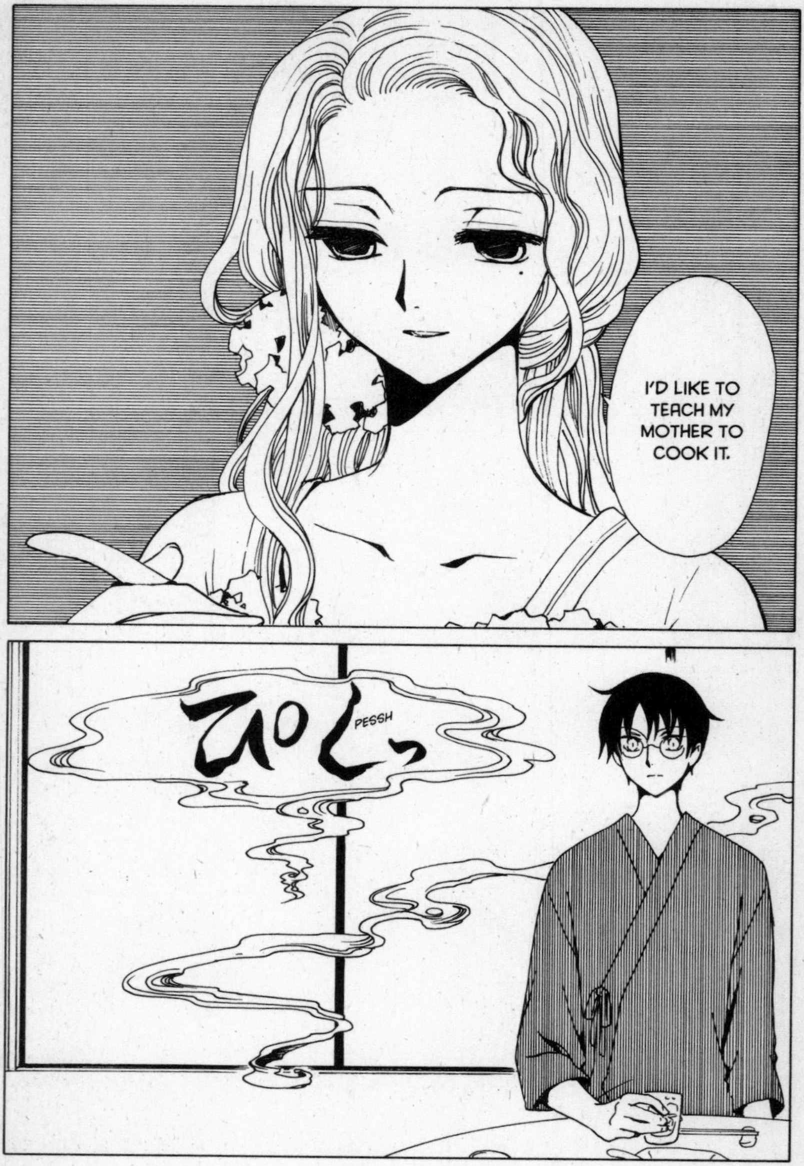
I'D LIKE TO TEACH MY MOTHER TO COOK IT.
ぴしっ
PESSH

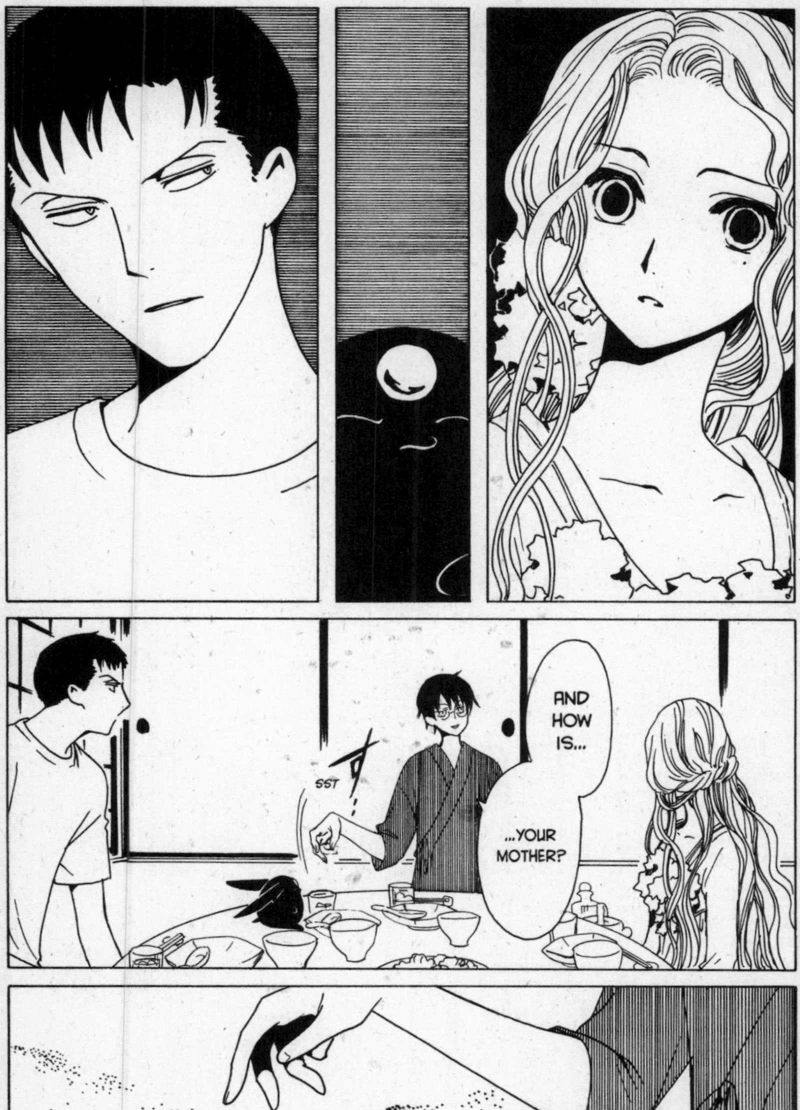
AND HOW IS...
...YOUR MOTHER?
SST

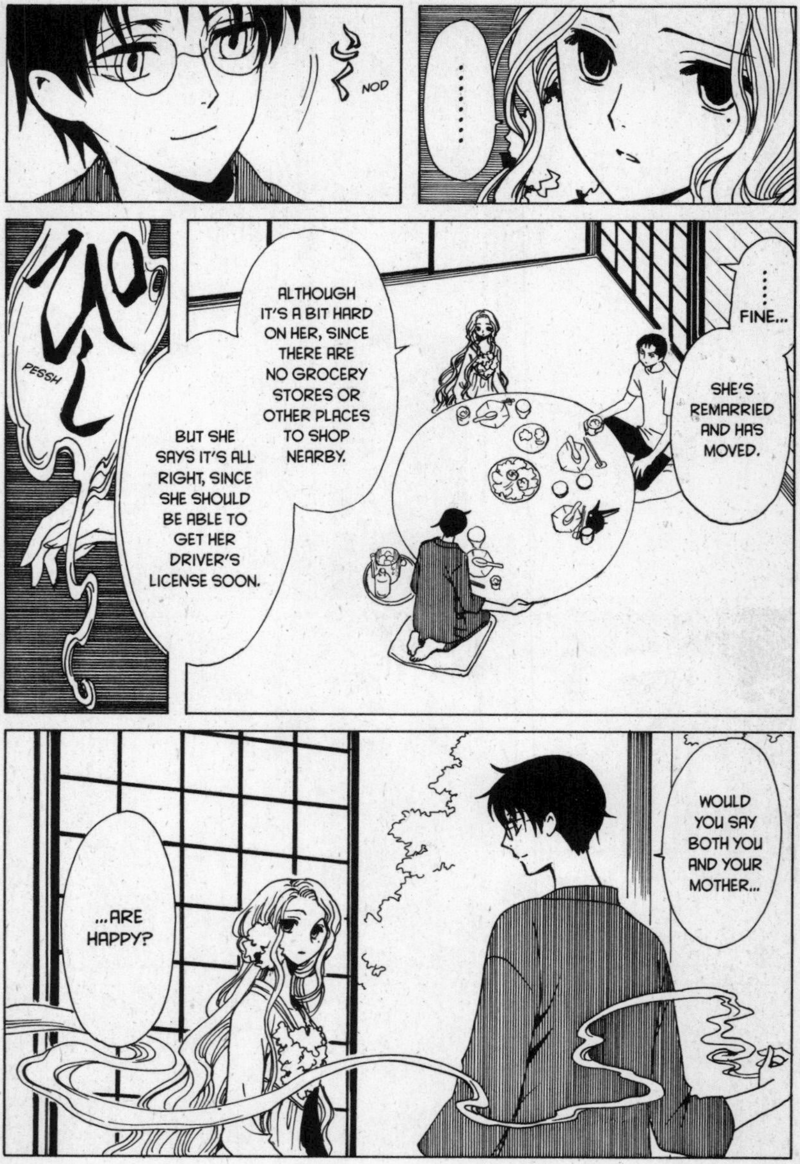
……
NOD
……FINE…
SHE'S REMARRIED AND HAS MOVED.
ALTHOUGH IT'S A BIT HARD ON HER, SINCE THERE ARE NO GROCERY STORES OR OTHER PLACES TO SHOP NEARBY.
BUT SHE SAYS IT'S ALL RIGHT, SINCE SHE SHOULD BE ABLE TO GET HER DRIVER'S LICENSE SOON.
PESSH
WOULD YOU SAY BOTH YOU AND YOUR MOTHER…
…ARE HAPPY?

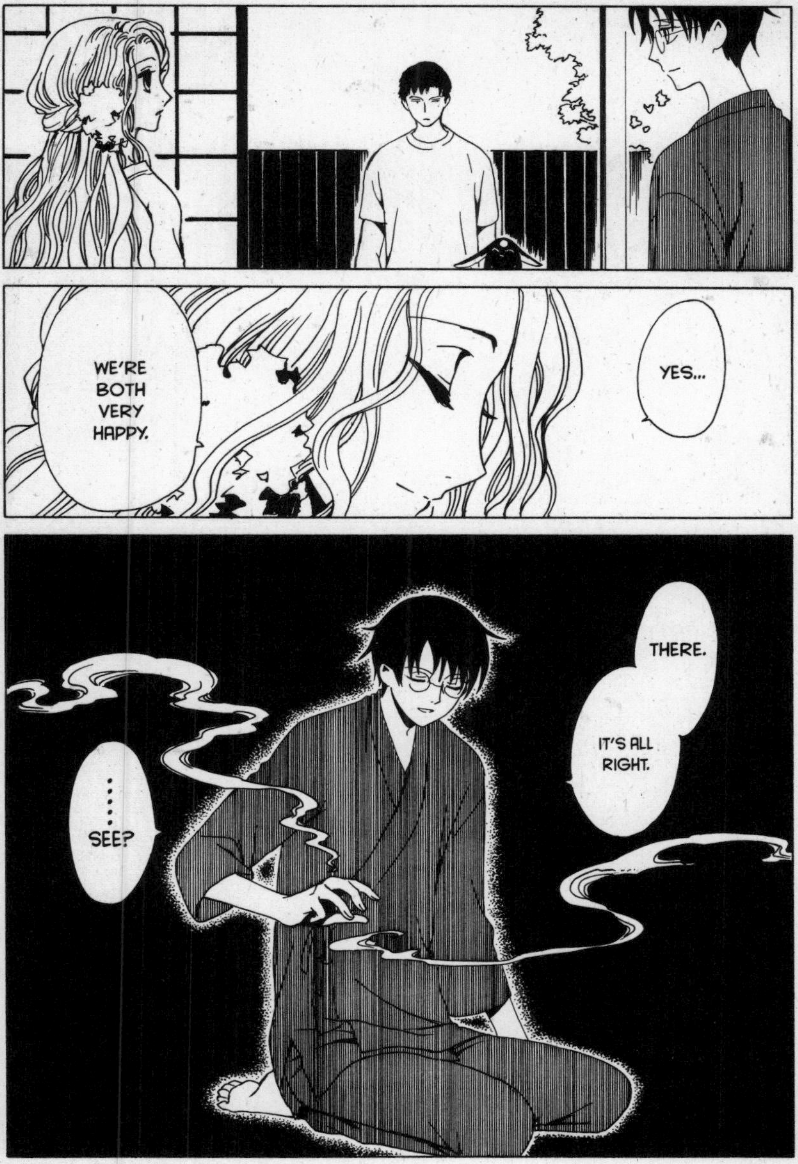
YES...
WE'RE BOTH VERY HAPPY.
THERE.
IT'S ALL RIGHT.
...SEE?

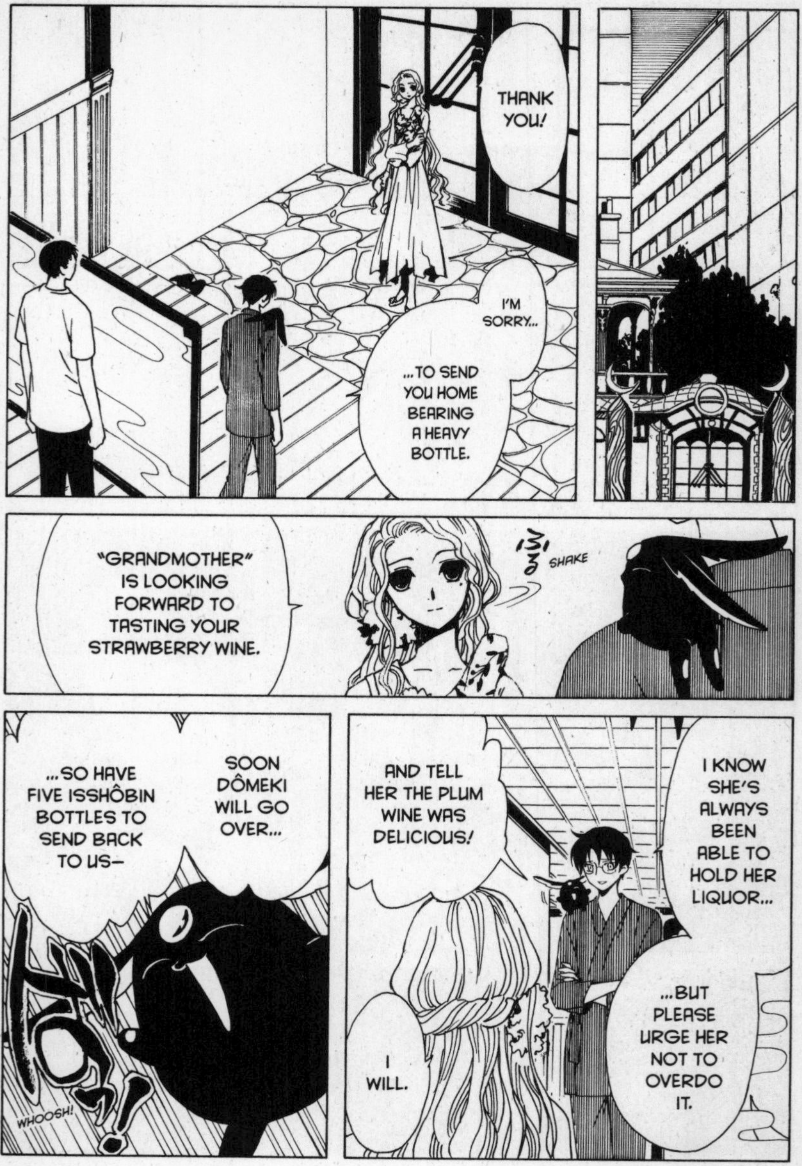
THANK YOU!
I'M SORRY...
...TO SEND YOU HOME BEARING A HEAVY BOTTLE.
SHAKE
"GRANDMOTHER" IS LOOKING FORWARD TO TASTING YOUR STRAWBERRY WINE.
I KNOW SHE'S ALWAYS BEEN ABLE TO HOLD HER LIQUOR...
...BUT PLEASE URGE HER NOT TO OVERDO IT.
AND TELL HER THE PLUM WINE WAS DELICIOUS!
I WILL.
SOON DÔMEKI WILL GO OVER...
...SO HAVE FIVE ISSHÔBIN BOTTLES TO SEND BACK TO US—
WHOOSH!

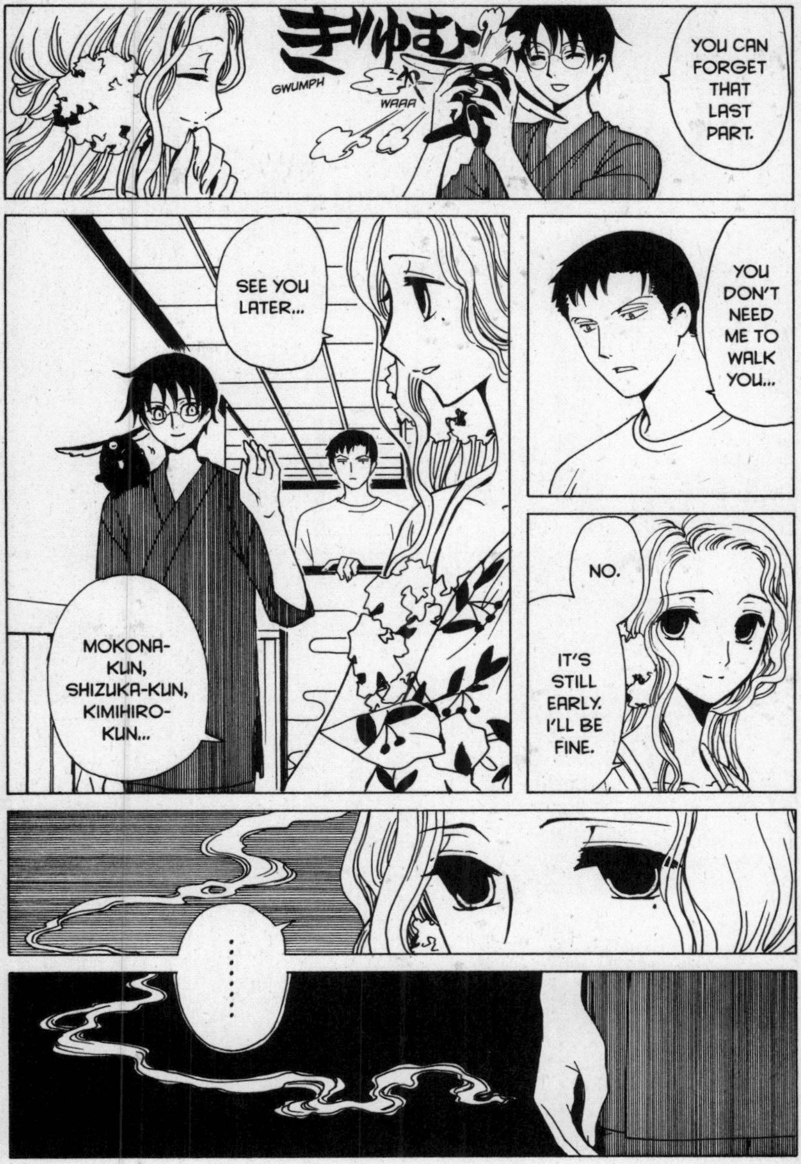
YOU CAN FORGET THAT LAST PART.
WAAA
GWUMPH
YOU DON'T NEED ME TO WALK YOU...
NO.
IT'S STILL EARLY. I'LL BE FINE.
SEE YOU LATER...
MOKONA-KUN, SHIZUKA-KUN, KIMIHIRO-KUN...
......

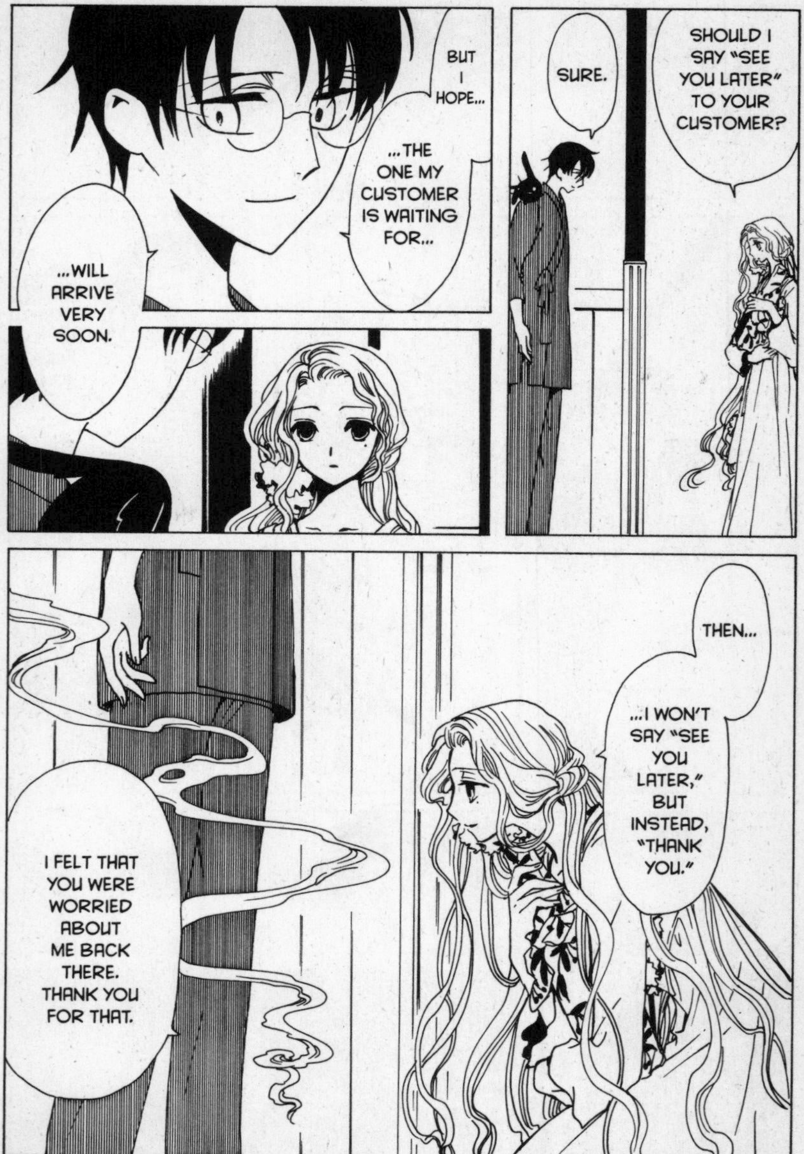
SHOULD I SAY "SEE YOU LATER" TO YOUR CUSTOMER?
SURE.
BUT I HOPE...
...THE ONE MY CUSTOMER IS WAITING FOR...
...WILL ARRIVE VERY SOON.
THEN...
...I WON'T SAY "SEE YOU LATER," BUT INSTEAD, "THANK YOU."
I FELT THAT YOU WERE WORRIED ABOUT ME BACK THERE. THANK YOU FOR THAT.

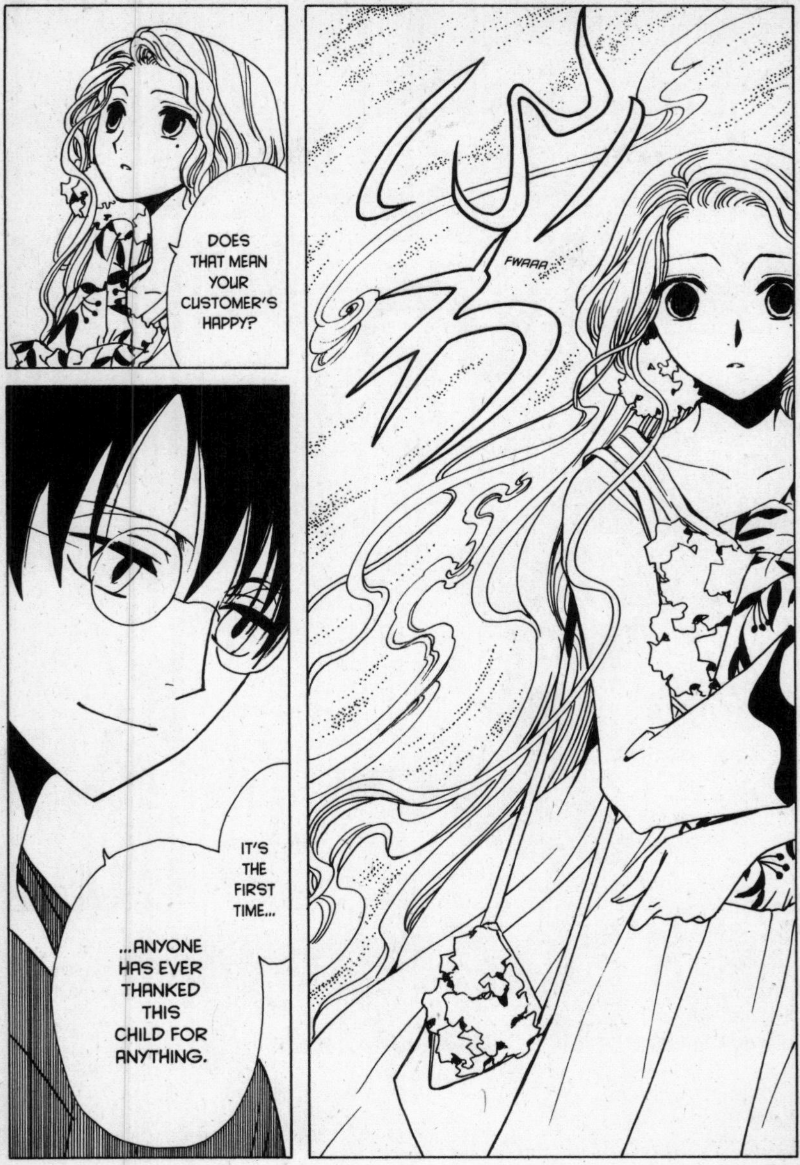
FWAAA
DOES THAT MEAN YOUR CUSTOMER'S HAPPY?
IT'S THE FIRST TIME...
...ANYONE HAS EVER THANKED THIS CHILD FOR ANYTHING.

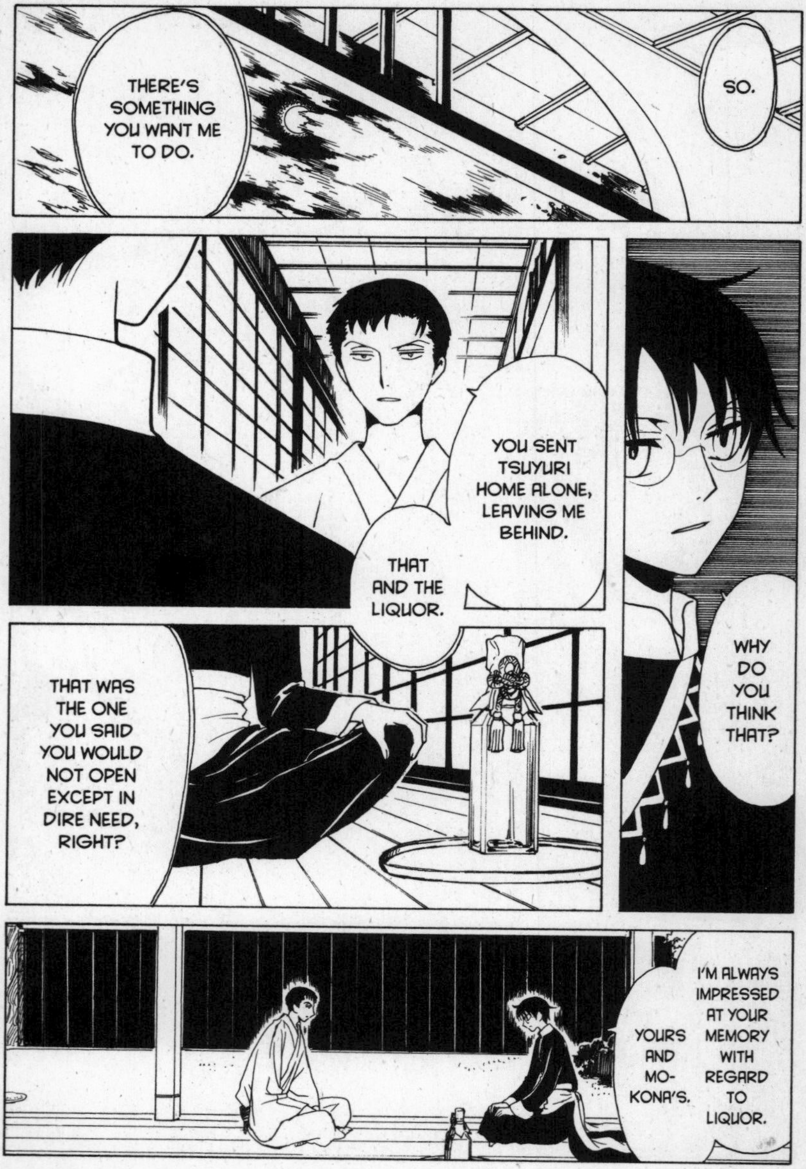
SO.
THERE'S SOMETHING YOU WANT ME TO DO.
WHY DO YOU THINK THAT?
YOU SENT TSUYURI HOME ALONE, LEAVING ME BEHIND.
THAT AND THE LIQUOR.
THAT WAS THE ONE YOU SAID YOU WOULD NOT OPEN EXCEPT IN DIRE NEED, RIGHT?
I'M ALWAYS IMPRESSED AT YOUR MEMORY WITH REGARD TO LIQUOR.
YOURS AND MO-KONA'S.

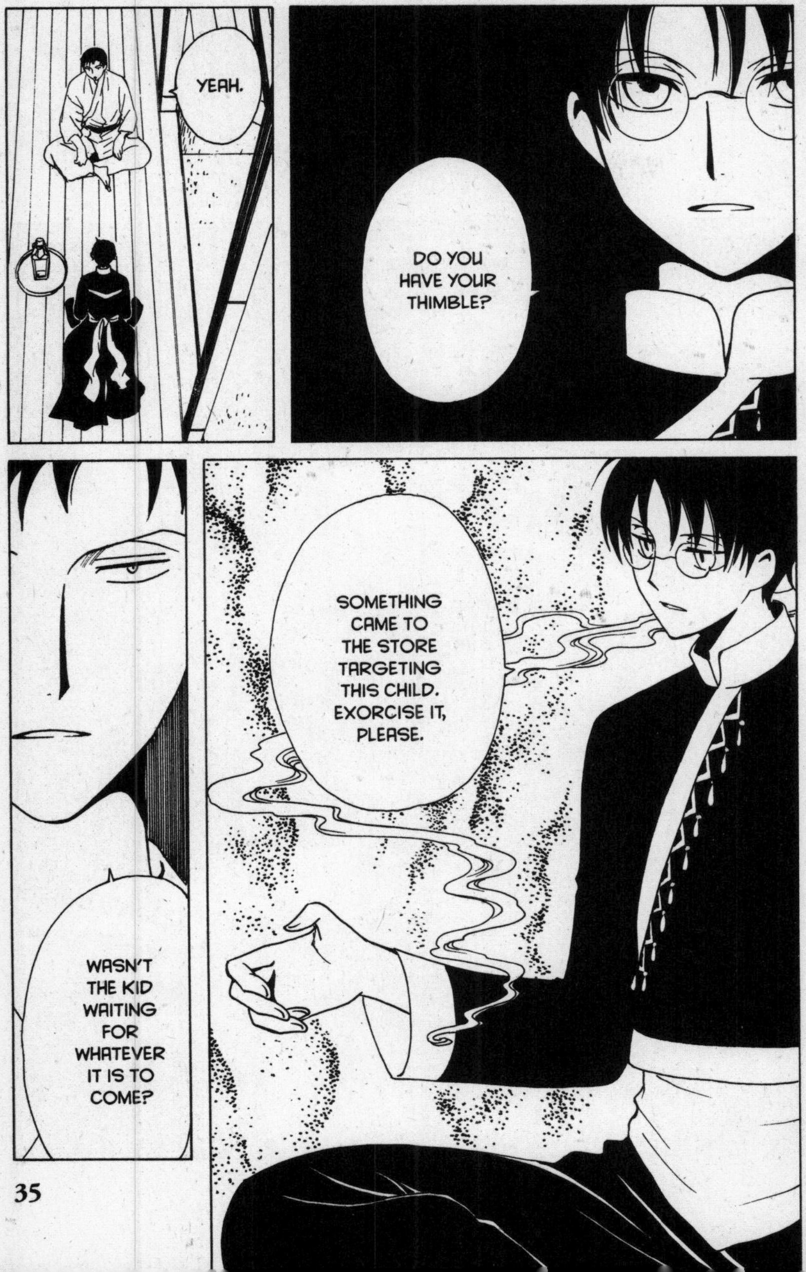
DO YOU HAVE YOUR THIMBLE?
YEAH.
SOMETHING CAME TO THE STORE TARGETING THIS CHILD. EXORCISE IT, PLEASE.
WASN'T THE KID WAITING FOR WHATEVER IT IS TO COME?

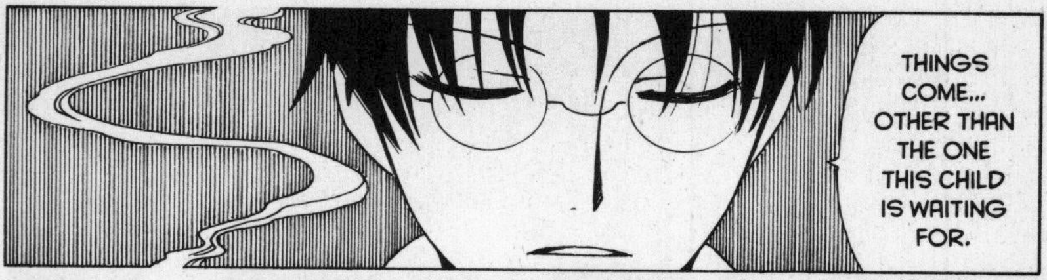
THINGS COME... OTHER THAN THE ONE THIS CHILD IS WAITING FOR.

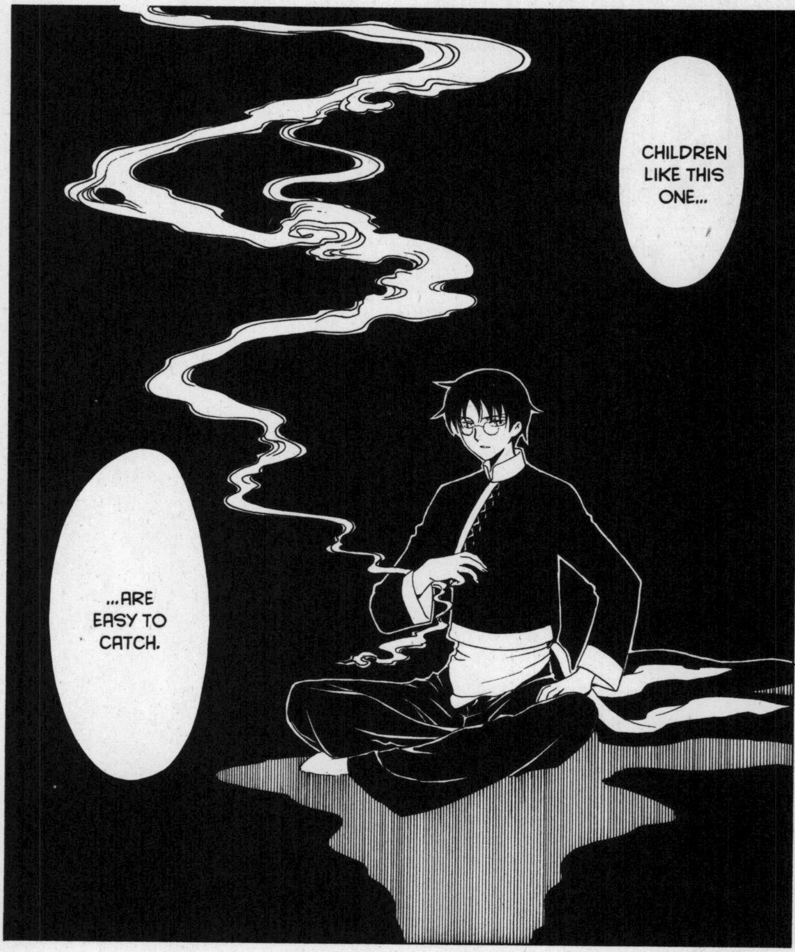
CHILDREN LIKE THIS ONE...
...ARE EASY TO CATCH.

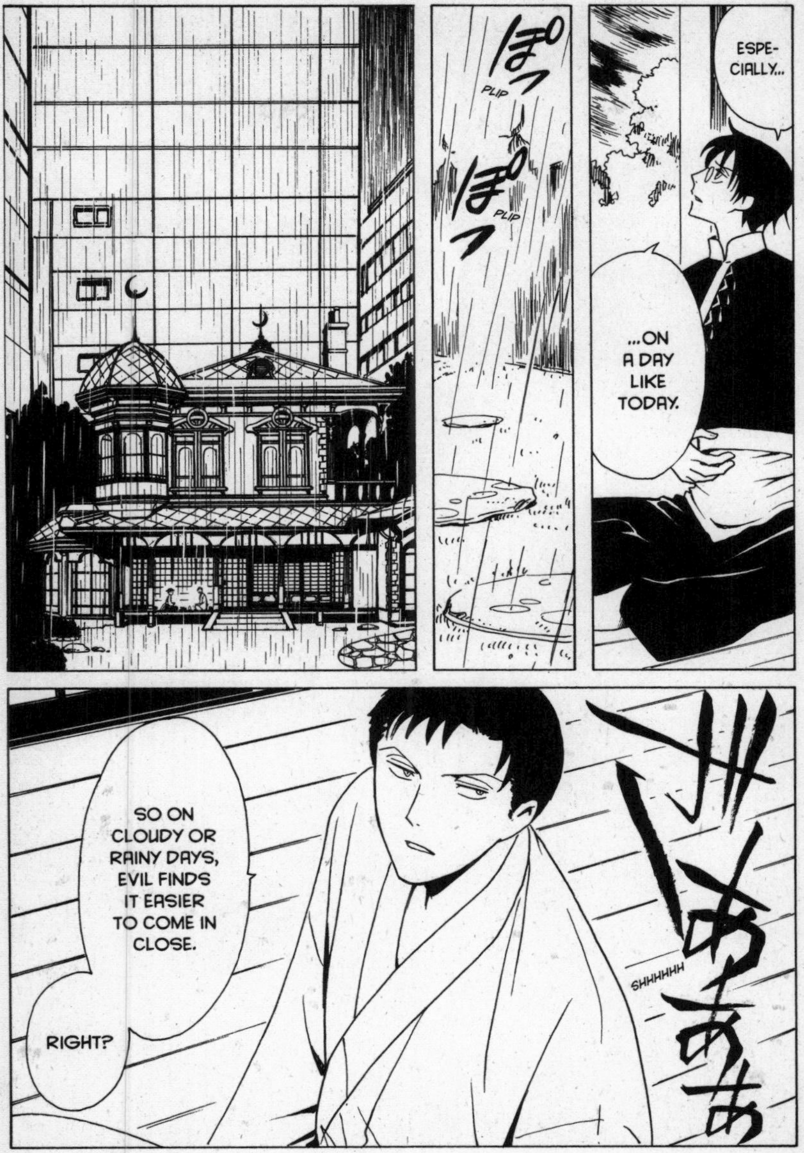
ESPE-CIALLY...
...ON A DAY LIKE TODAY.
ぽつ
PLIP
ぽつ
PLIP
ザーああああ
SHHHHHH
SO ON CLOUDY OR RAINY DAYS, EVIL FINDS IT EASIER TO COME IN CLOSE.
RIGHT?

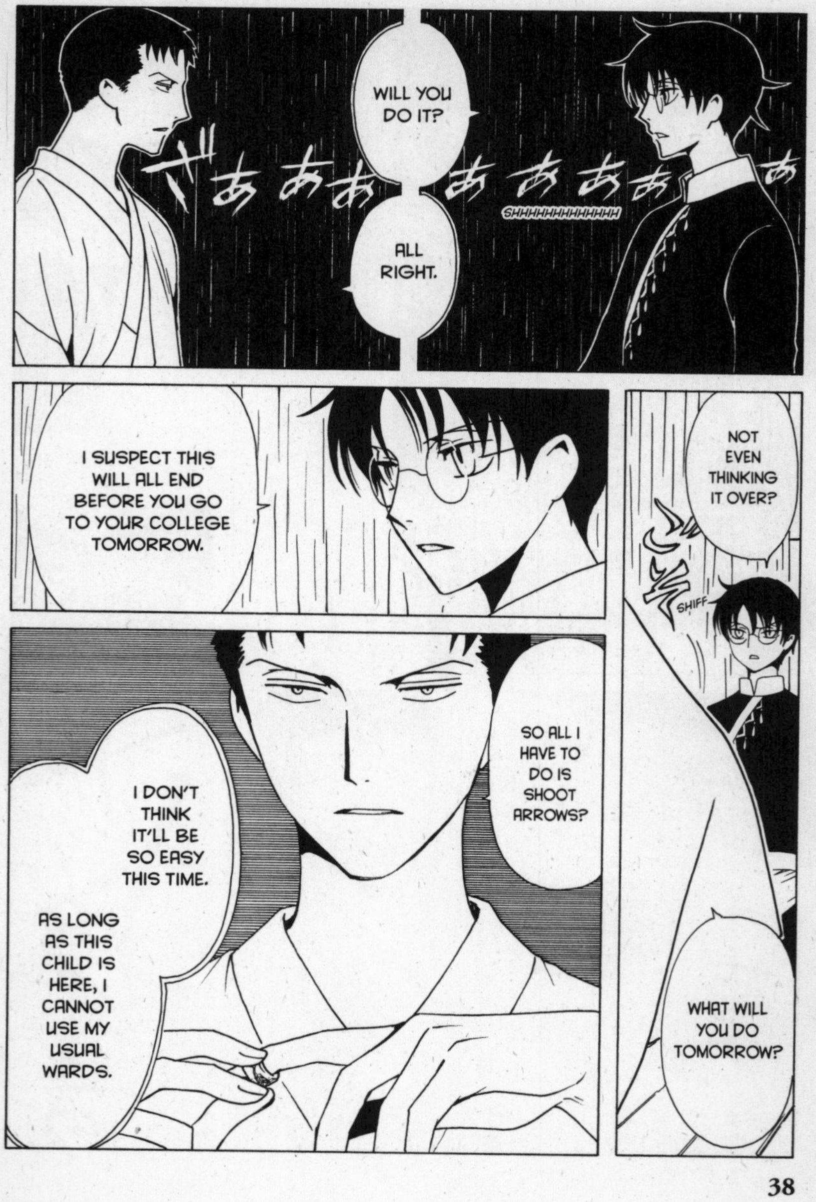
WILL YOU DO IT?
ザあああああああああ
SHHHHHHHHHHHHHH
ALL RIGHT.
NOT EVEN THINKING IT OVER?
SHIFF
WHAT WILL YOU DO TOMORROW?
I SUSPECT THIS WILL ALL END BEFORE YOU GO TO YOUR COLLEGE TOMORROW.
SO ALL I HAVE TO DO IS SHOOT ARROWS?
I DON'T THINK IT'LL BE SO EASY THIS TIME.
AS LONG AS THIS CHILD IS HERE, I CANNOT USE MY USUAL WARDS.

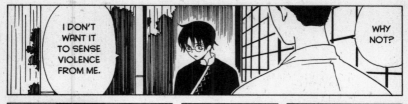

WHY NOT?
I DON'T WANT IT TO SENSE VIOLENCE FROM ME.
LET'S GO INSIDE.
SST
YOU DON'T WANT TO?
FWAA
BUT INSIDE IS SAFER THAN OUTSIDE.
THE WARDS ARE MORE EFFECTIVE THERE...
THERE'S NO WAY...
...I CAN CONVINCE YOU?
...I SEE.
I'M HAPPY THAT YOU LIKE MY GARDEN SO MUCH.
BE-SIDES...

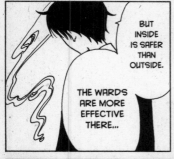

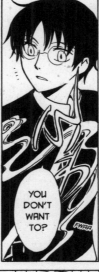

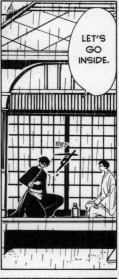

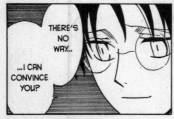

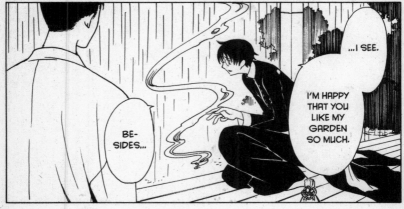

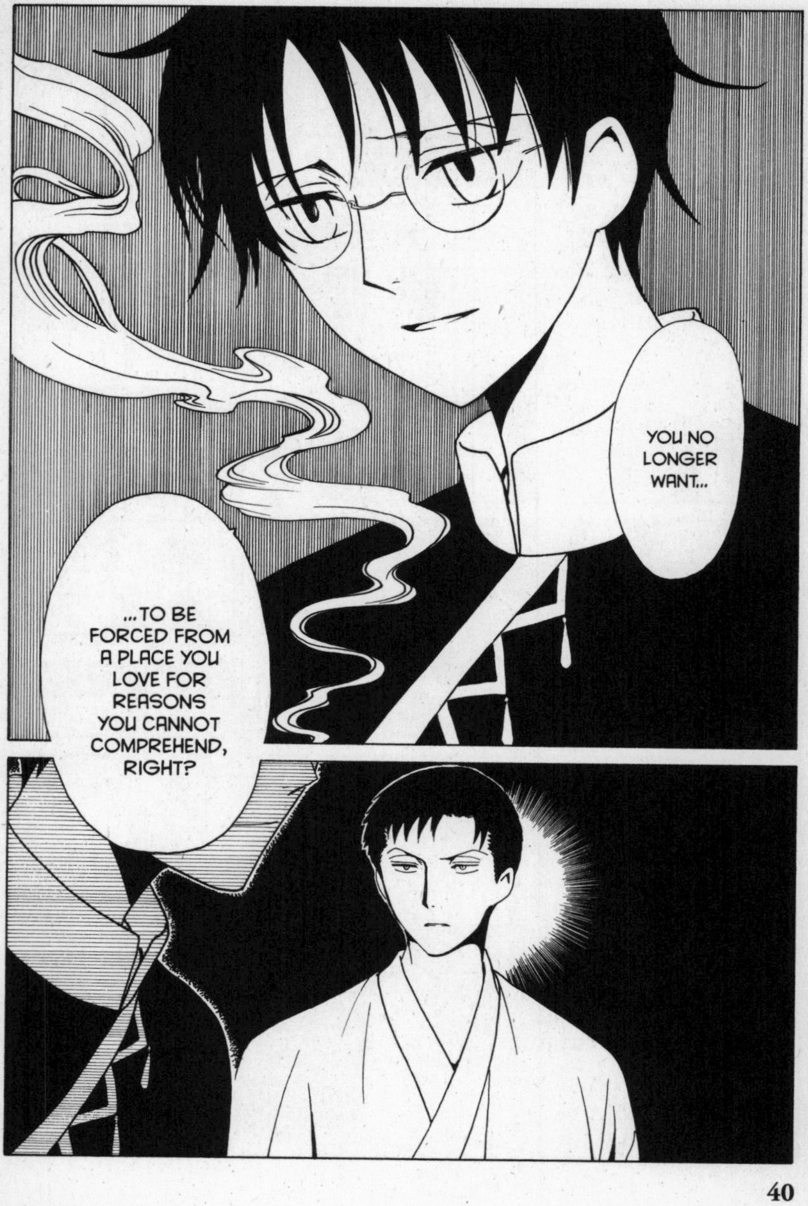
YOU NO LONGER WANT...
...TO BE FORCED FROM A PLACE YOU LOVE FOR REASONS YOU CANNOT COMPREHEND, RIGHT?

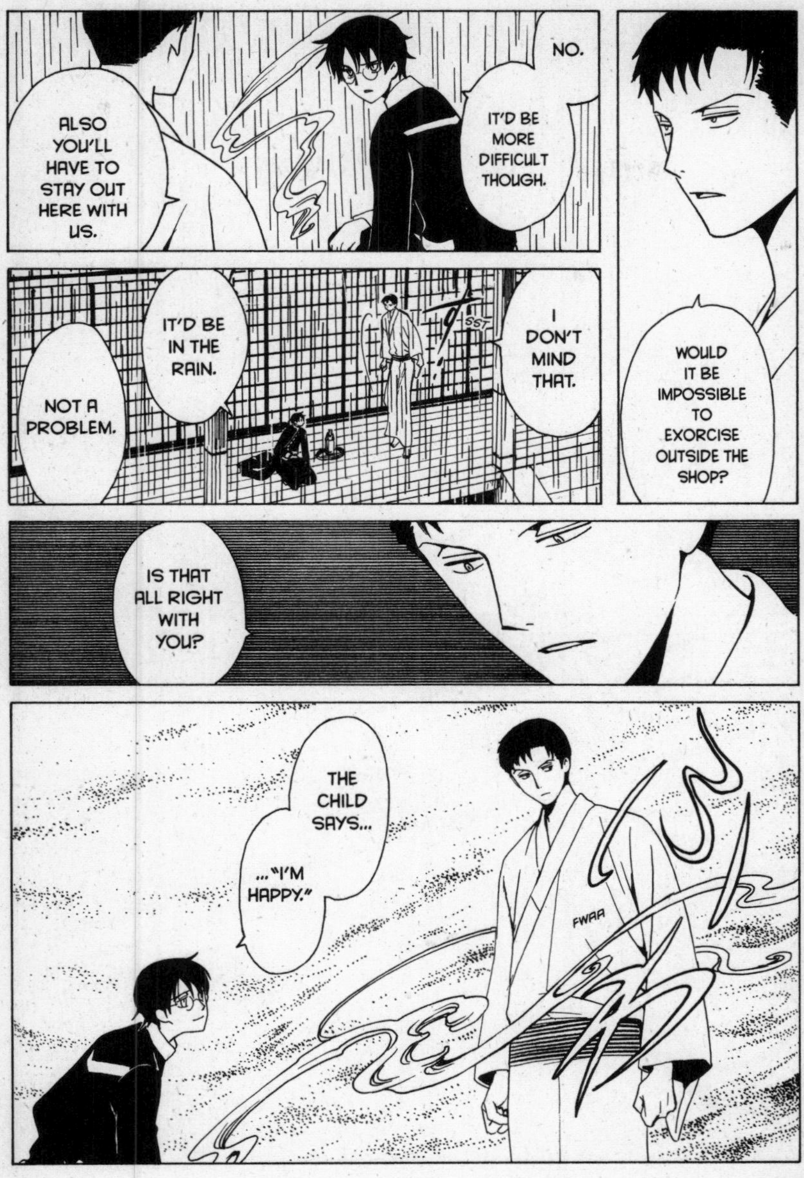
WOULD IT BE IMPOSSIBLE TO EXORCISE OUTSIDE THE SHOP?
NO.
IT'D BE MORE DIFFICULT THOUGH.
ALSO YOU'LL HAVE TO STAY OUT HERE WITH US.
I DON'T MIND THAT.
SST
IT'D BE IN THE RAIN.
NOT A PROBLEM.
IS THAT ALL RIGHT WITH YOU?
FWAA
THE CHILD SAYS...
..."I'M HAPPY."

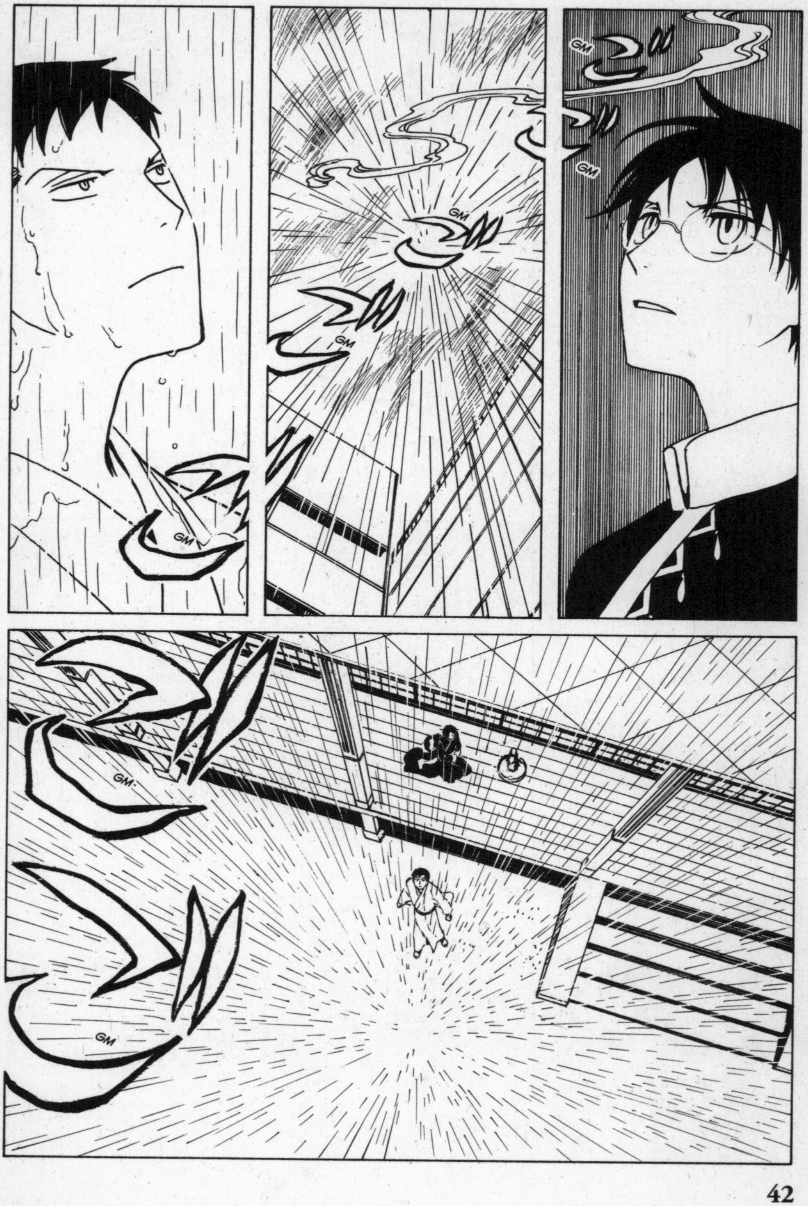
GM
GM
GM
GM
GM
GM
GM

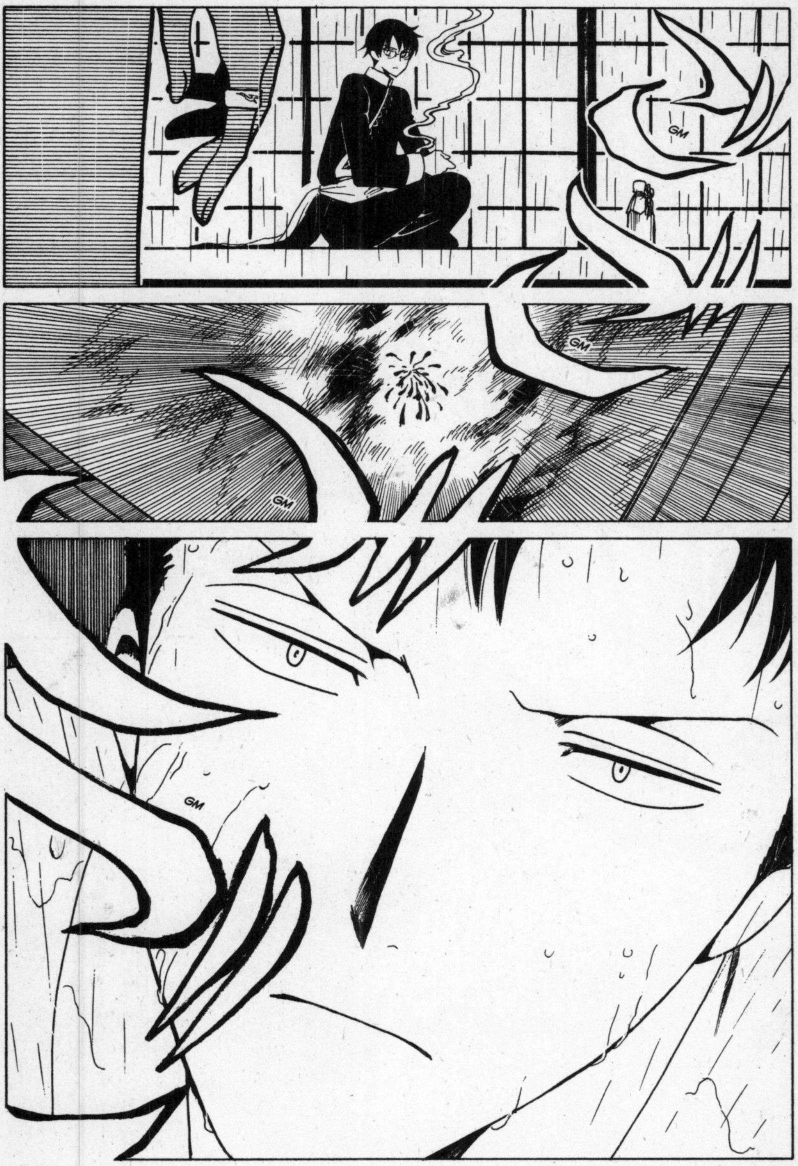
GM
GM
GM
GM

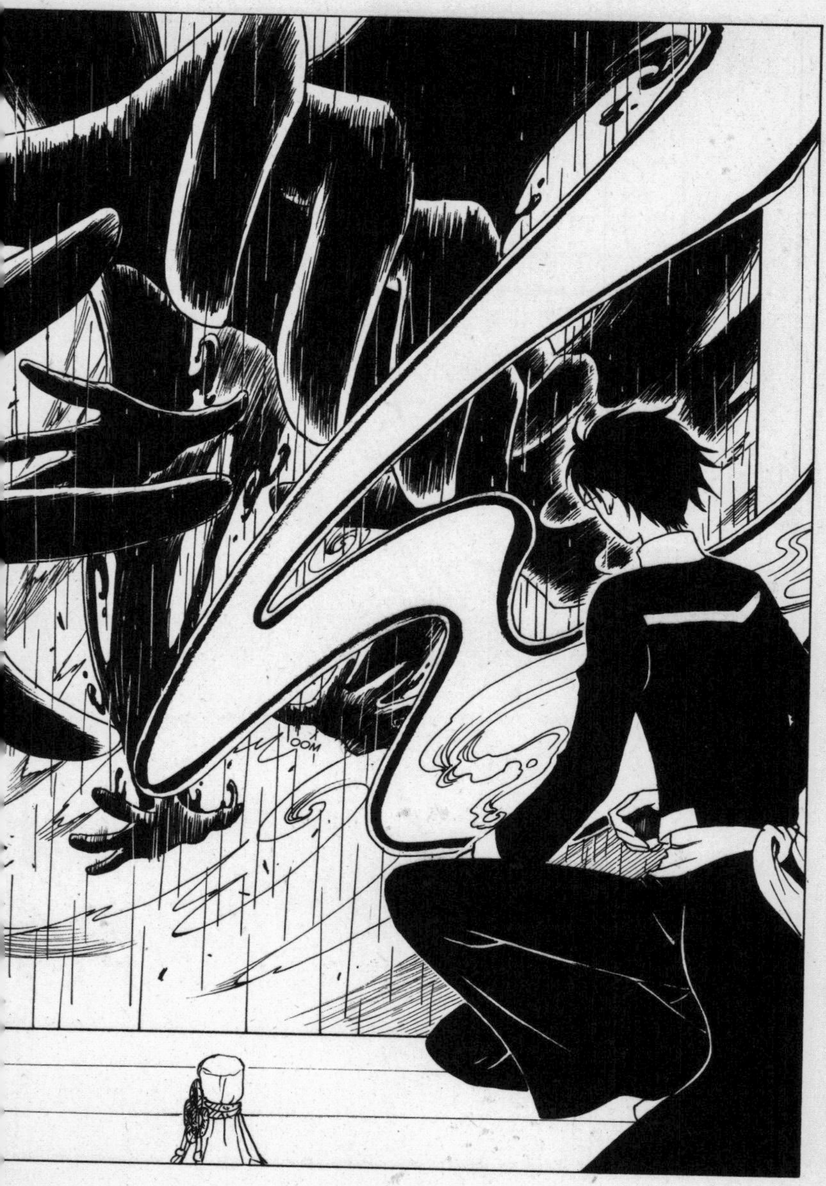
OOM

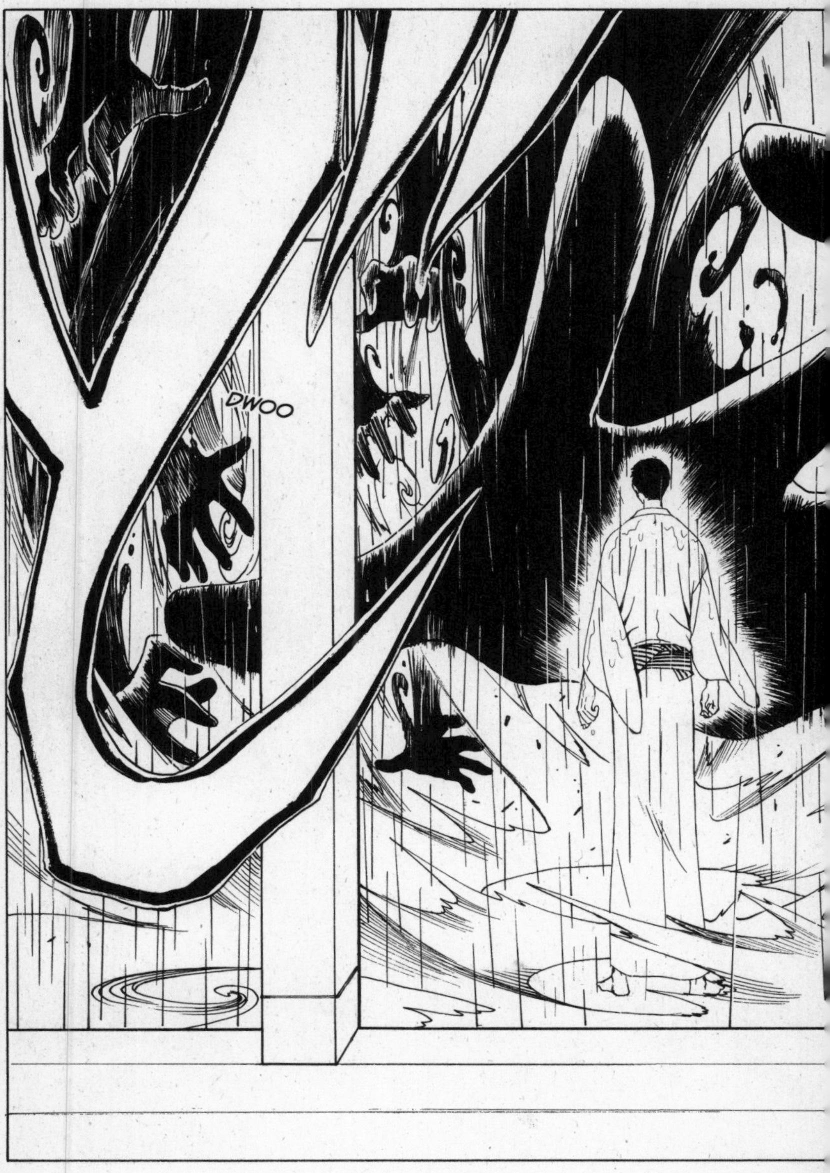
DWOO

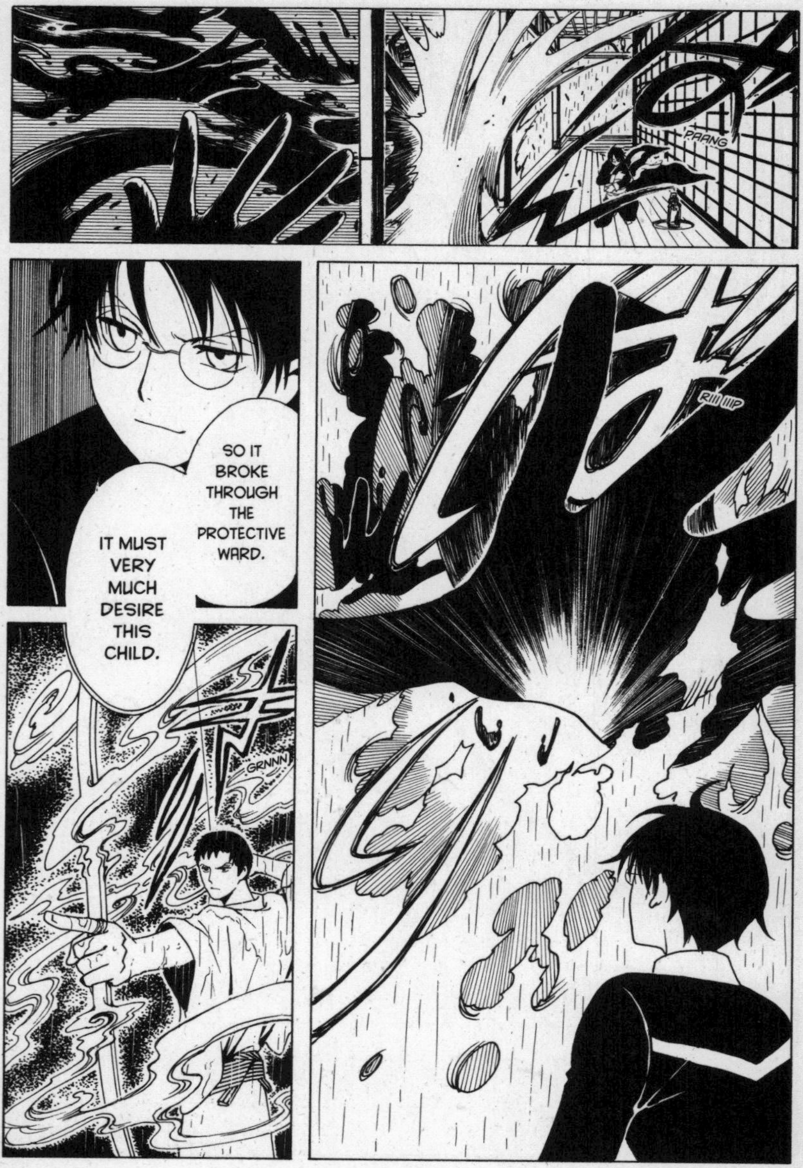
PAANG
RIIIIIP
SO IT BROKE THROUGH THE PROTECTIVE WARD.
IT MUST VERY MUCH DESIRE THIS CHILD.
GRNNN

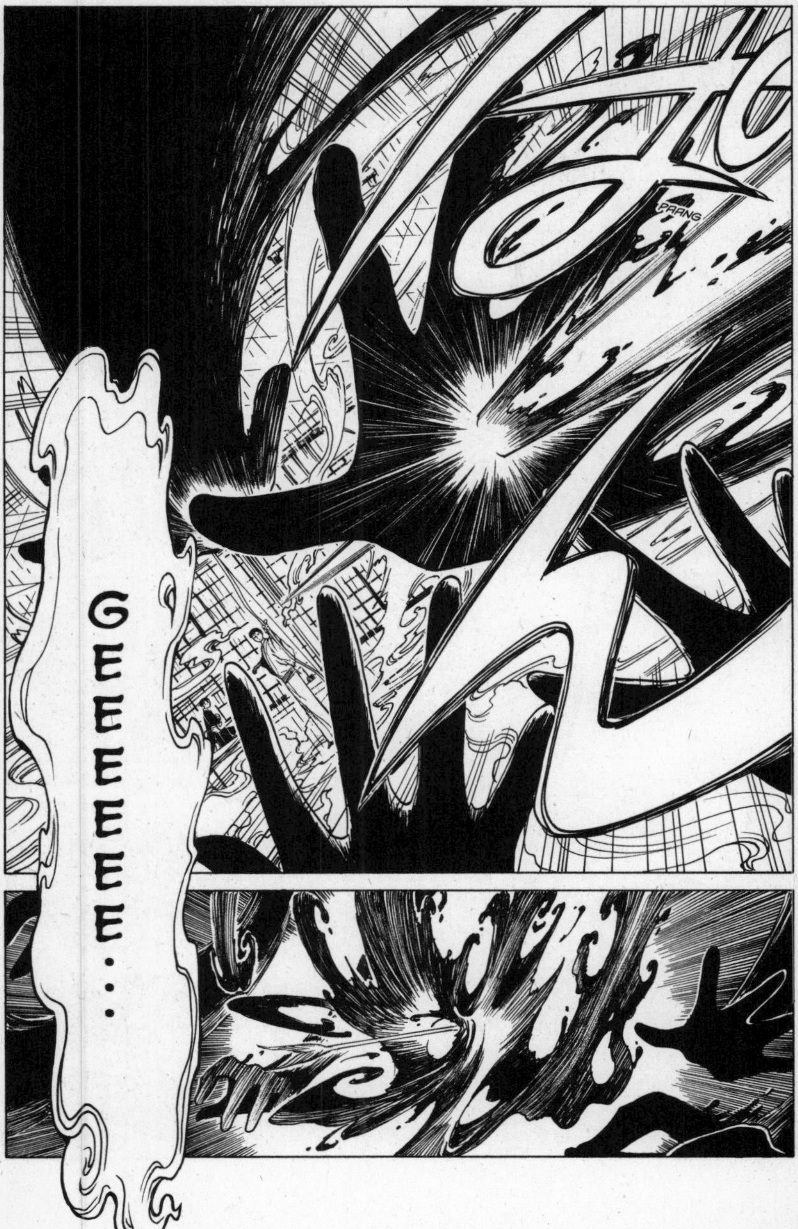
PAANG
GEEEEEEE...

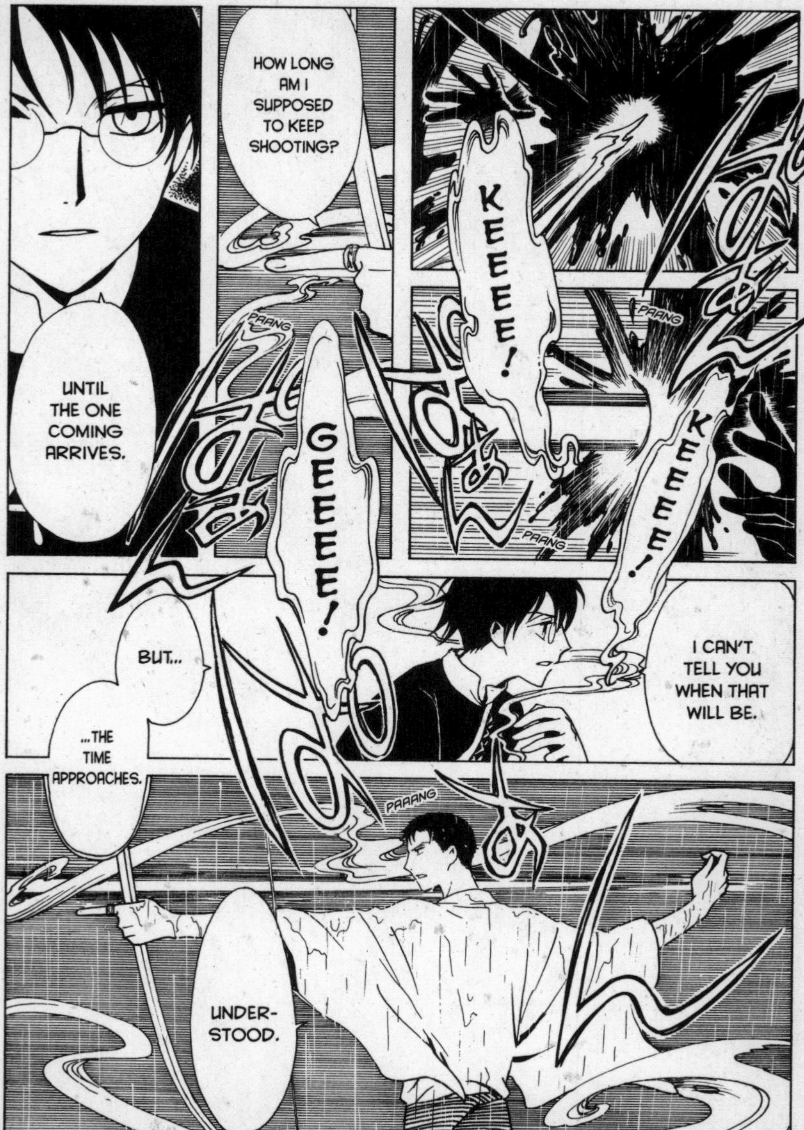
KEEEE!
PAANG
KEEEE!
PAANG
HOW LONG AM I SUPPOSED TO KEEP SHOOTING?
PAANG
GEEEE!
UNTIL THE ONE COMING ARRIVES.
I CAN'T TELL YOU WHEN THAT WILL BE.
BUT...
...THE TIME APPROACHES.
PAAANG
UNDER-STOOD.

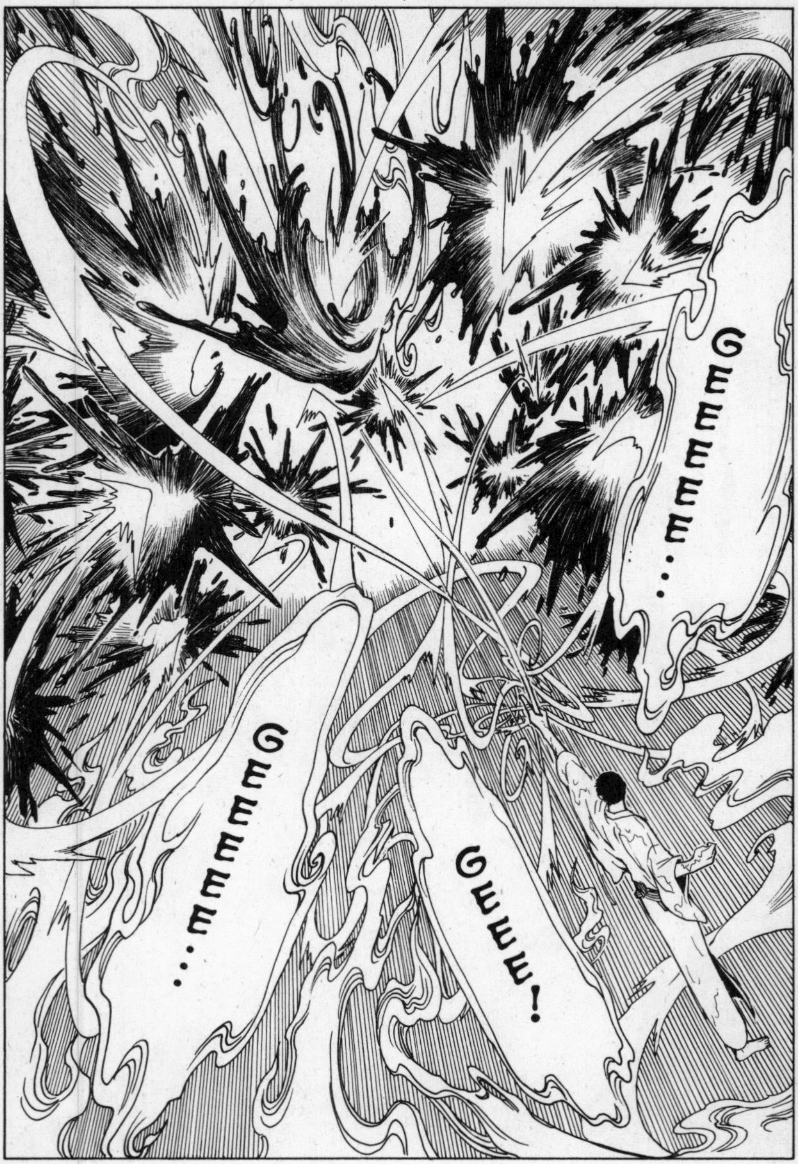
GEEEEEE...
GEEEE!
GEEEEEE...

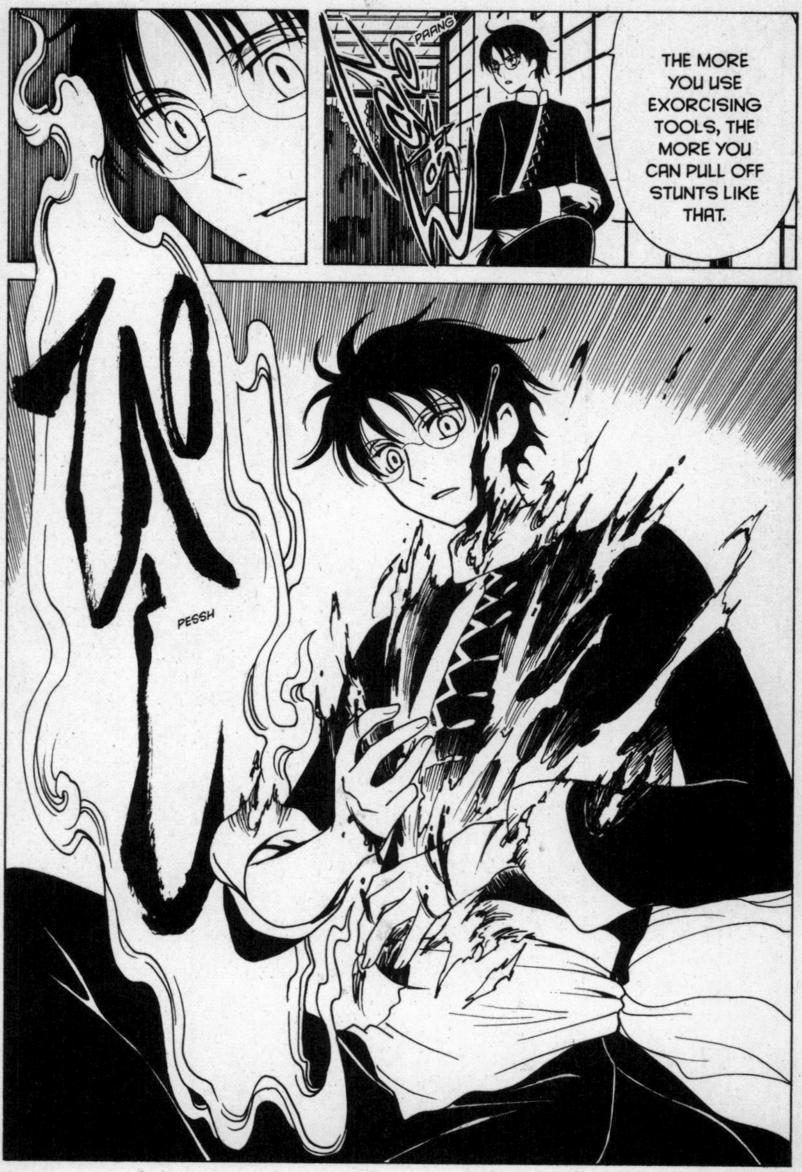
THE MORE YOU USE EXORCISING TOOLS, THE MORE YOU CAN PULL OFF STUNTS LIKE THAT.
PRANG
PESSH

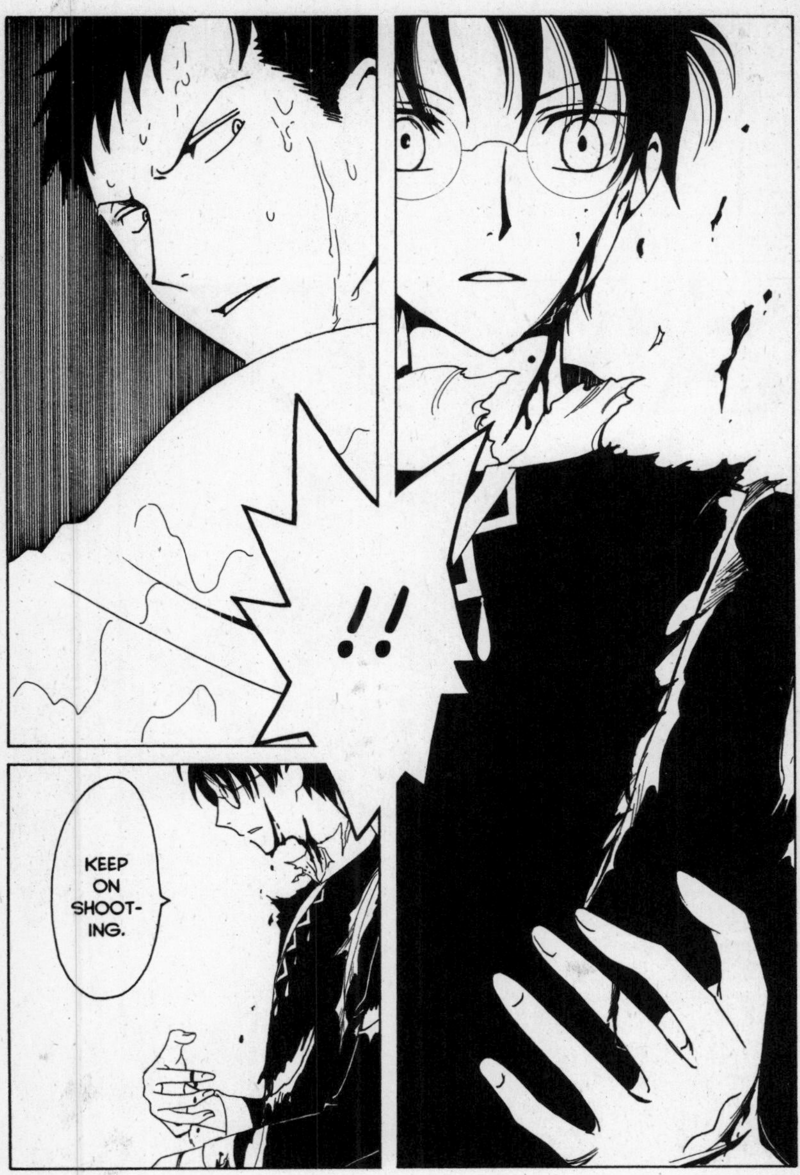
!!
KEEP ON SHOOT-ING.

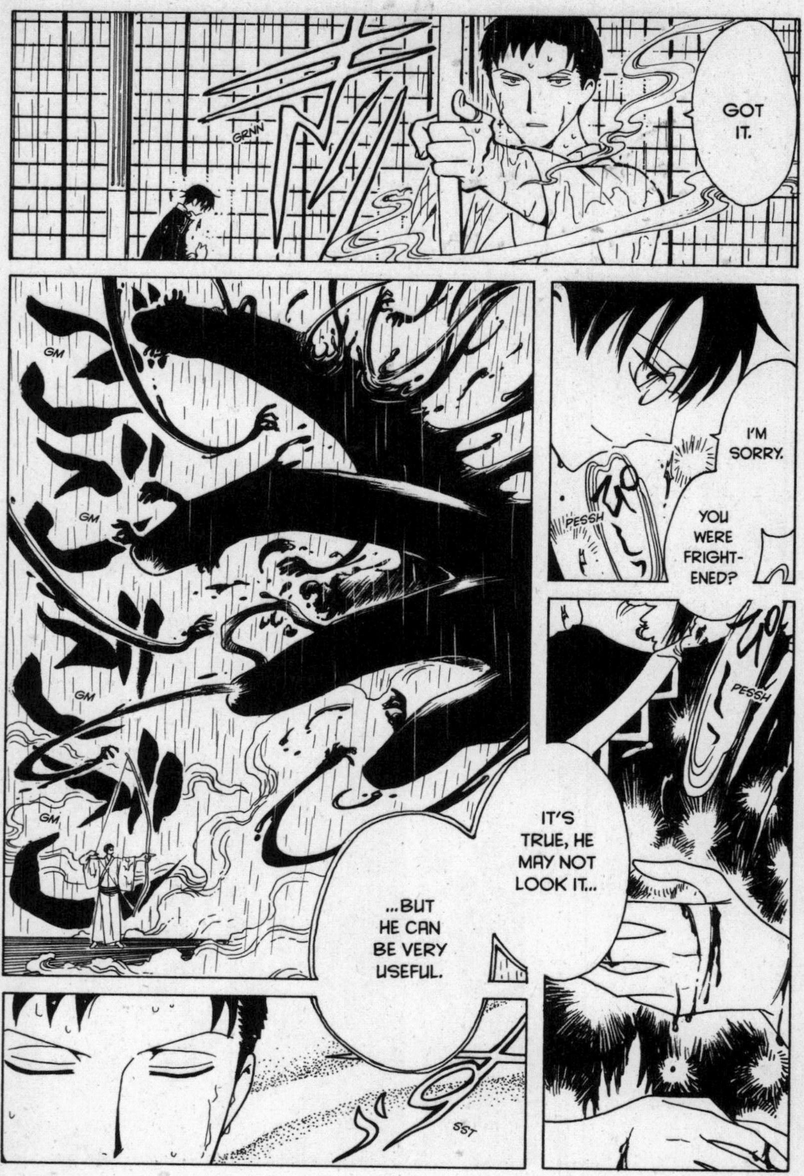
GOT IT.
GRNN
I'M SORRY.
YOU WERE FRIGHTENED?
PESSH
PESSH
IT'S TRUE, HE MAY NOT LOOK IT...
...BUT HE CAN BE VERY USEFUL.
GM
GM
GM
GM
SST

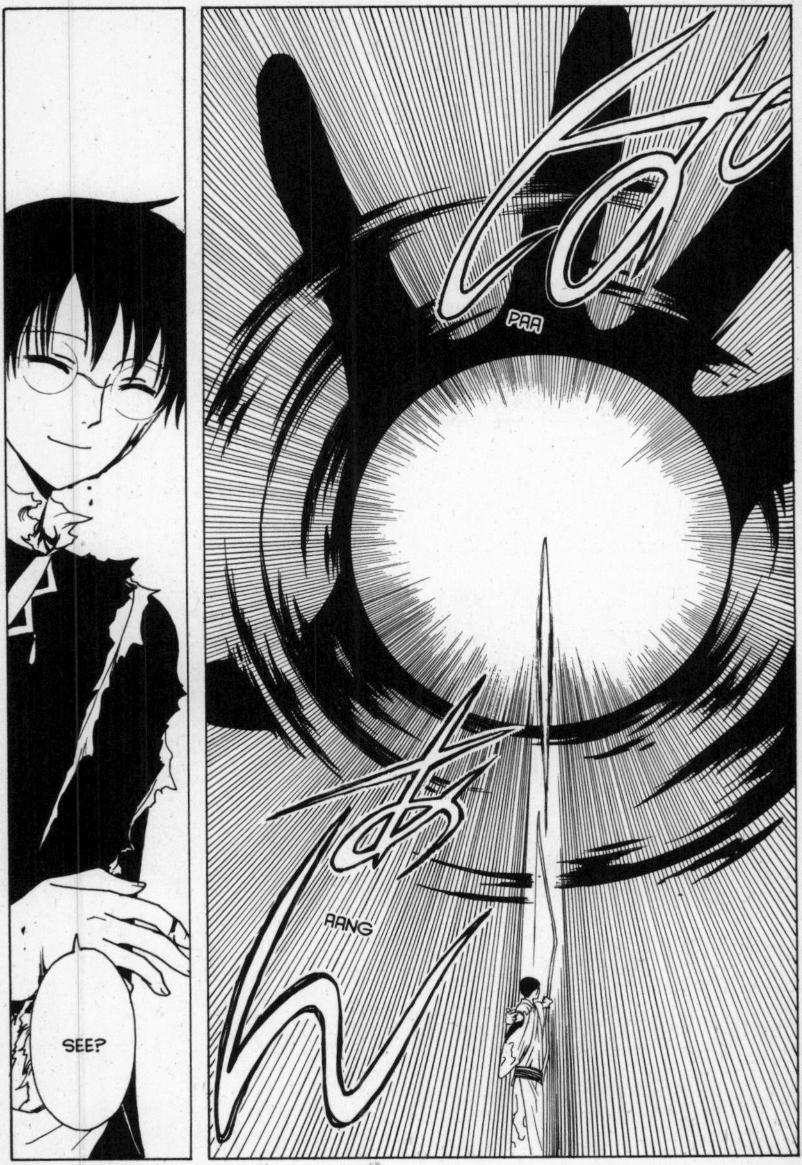
PAA
AANG
SEE?

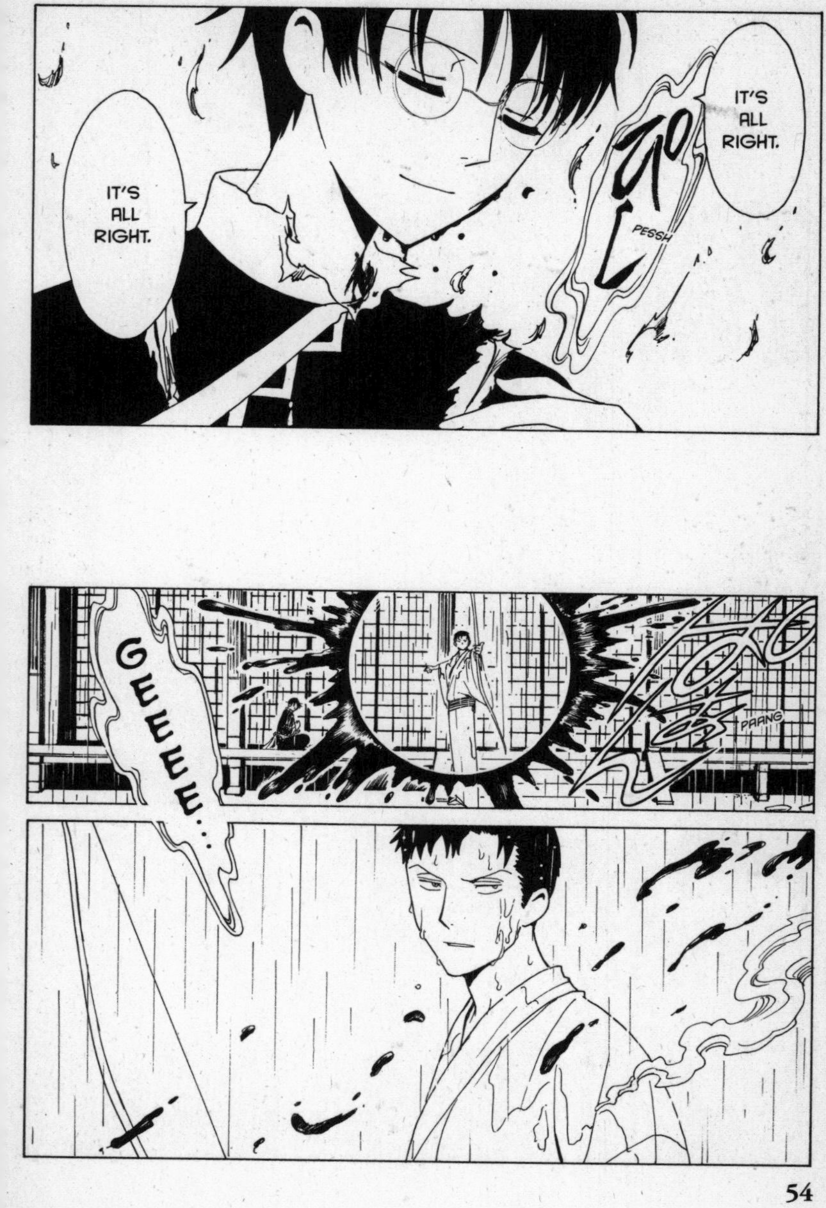
IT'S ALL RIGHT.
PESSH
IT'S ALL RIGHT.
PAANG
GEEEE...

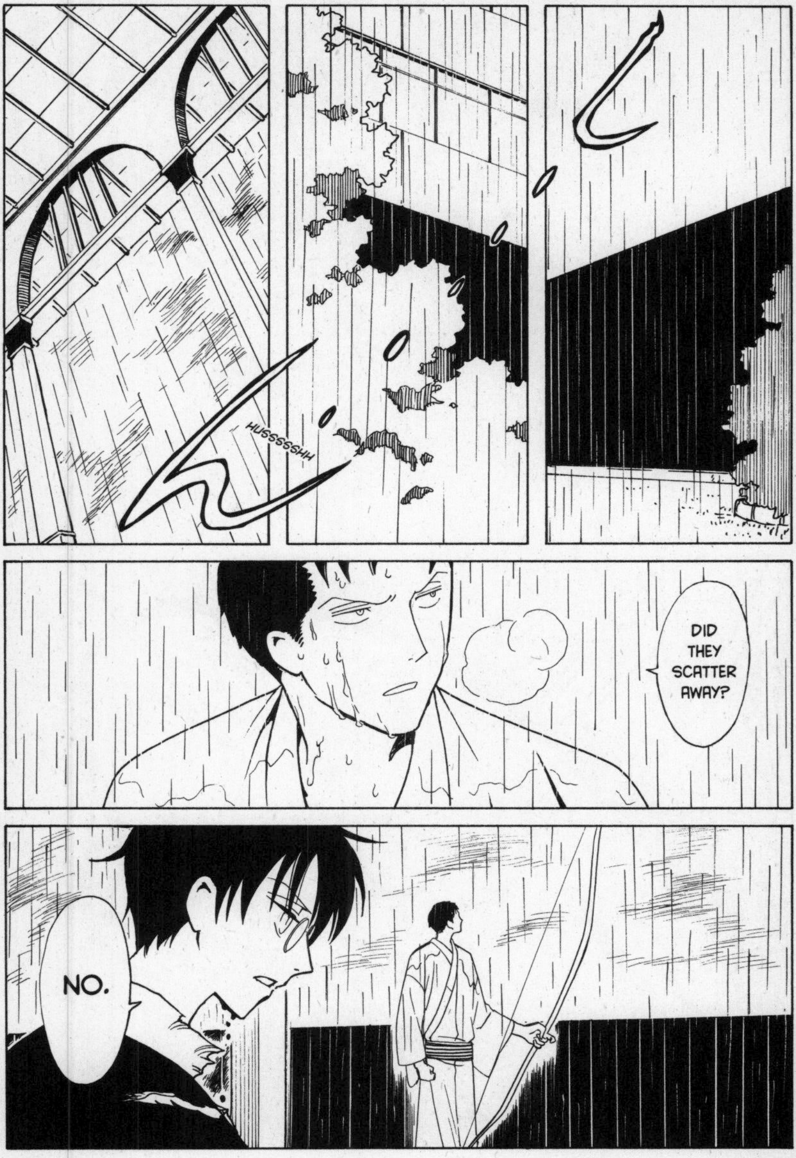
HUSSSSSHH
DID THEY SCATTER AWAY?
NO.

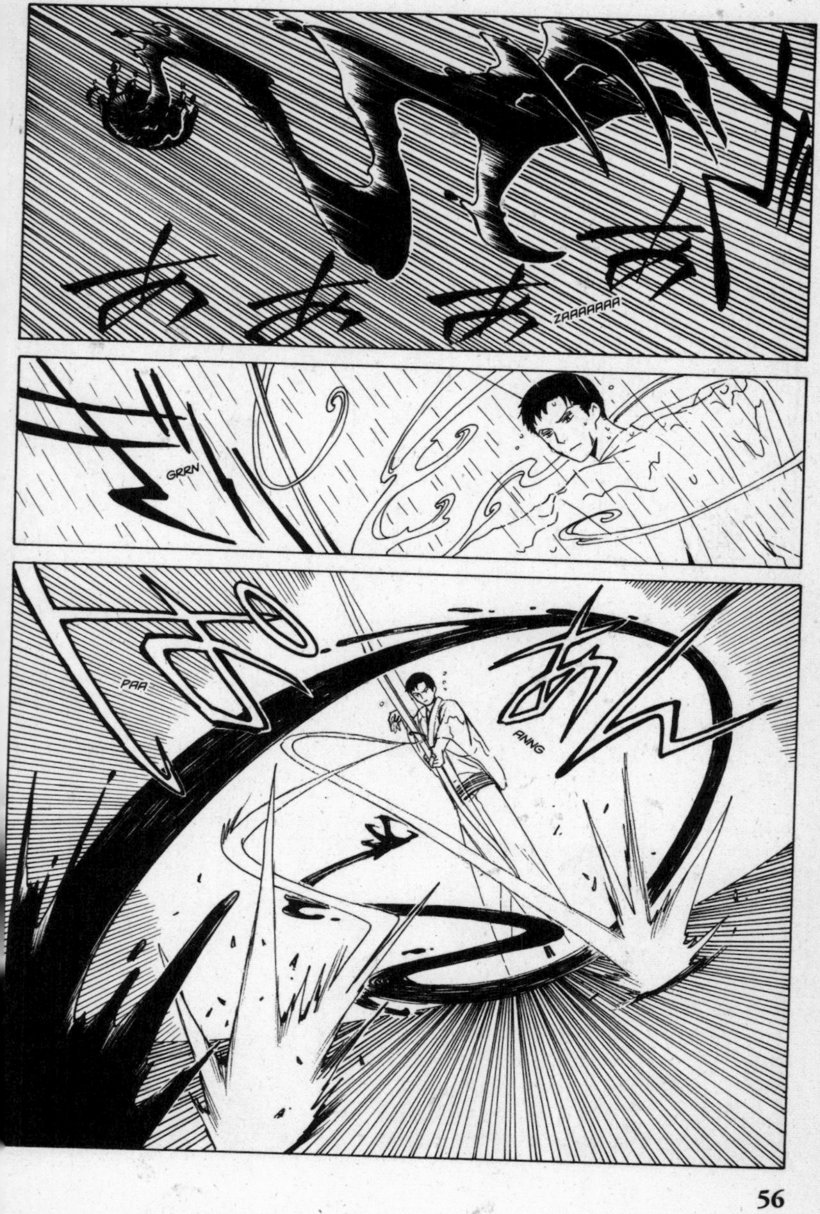
ZAAAAAAA
GRRN
PAA
ANNG

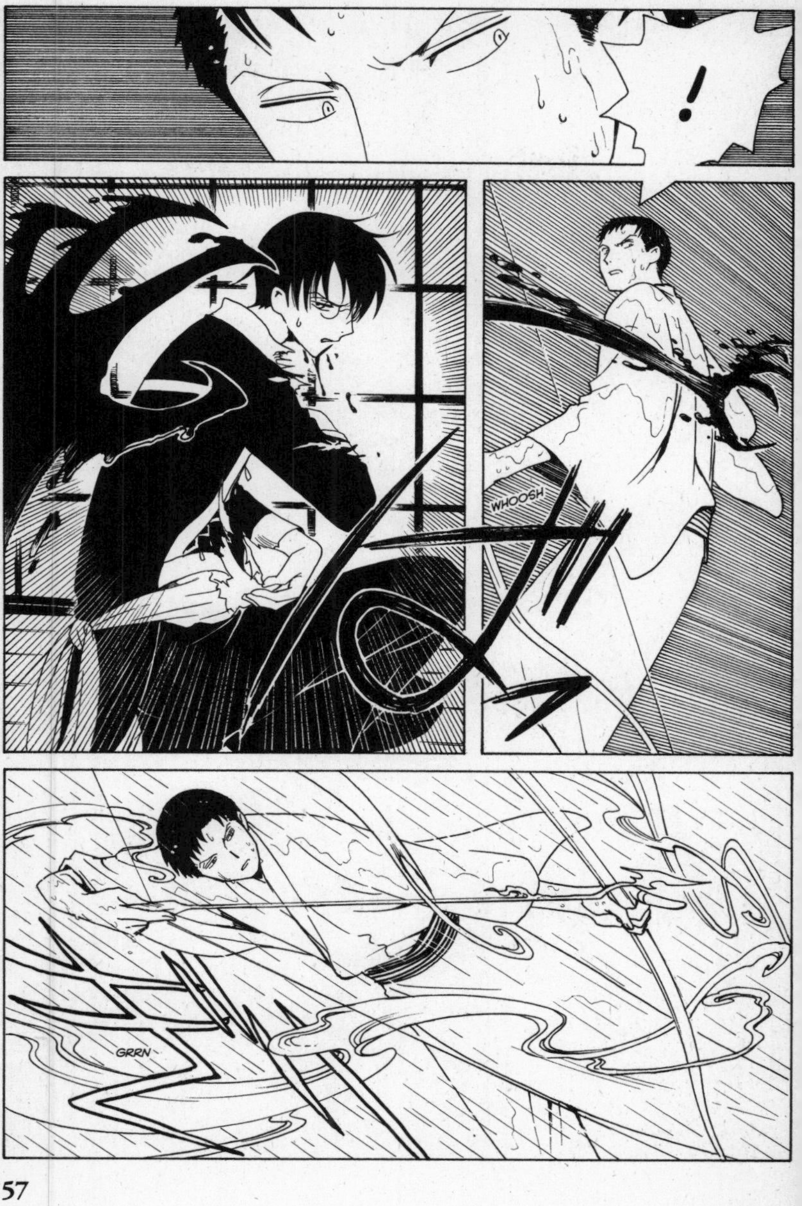
!
WHOOSH
GRRN

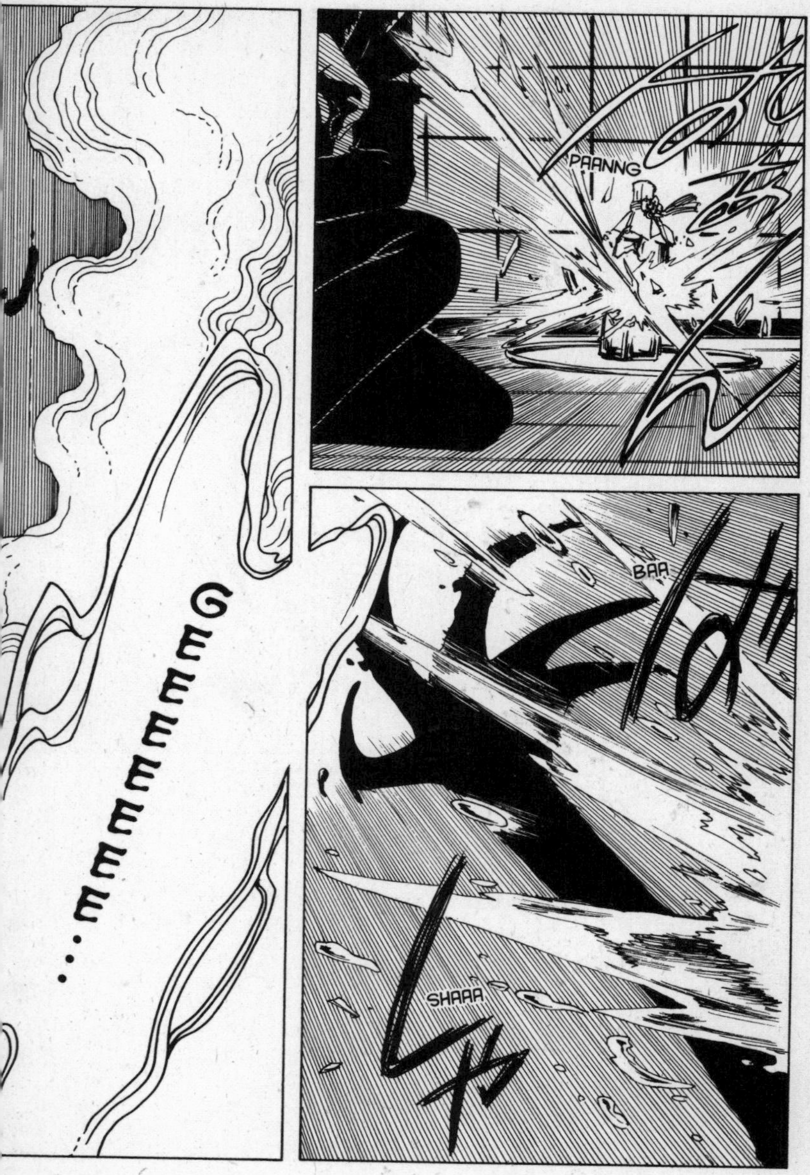
PAANNG
BAA
SHAAA
GEEEEEEE...

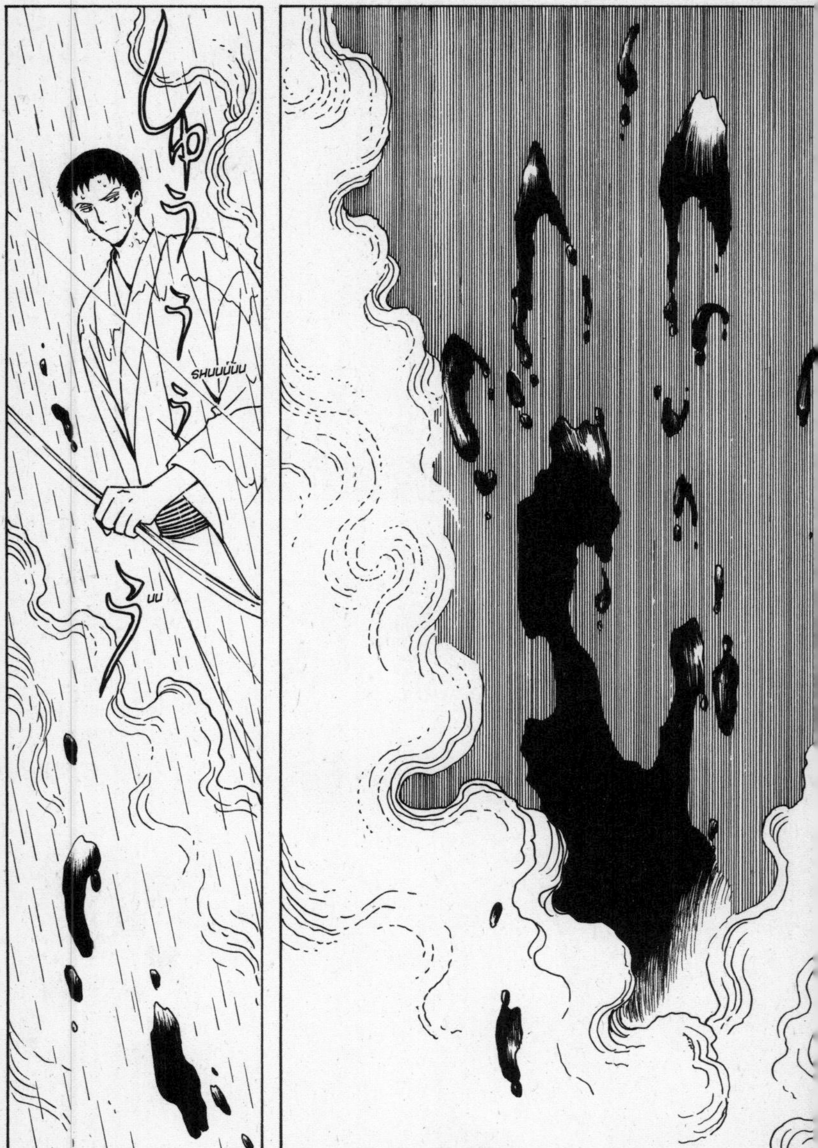
SHUUUUUU
UU

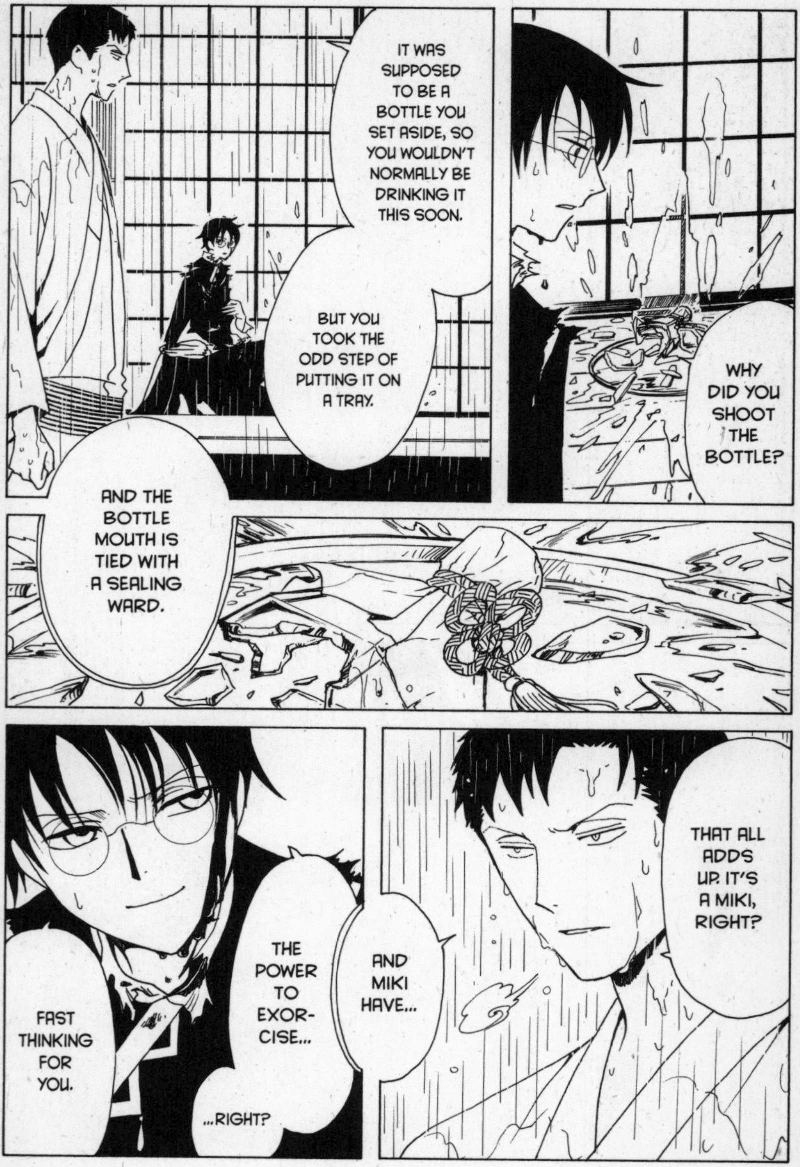
WHY DID YOU SHOOT THE BOTTLE?
IT WAS SUPPOSED TO BE A BOTTLE YOU SET ASIDE, SO YOU WOULDN'T NORMALLY BE DRINKING IT THIS SOON.
BUT YOU TOOK THE ODD STEP OF PUTTING IT ON A TRAY.
AND THE BOTTLE MOUTH IS TIED WITH A SEALING WARD.
THAT ALL ADDS UP. IT'S A MIKI, RIGHT?
AND MIKI HAVE...
THE POWER TO EXOR-CISE...
...RIGHT?
FAST THINKING FOR YOU.

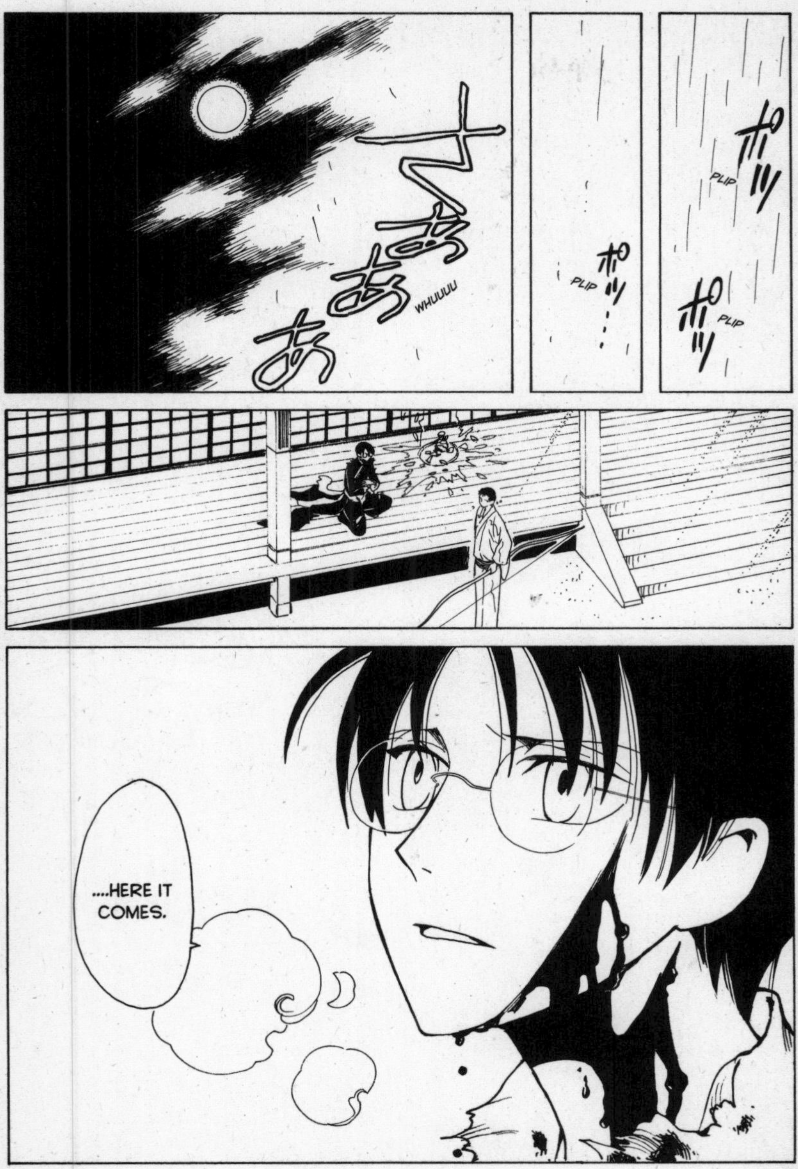

ポツ
PLIP
ポツ
PLIP
ポツ…
PLIP
さああ
WHUUUU
....HERE IT COMES.

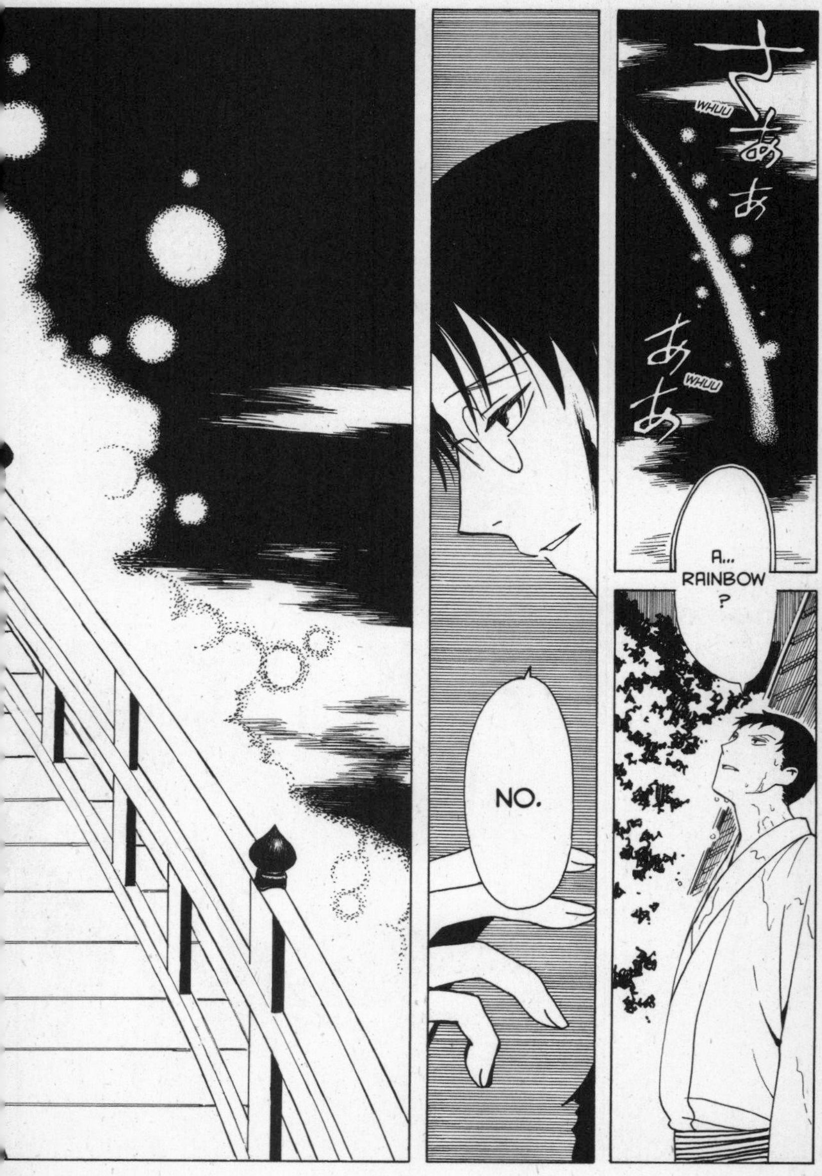
さああ
WHUU
ああ
WHUU
A... RAINBOW?
NO.

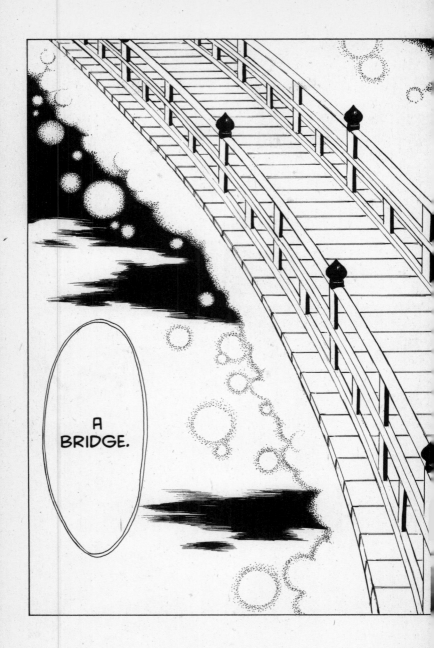

A
BRIDGE.

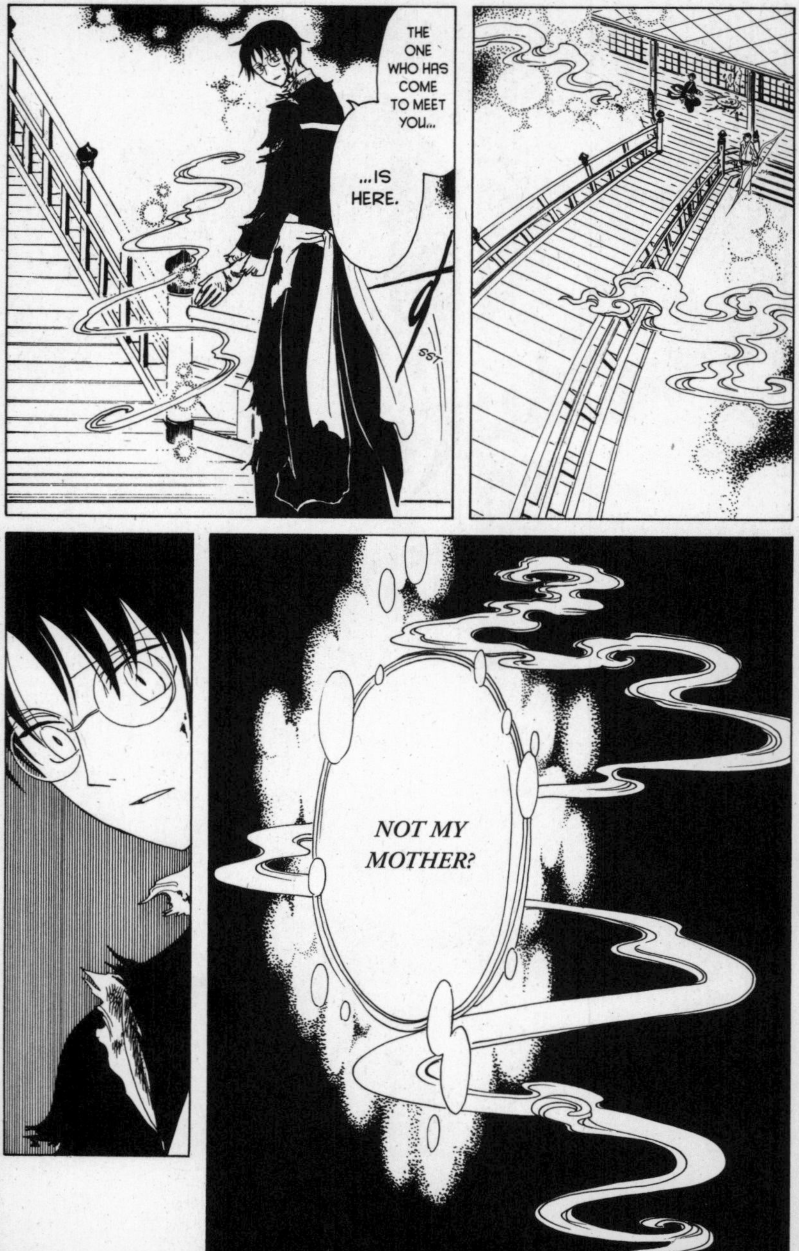
THE ONE WHO HAS COME TO MEET YOU...
...IS HERE.
SST
NOT MY MOTHER?

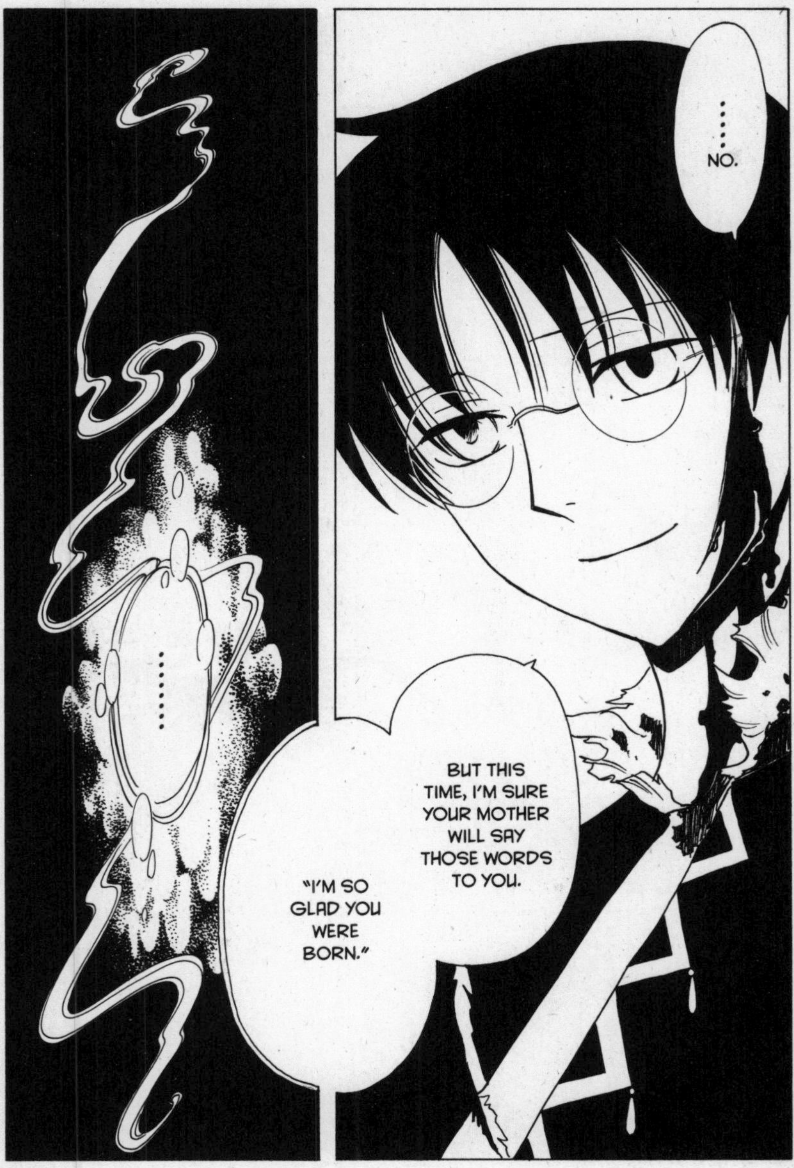
......NO.
BUT THIS TIME, I'M SURE YOUR MOTHER WILL SAY THOSE WORDS TO YOU.
"I'M SO GLAD YOU WERE BORN."
......

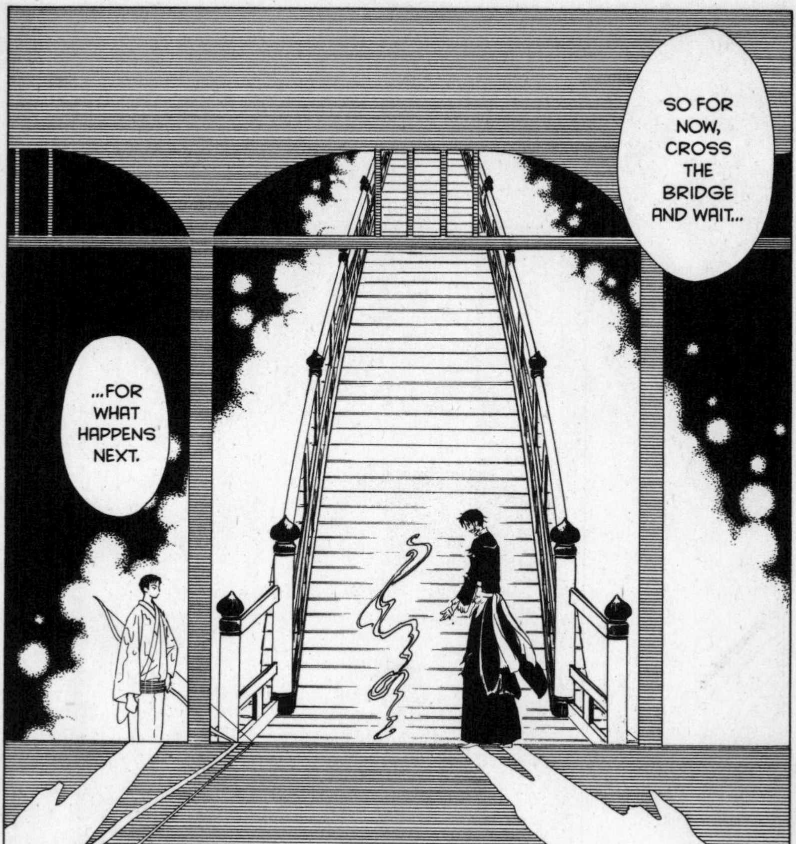
SO FOR NOW, CROSS THE BRIDGE AND WAIT...
...FOR WHAT HAPPENS NEXT.
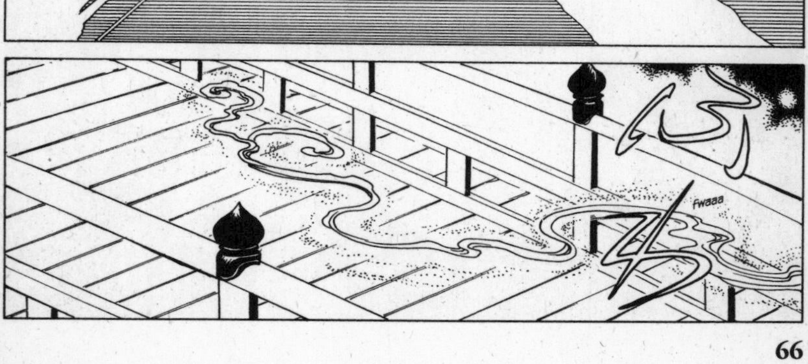
fwaaa

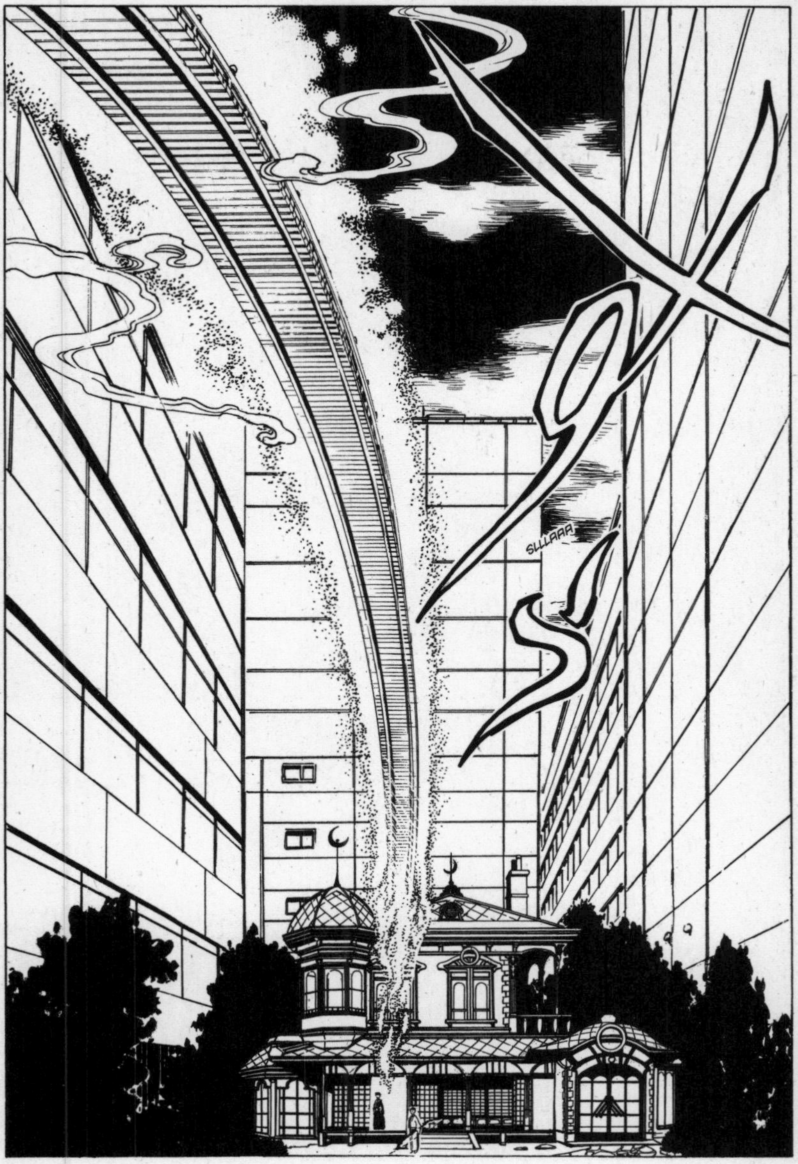
SLLLAAA

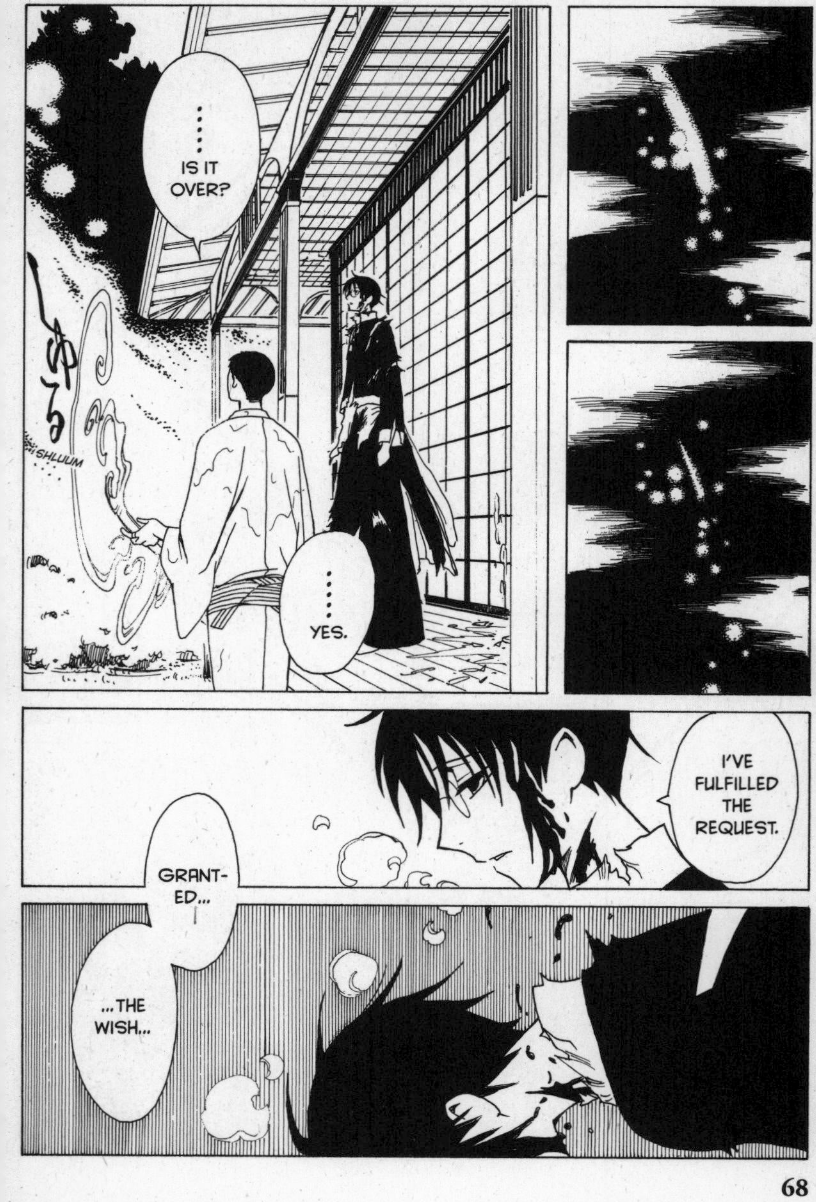
......
IS IT OVER?
しゅる
SHLUUM
......
YES.
I'VE FULFILLED THE REQUEST.
GRANT-ED...
...THE WISH...

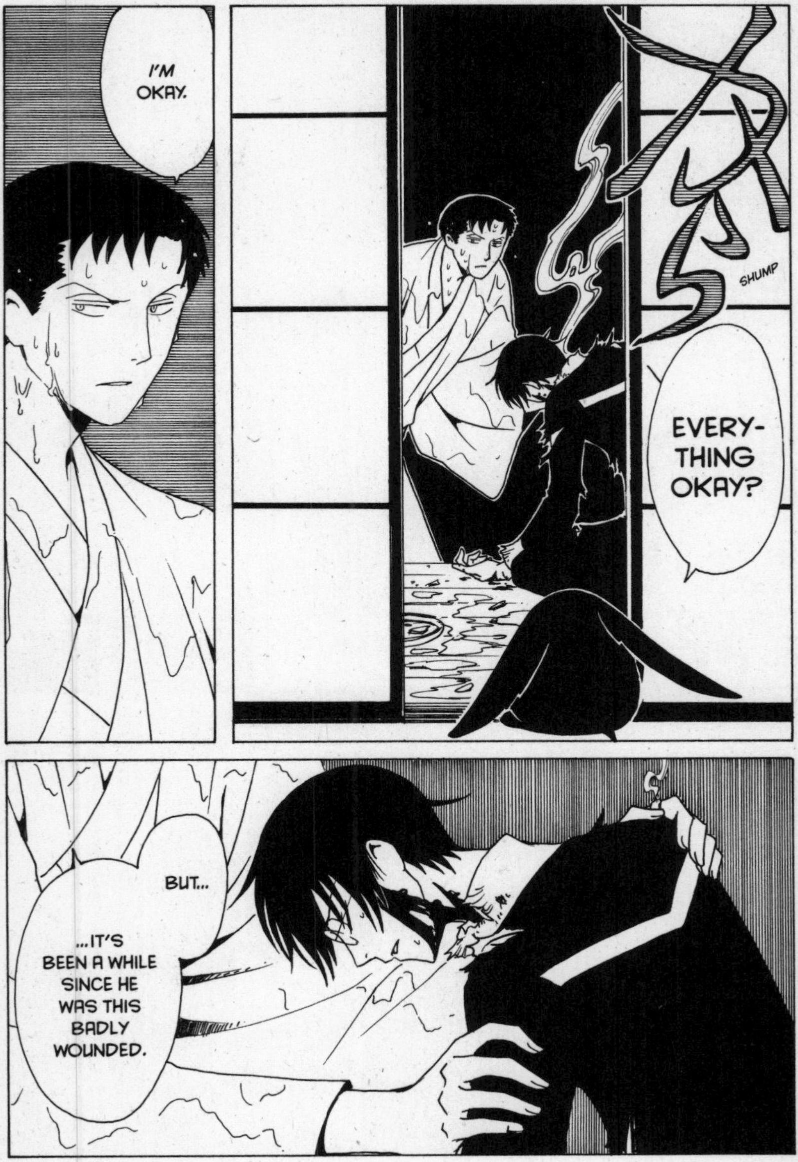
SHUMP
EVERYTHING OKAY?
I'M OKAY.
BUT...
...IT'S BEEN A WHILE SINCE HE WAS THIS BADLY WOUNDED.

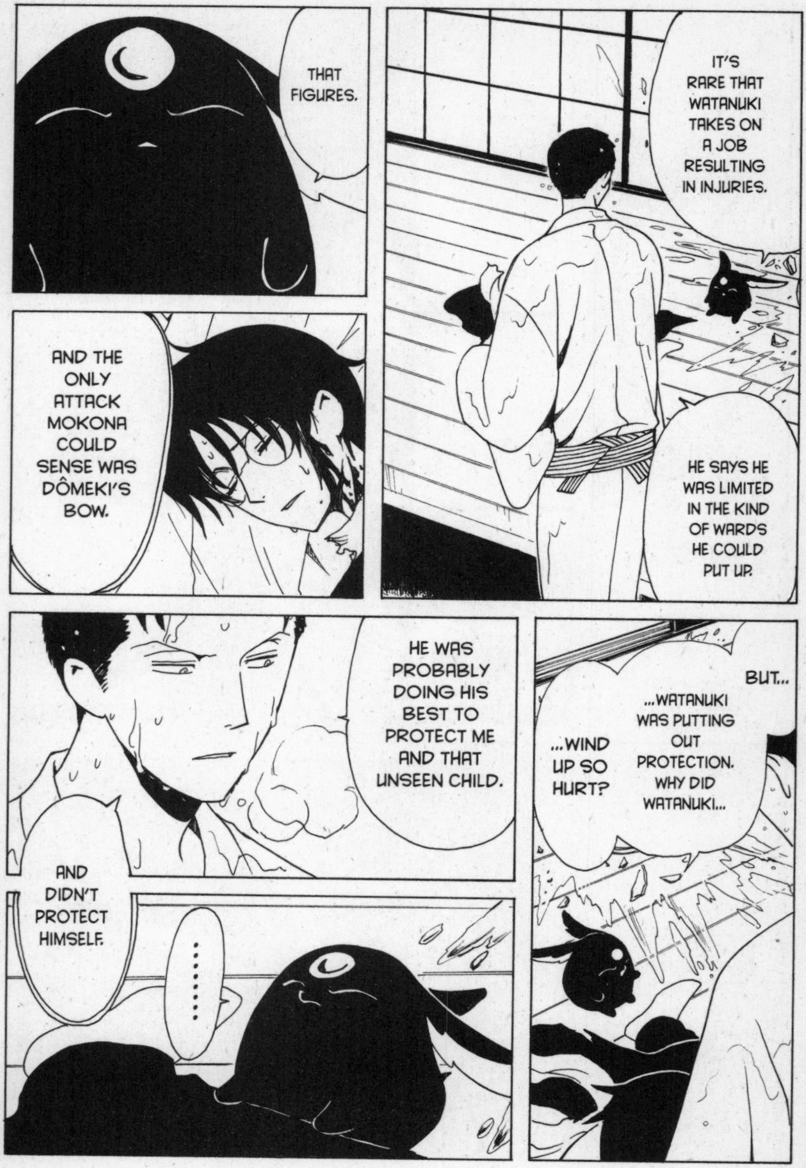
IT'S RARE THAT WATANUKI TAKES ON A JOB RESULTING IN INJURIES.
HE SAYS HE WAS LIMITED IN THE KIND OF WARDS HE COULD PUT UP.
THAT FIGURES.
AND THE ONLY ATTACK MOKONA COULD SENSE WAS DÔMEKI'S BOW.
BUT...
...WATANUKI WAS PUTTING OUT PROTECTION. WHY DID WATANUKI...
...WIND UP SO HURT?
HE WAS PROBABLY DOING HIS BEST TO PROTECT ME AND THAT UNSEEN CHILD.
AND DIDN'T PROTECT HIMSELF.
......

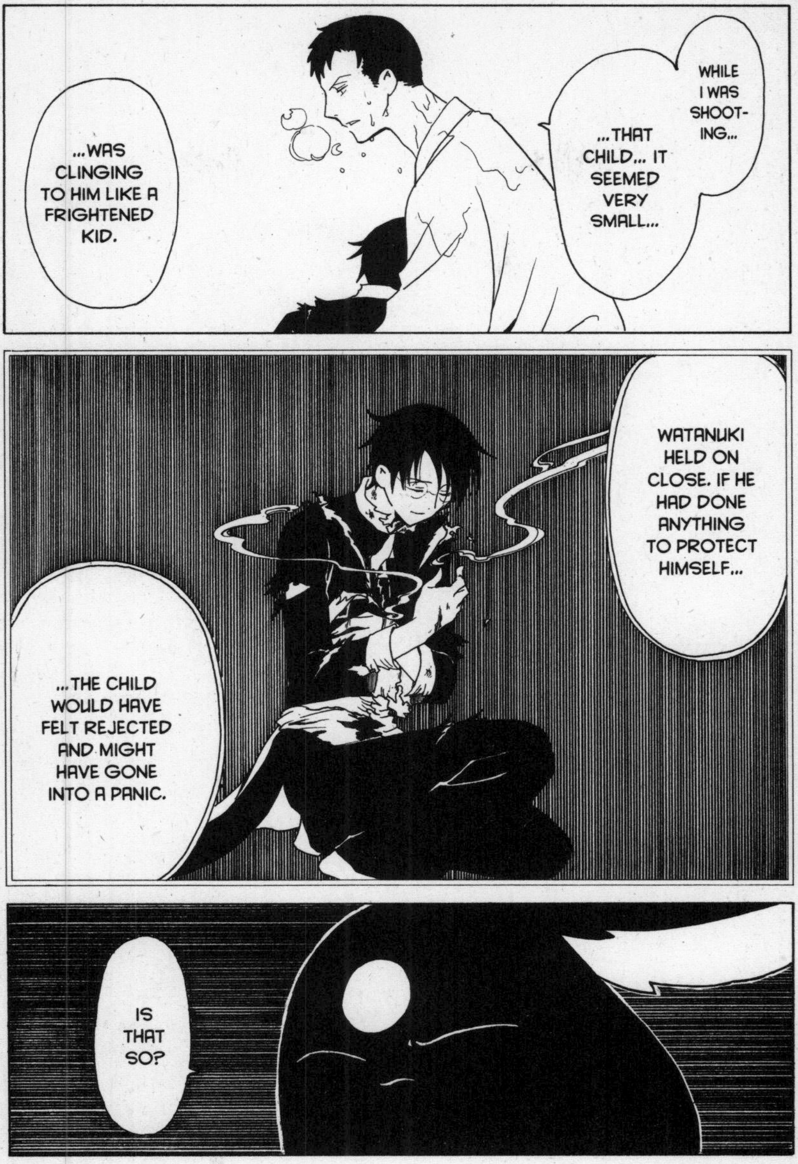
WHILE I WAS SHOOTING...
...THAT CHILD... IT SEEMED VERY SMALL...
...WAS CLINGING TO HIM LIKE A FRIGHTENED KID.
WATANUKI HELD ON CLOSE. IF HE HAD DONE ANYTHING TO PROTECT HIMSELF...
...THE CHILD WOULD HAVE FELT REJECTED AND MIGHT HAVE GONE INTO A PANIC.
IS THAT SO?

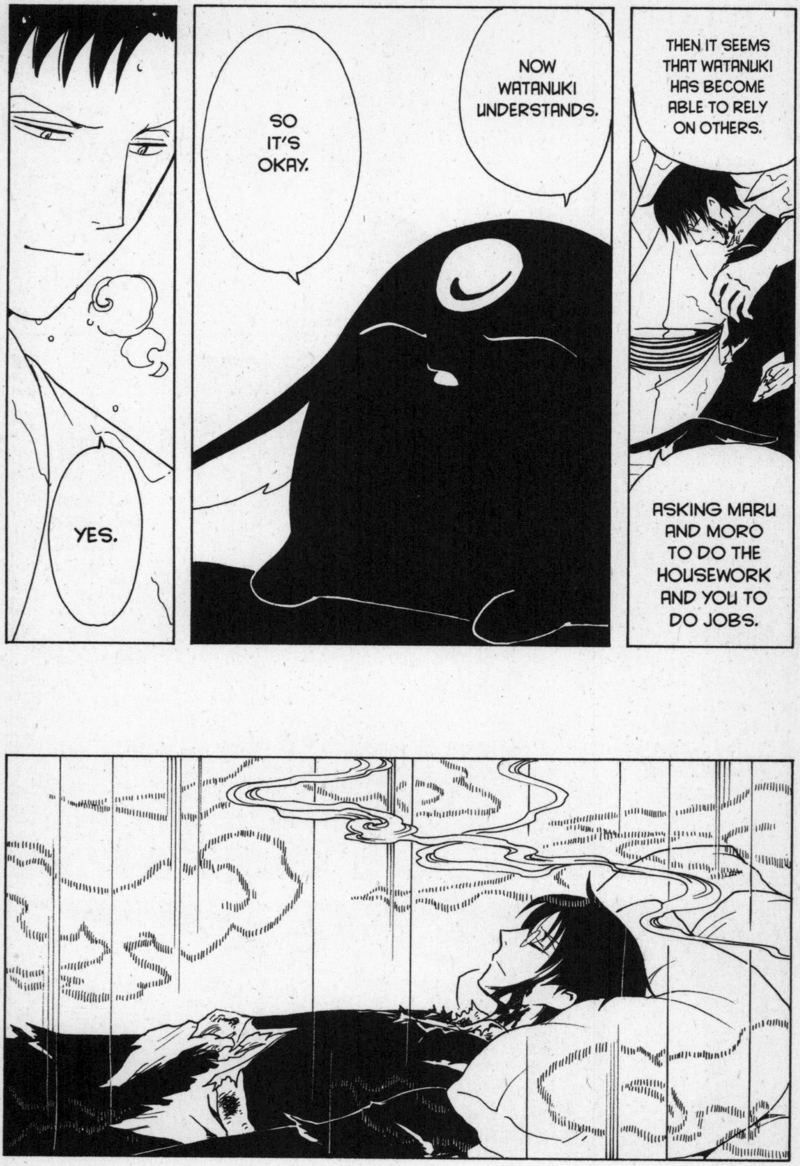
THEN IT SEEMS THAT WATANUKI HAS BECOME ABLE TO RELY ON OTHERS.
ASKING MARU AND MORO TO DO THE HOUSEWORK AND YOU TO DO JOBS.
NOW WATANUKI UNDERSTANDS.
SO IT'S OKAY.
YES.

I'M SORRY.

I GOT HIM WOUNDED.

WATANUKI!

WATANUKI!

THANK YOU!

HUGS

SHAKE

SHAKE

SHAKE

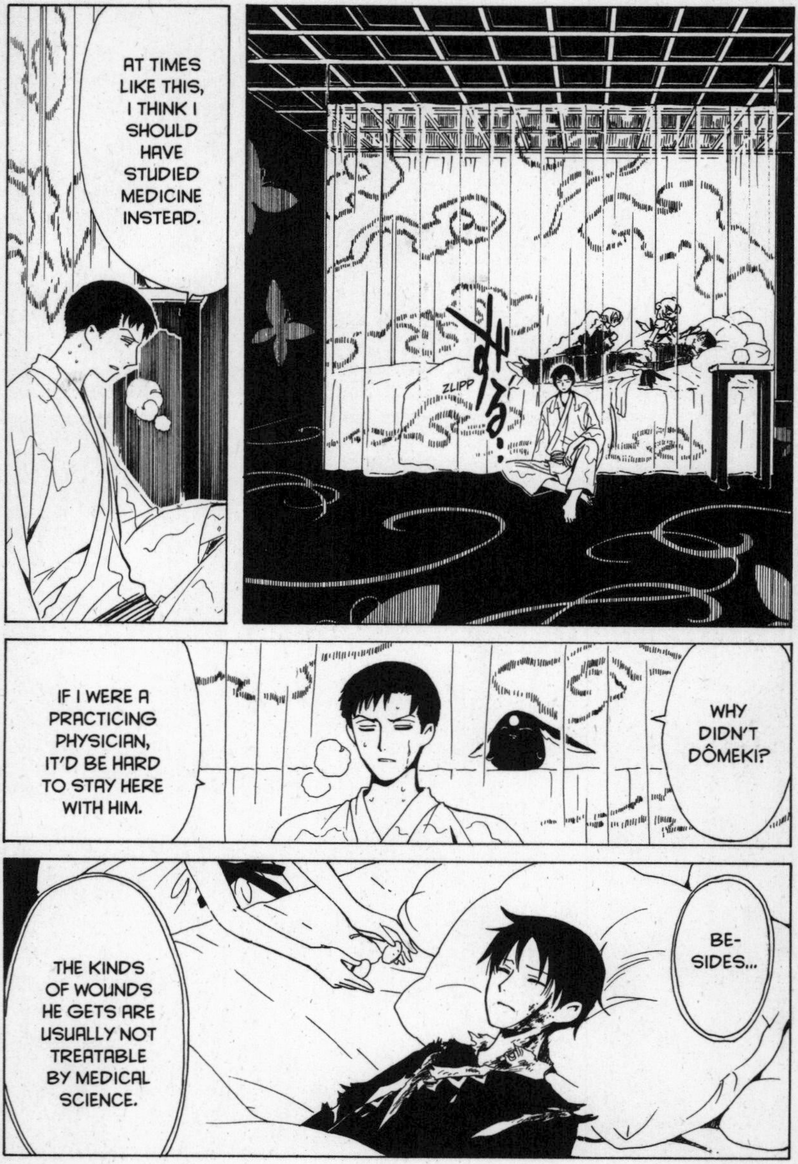

ずる!
ZLIPP
AT TIMES LIKE THIS, I THINK I SHOULD HAVE STUDIED MEDICINE INSTEAD.
WHY DIDN'T DÔMEKI?
IF I WERE A PRACTICING PHYSICIAN, IT'D BE HARD TO STAY HERE WITH HIM.
BE-SIDES...
THE KINDS OF WOUNDS HE GETS ARE USUALLY NOT TREATABLE BY MEDICAL SCIENCE.

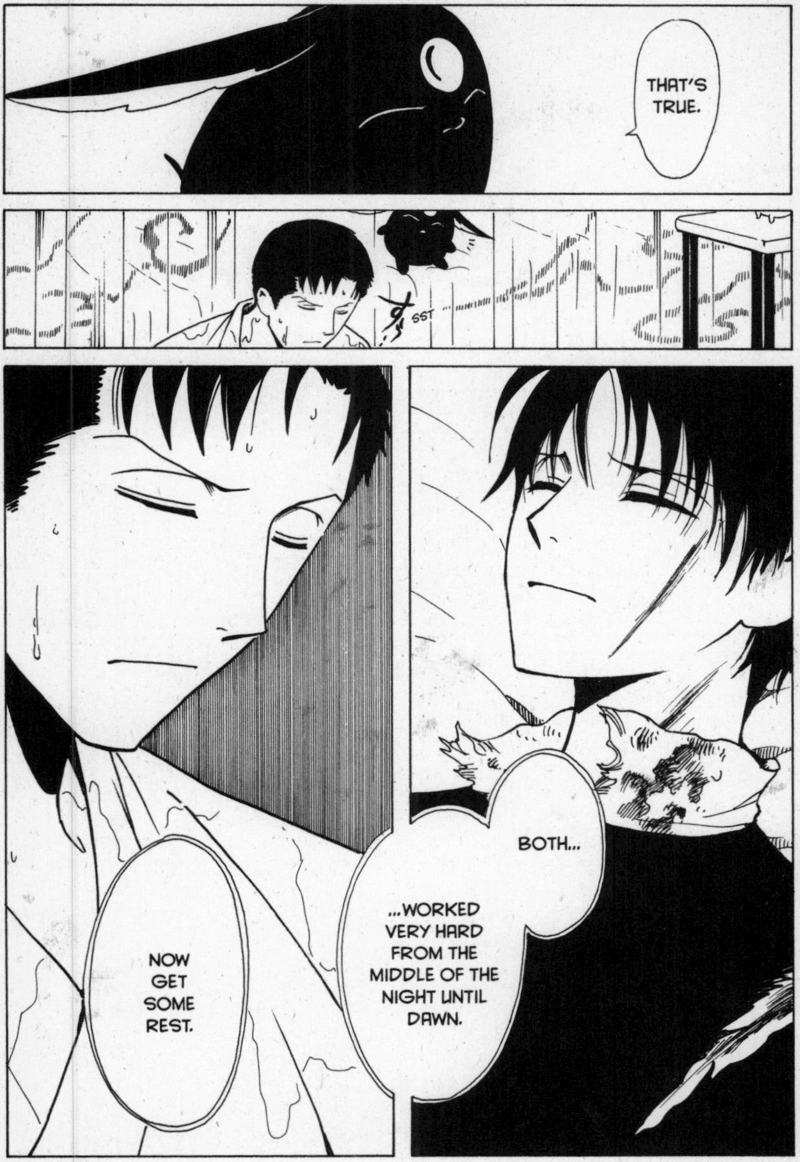
THAT'S TRUE.
SST
BOTH...
...WORKED VERY HARD FROM THE MIDDLE OF THE NIGHT UNTIL DAWN.
NOW GET SOME REST.

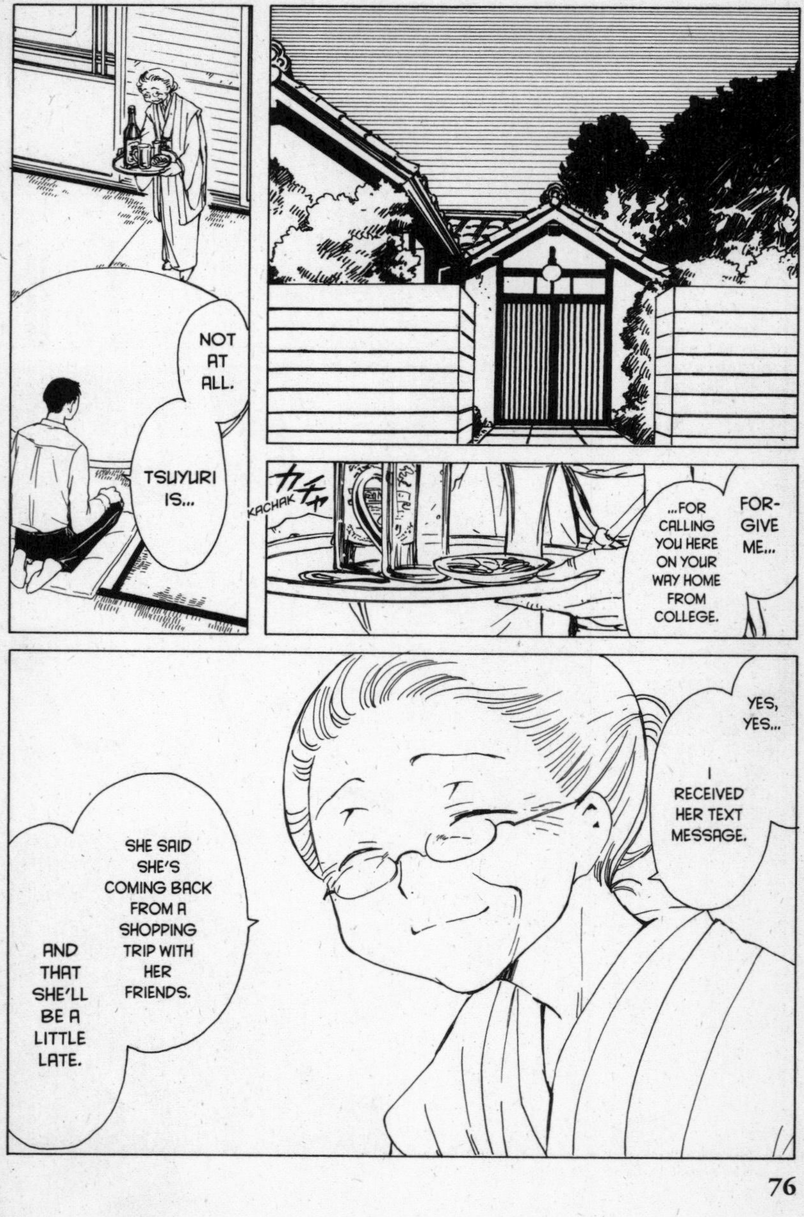
カチャ
KACHAK
FOR-GIVE ME...
...FOR CALLING YOU HERE ON YOUR WAY HOME FROM COLLEGE.
NOT AT ALL.
TSUYURI IS...
YES, YES...
I RECEIVED HER TEXT MESSAGE.
SHE SAID SHE'S COMING BACK FROM A SHOPPING TRIP WITH HER FRIENDS.
AND THAT SHE'LL BE A LITTLE LATE.

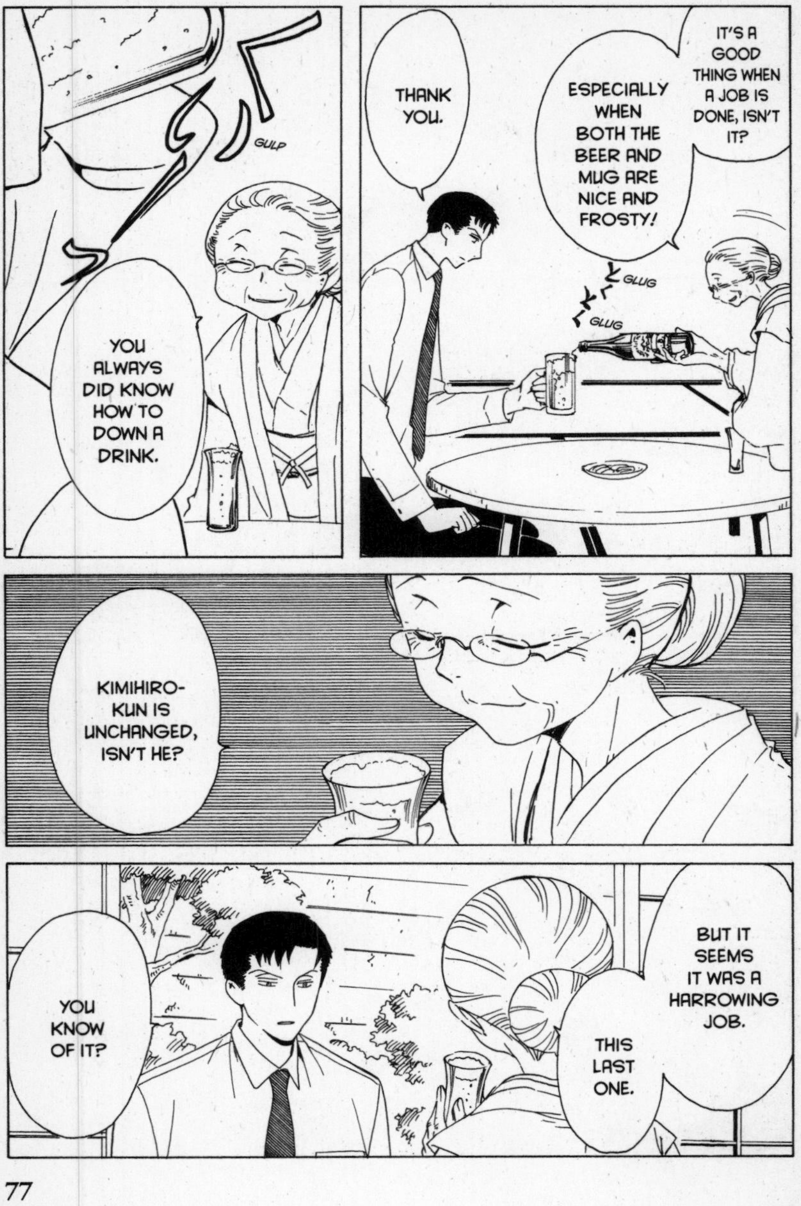
IT'S A GOOD THING WHEN A JOB IS DONE, ISN'T IT?
ESPECIALLY WHEN BOTH THE BEER AND MUG ARE NICE AND FROSTY!
GLUG
GLUG
THANK YOU.
GULP
YOU ALWAYS DID KNOW HOW TO DOWN A DRINK.
KIMIHIRO-KUN IS UNCHANGED, ISN'T HE?
BUT IT SEEMS IT WAS A HARROWING JOB.
THIS LAST ONE.
YOU KNOW OF IT?

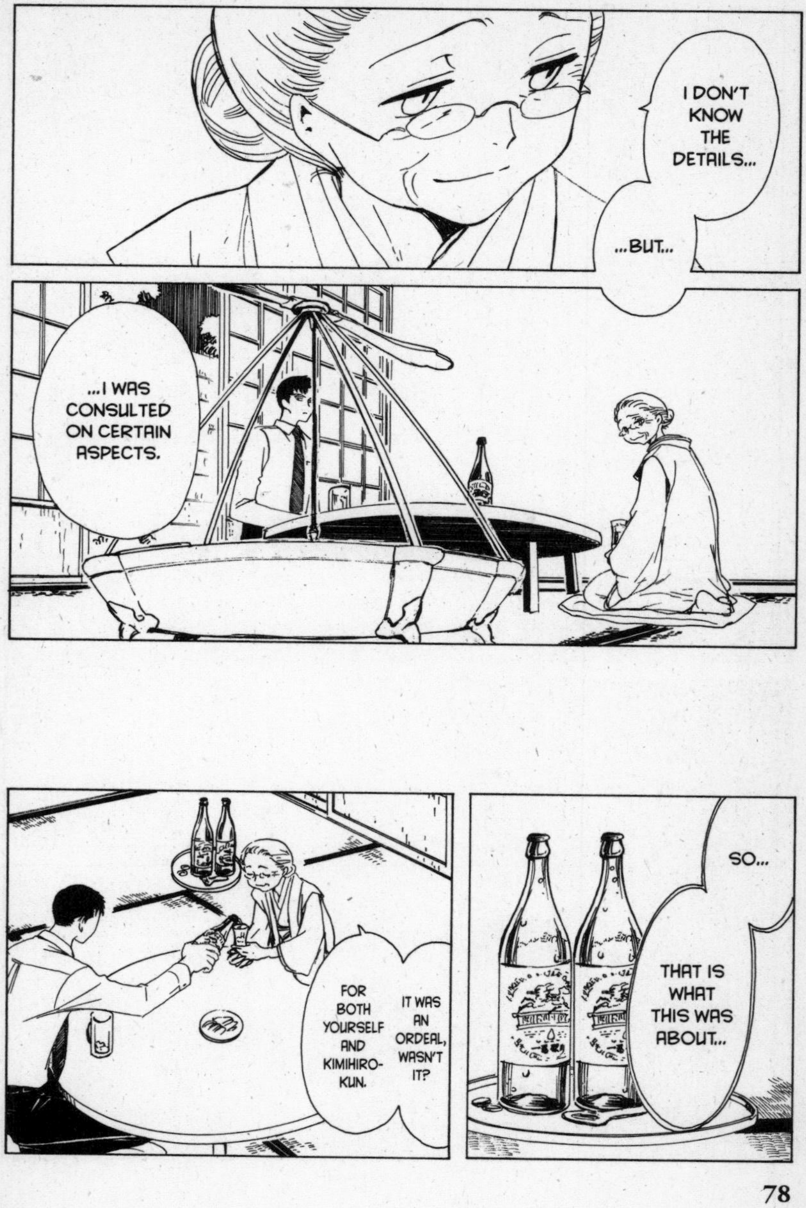
I DON'T KNOW THE DETAILS...
...BUT...
...I WAS CONSULTED ON CERTAIN ASPECTS.
SO...
THAT IS WHAT THIS WAS ABOUT...
IT WAS AN ORDEAL, WASN'T IT?
FOR BOTH YOURSELF AND KIMIHIRO-KUN.

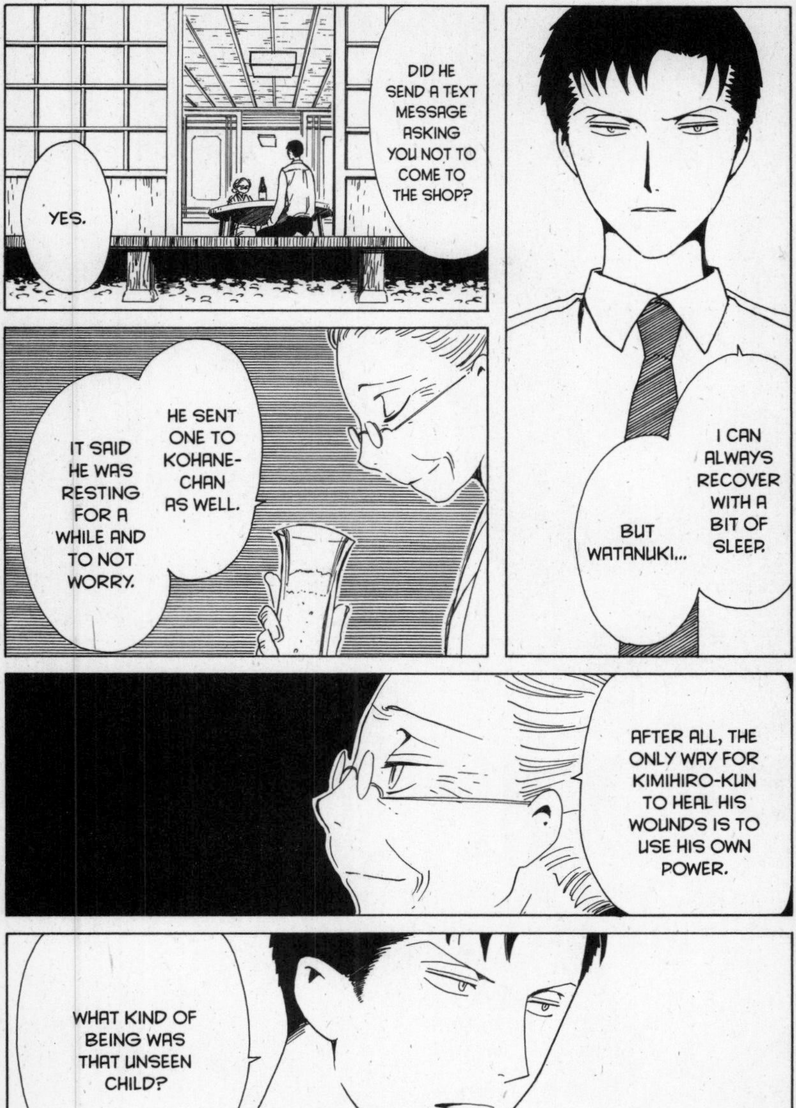
I CAN ALWAYS RECOVER WITH A BIT OF SLEEP.
BUT WATANUKI...
DID HE SEND A TEXT MESSAGE ASKING YOU NOT TO COME TO THE SHOP?
YES.
HE SENT ONE TO KOHANE-CHAN AS WELL.
IT SAID HE WAS RESTING FOR A WHILE AND TO NOT WORRY.
AFTER ALL, THE ONLY WAY FOR KIMIHIRO-KUN TO HEAL HIS WOUNDS IS TO USE HIS OWN POWER.
WHAT KIND OF BEING WAS THAT UNSEEN CHILD?

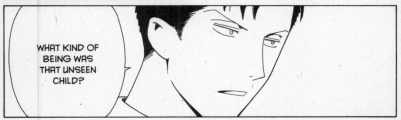

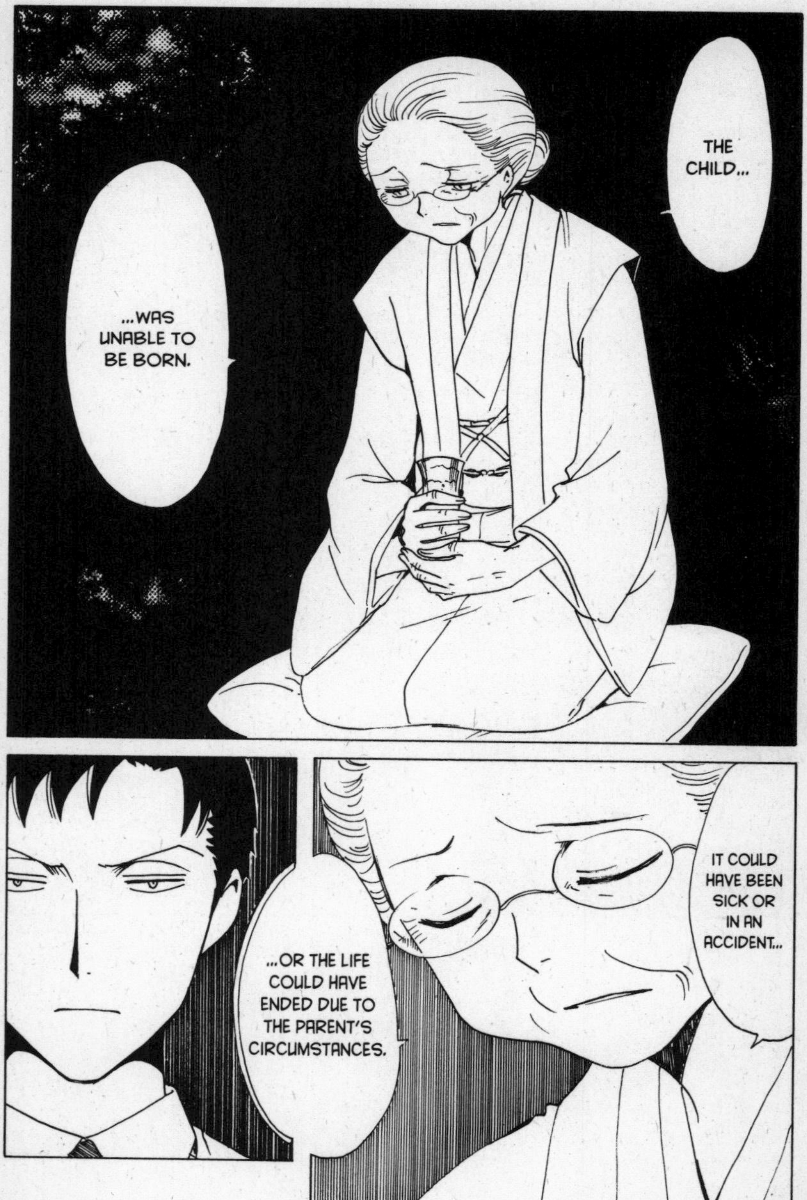
THE CHILD...
...WAS UNABLE TO BE BORN.
IT COULD HAVE BEEN SICK OR IN AN ACCIDENT...
...OR THE LIFE COULD HAVE ENDED DUE TO THE PARENT'S CIRCUMSTANCES.

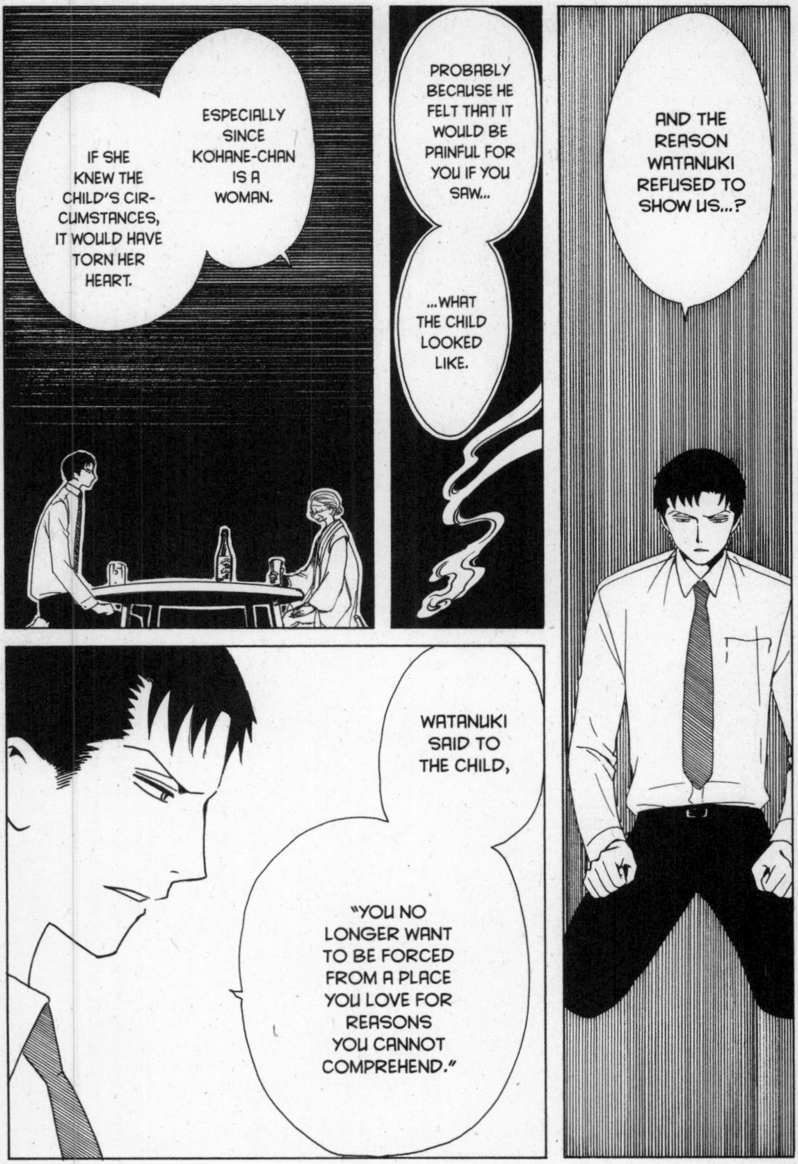
AND THE REASON WATANUKI REFUSED TO SHOW US...?
PROBABLY BECAUSE HE FELT THAT IT WOULD BE PAINFUL FOR YOU IF YOU SAW...
...WHAT THE CHILD LOOKED LIKE.
IF SHE KNEW THE CHILD'S CIR-CUMSTANCES, IT WOULD HAVE TORN HER HEART.
ESPECIALLY SINCE KOHANE-CHAN IS A WOMAN.
WATANUKI SAID TO THE CHILD,
"YOU NO LONGER WANT TO BE FORCED FROM A PLACE YOU LOVE FOR REASONS YOU CANNOT COMPREHEND."

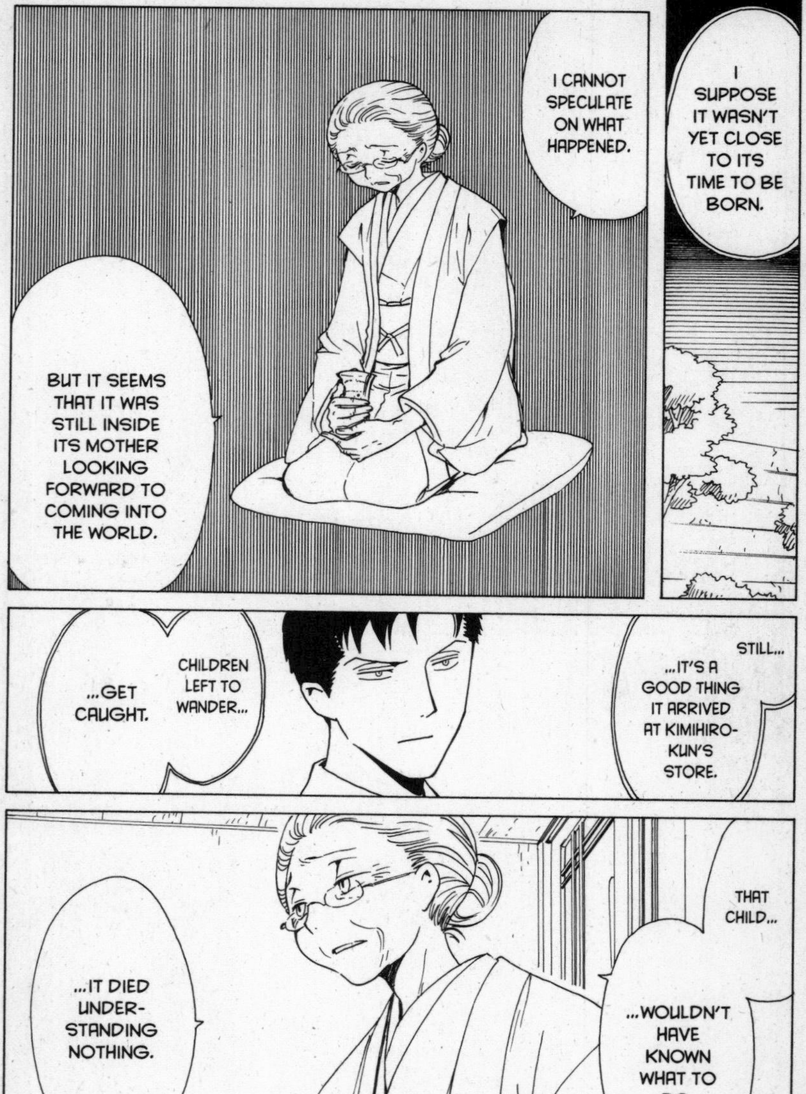
I SUPPOSE IT WASN'T YET CLOSE TO ITS TIME TO BE BORN.
I CANNOT SPECULATE ON WHAT HAPPENED.
BUT IT SEEMS THAT IT WAS STILL INSIDE ITS MOTHER LOOKING FORWARD TO COMING INTO THE WORLD.
STILL...
...IT'S A GOOD THING IT ARRIVED AT KIMIHIRO-KUN'S STORE.
CHILDREN LEFT TO WANDER...
...GET CAUGHT.
THAT CHILD...
...WOULDN'T HAVE KNOWN WHAT TO DO.
...IT DIED UNDER-STANDING NOTHING.

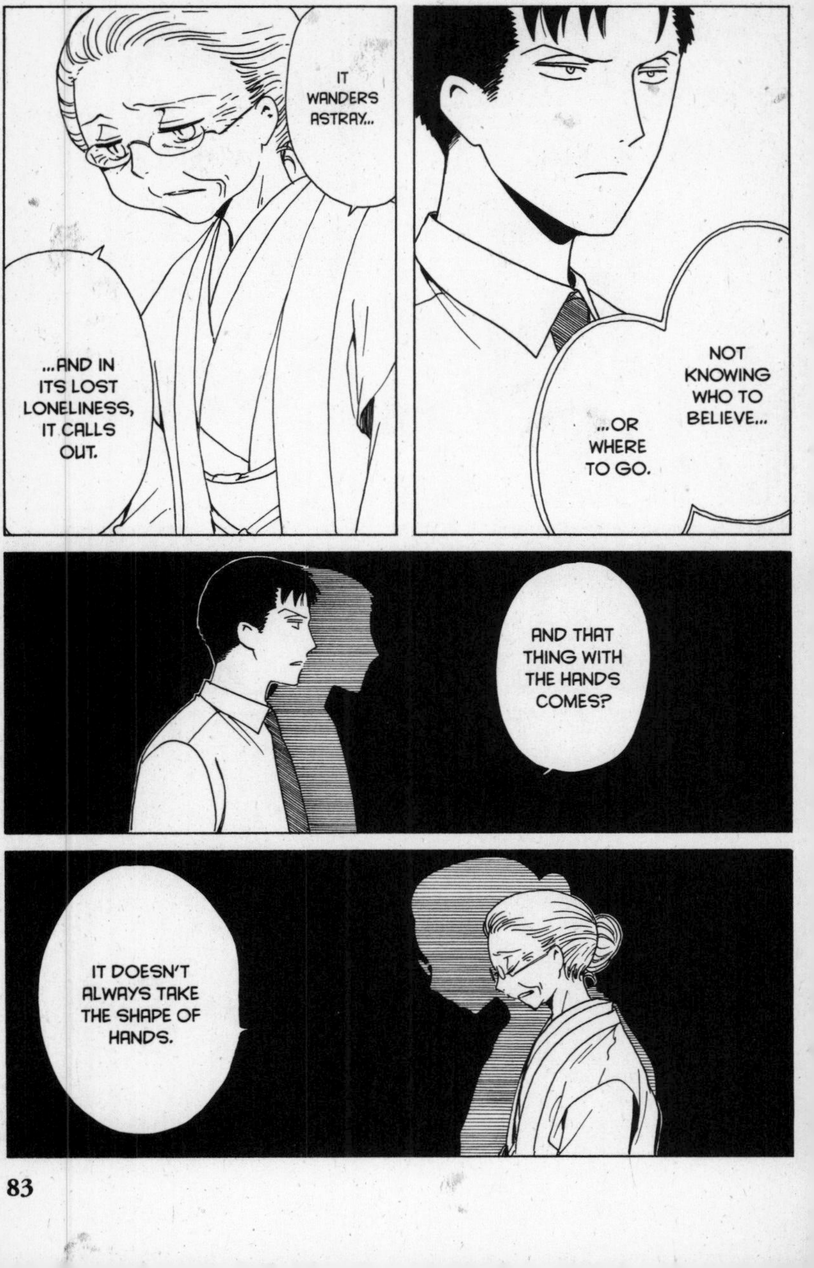
NOT KNOWING WHO TO BELIEVE...
...OR WHERE TO GO.
IT WANDERS ASTRAY...
...AND IN ITS LOST LONELINESS, IT CALLS OUT.
AND THAT THING WITH THE HANDS COMES?
IT DOESN'T ALWAYS TAKE THE SHAPE OF HANDS.

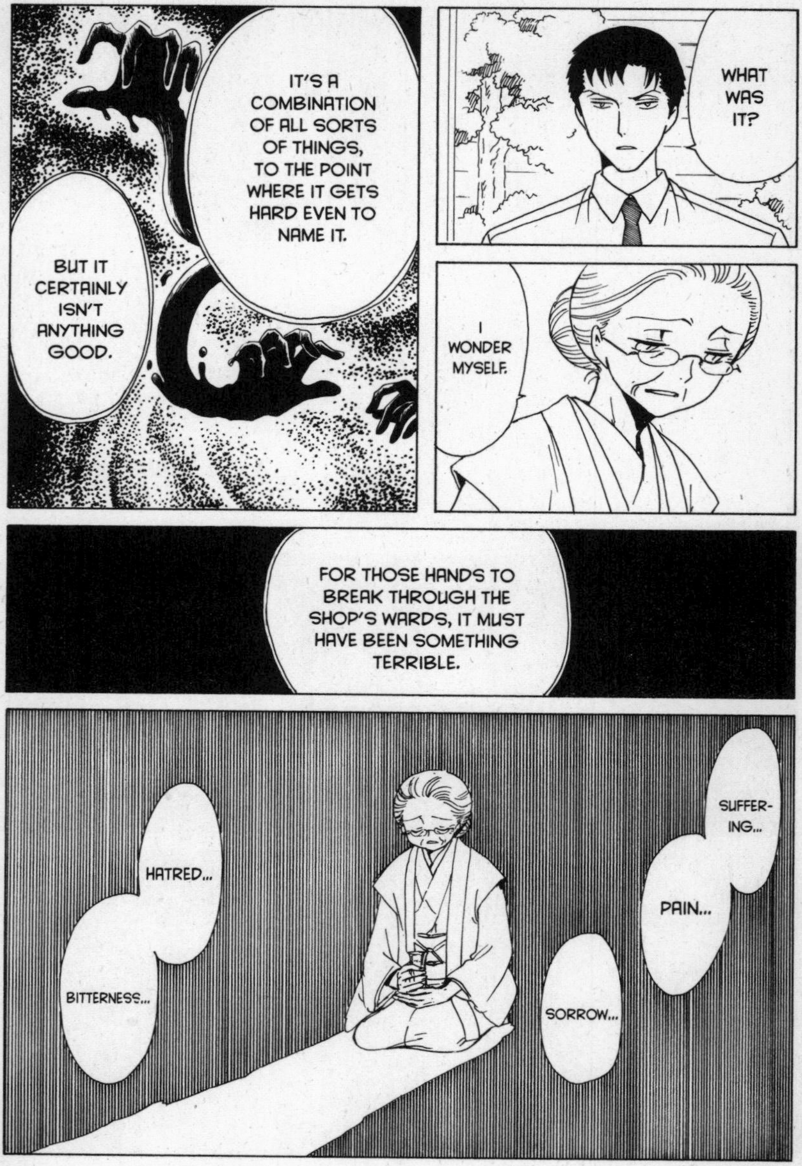
WHAT WAS IT?
I WONDER MYSELF.
IT'S A COMBINATION OF ALL SORTS OF THINGS, TO THE POINT WHERE IT GETS HARD EVEN TO NAME IT.
BUT IT CERTAINLY ISN'T ANYTHING GOOD.
FOR THOSE HANDS TO BREAK THROUGH THE SHOP'S WARDS, IT MUST HAVE BEEN SOMETHING TERRIBLE.
SUFFER-ING...
PAIN...
SORROW...
HATRED...
BITTERNESS...

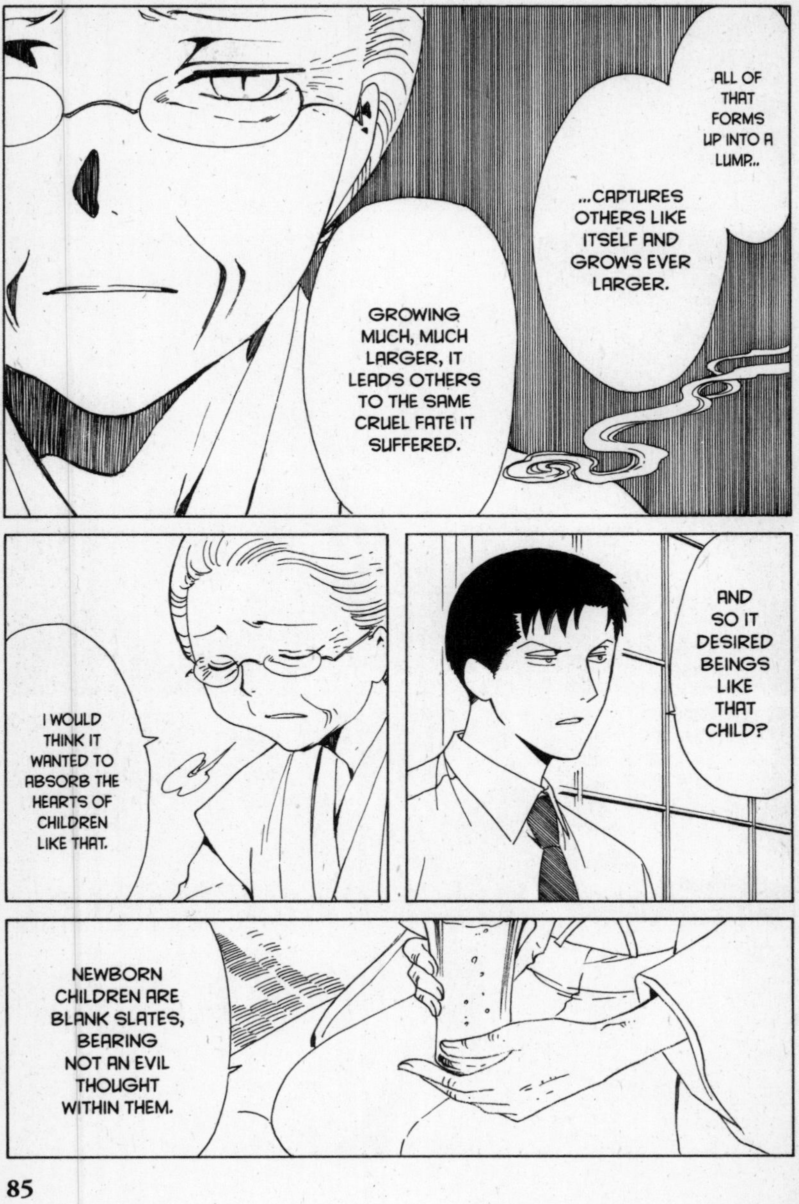
ALL OF THAT FORMS UP INTO A LUMP...
...CAPTURES OTHERS LIKE ITSELF AND GROWS EVER LARGER.
GROWING MUCH, MUCH LARGER, IT LEADS OTHERS TO THE SAME CRUEL FATE IT SUFFERED.
AND SO IT DESIRED BEINGS LIKE THAT CHILD?
I WOULD THINK IT WANTED TO ABSORB THE HEARTS OF CHILDREN LIKE THAT.
NEWBORN CHILDREN ARE BLANK SLATES, BEARING NOT AN EVIL THOUGHT WITHIN THEM.

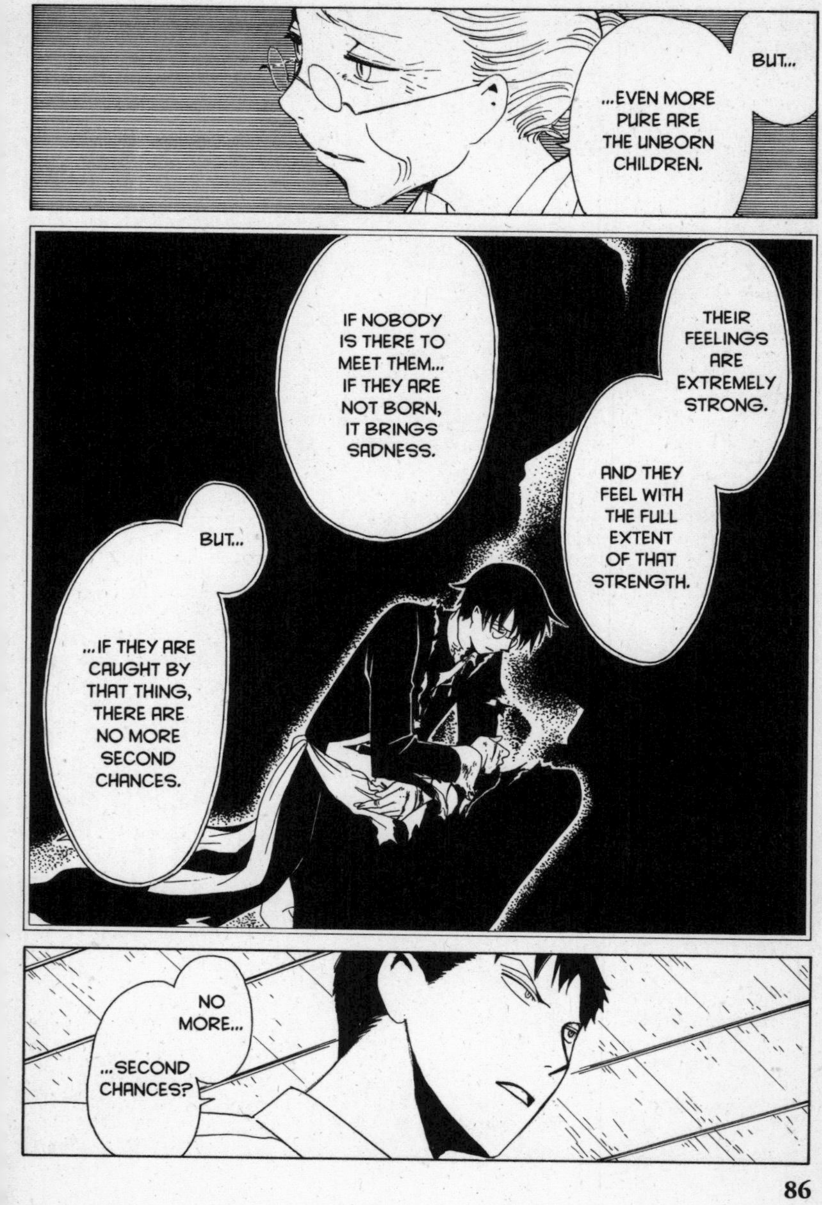
BUT...
...EVEN MORE PURE ARE THE UNBORN CHILDREN.
THEIR FEELINGS ARE EXTREMELY STRONG.
AND THEY FEEL WITH THE FULL EXTENT OF THAT STRENGTH.
IF NOBODY IS THERE TO MEET THEM... IF THEY ARE NOT BORN, IT BRINGS SADNESS.
BUT...
...IF THEY ARE CAUGHT BY THAT THING, THERE ARE NO MORE SECOND CHANCES.
NO MORE...
...SECOND CHANCES?

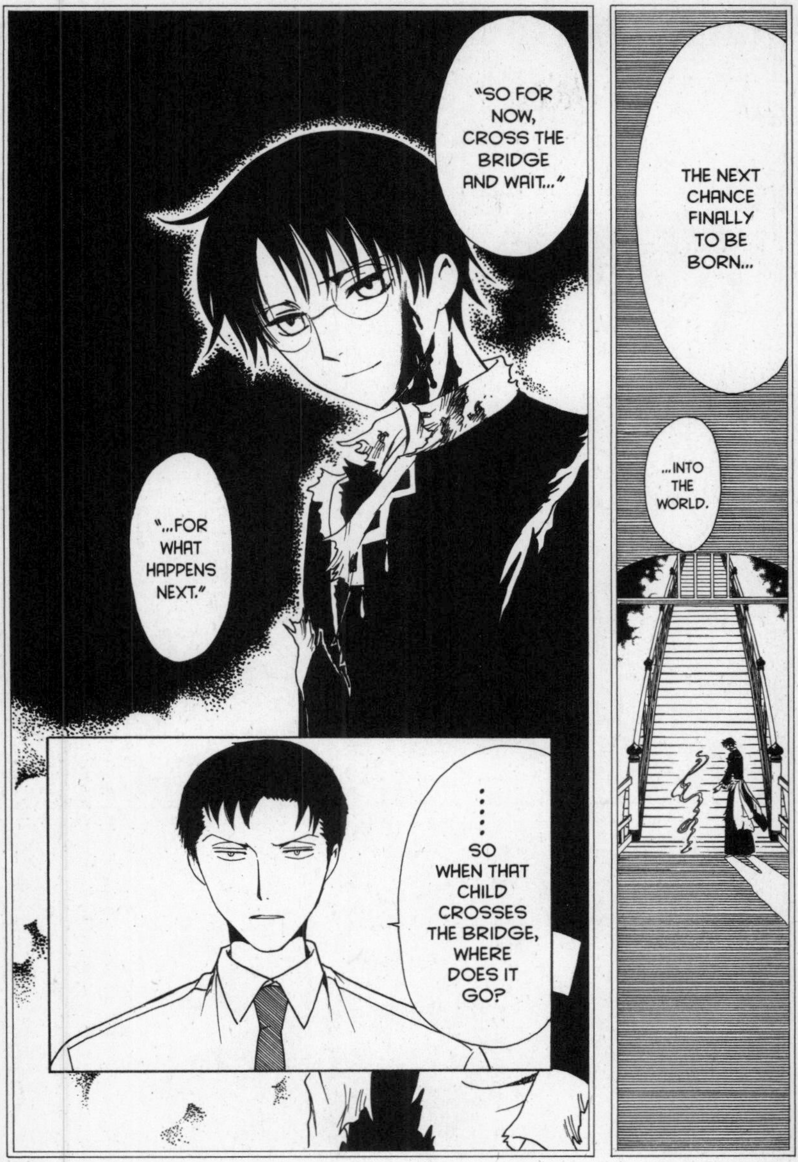
THE NEXT CHANCE FINALLY TO BE BORN...
...INTO THE WORLD.
"SO FOR NOW, CROSS THE BRIDGE AND WAIT..."
"...FOR WHAT HAPPENS NEXT."
...... SO WHEN THAT CHILD CROSSES THE BRIDGE, WHERE DOES IT GO?

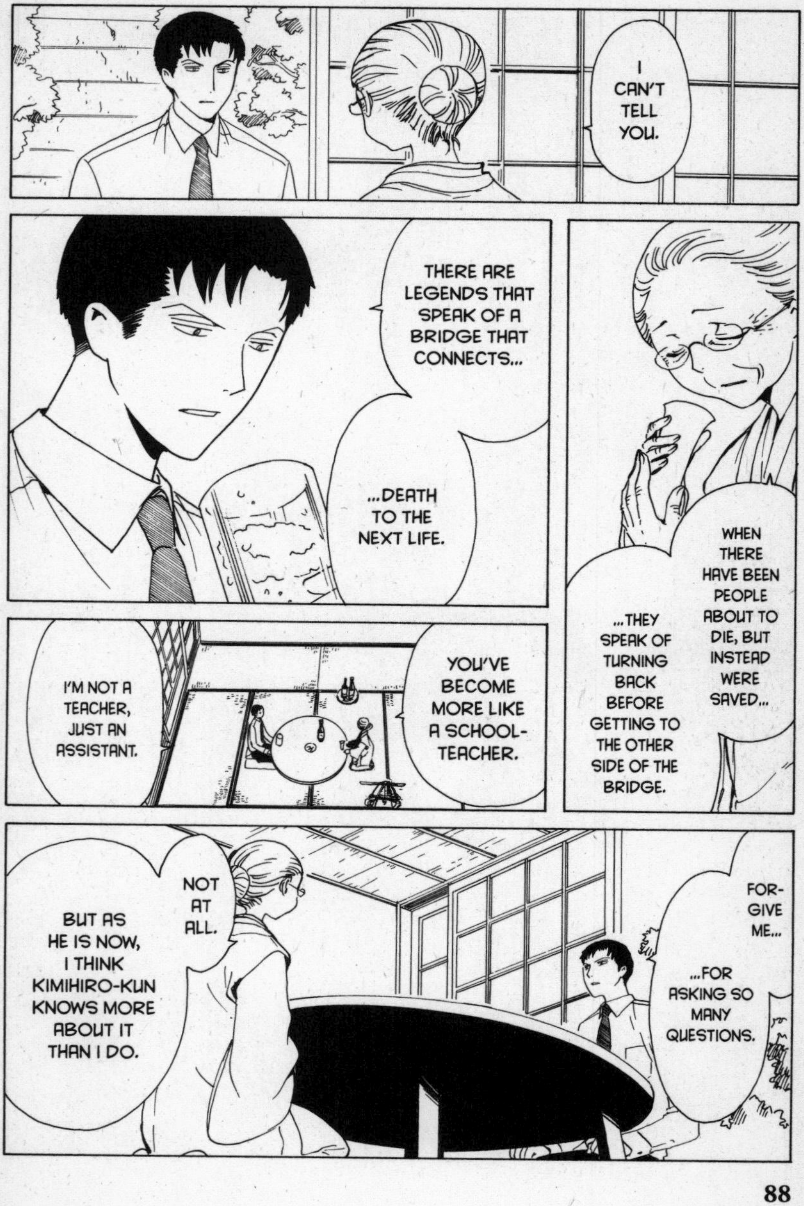
I CAN'T TELL YOU.
THERE ARE LEGENDS THAT SPEAK OF A BRIDGE THAT CONNECTS...
...DEATH TO THE NEXT LIFE.
WHEN THERE HAVE BEEN PEOPLE ABOUT TO DIE, BUT INSTEAD WERE SAVED...
...THEY SPEAK OF TURNING BACK BEFORE GETTING TO THE OTHER SIDE OF THE BRIDGE.
YOU'VE BECOME MORE LIKE A SCHOOL-TEACHER.
I'M NOT A TEACHER, JUST AN ASSISTANT.
FOR-GIVE ME...
...FOR ASKING SO MANY QUESTIONS.
NOT AT ALL.
BUT AS HE IS NOW, I THINK KIMIHIRO-KUN KNOWS MORE ABOUT IT THAN I DO.

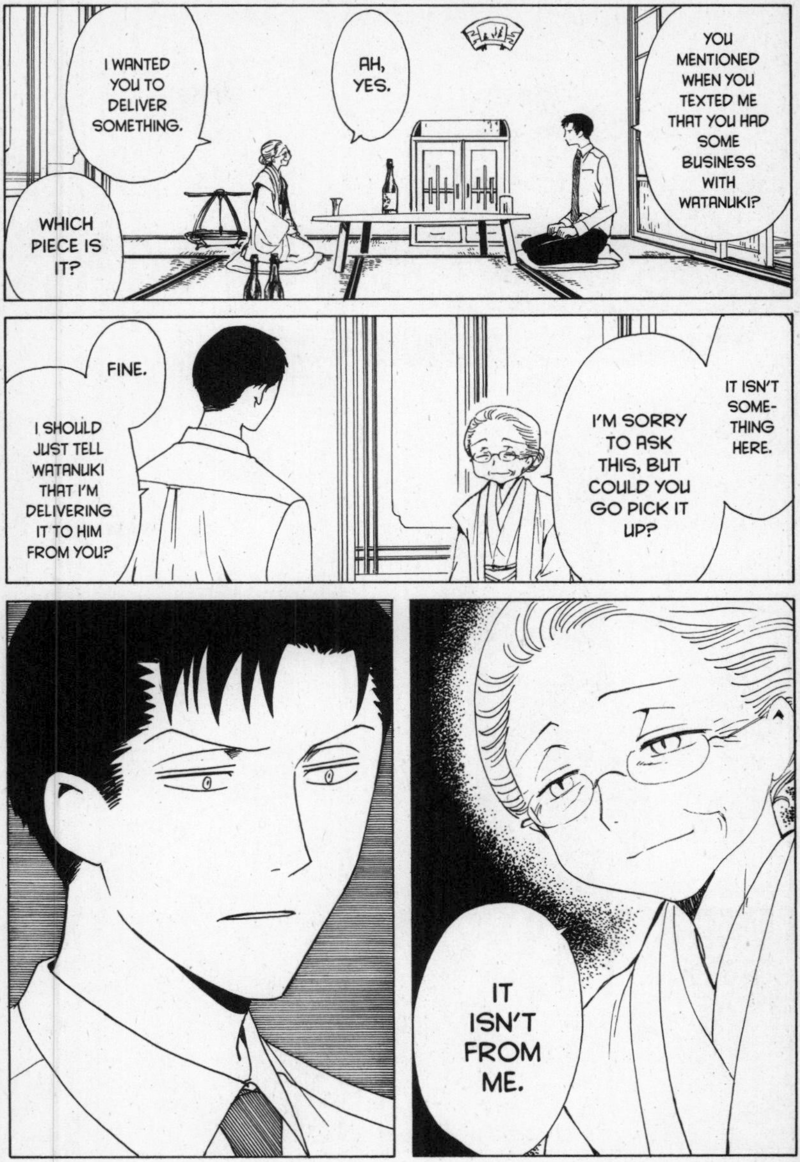
YOU MENTIONED WHEN YOU TEXTED ME THAT YOU HAD SOME BUSINESS WITH WATANUKI?
AH, YES.
I WANTED YOU TO DELIVER SOMETHING.
WHICH PIECE IS IT?
IT ISN'T SOME-THING HERE.
I'M SORRY TO ASK THIS, BUT COULD YOU GO PICK IT UP?
FINE.
I SHOULD JUST TELL WATANUKI THAT I'M DELIVERING IT TO HIM FROM YOU?
IT ISN'T FROM ME.

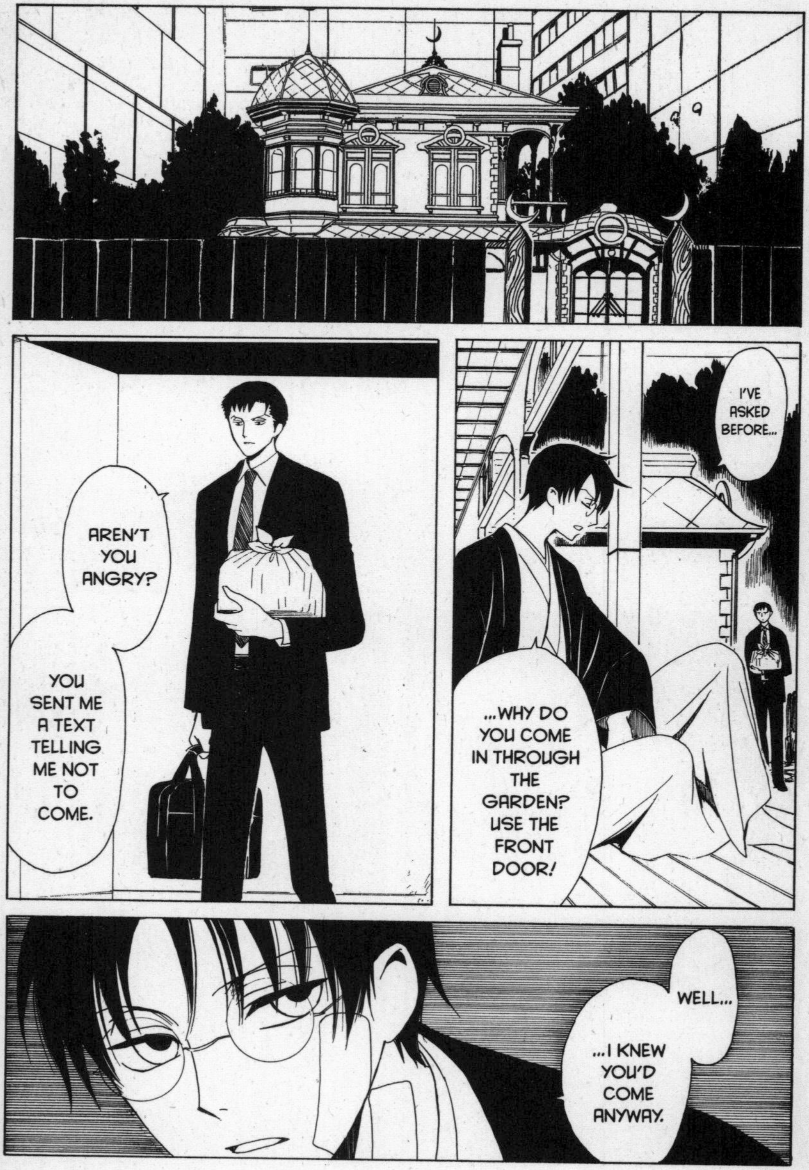
I'VE ASKED BEFORE...
...WHY DO YOU COME IN THROUGH THE GARDEN? USE THE FRONT DOOR!
AREN'T YOU ANGRY?
YOU SENT ME A TEXT TELLING ME NOT TO COME.
WELL...
...I KNEW YOU'D COME ANYWAY.

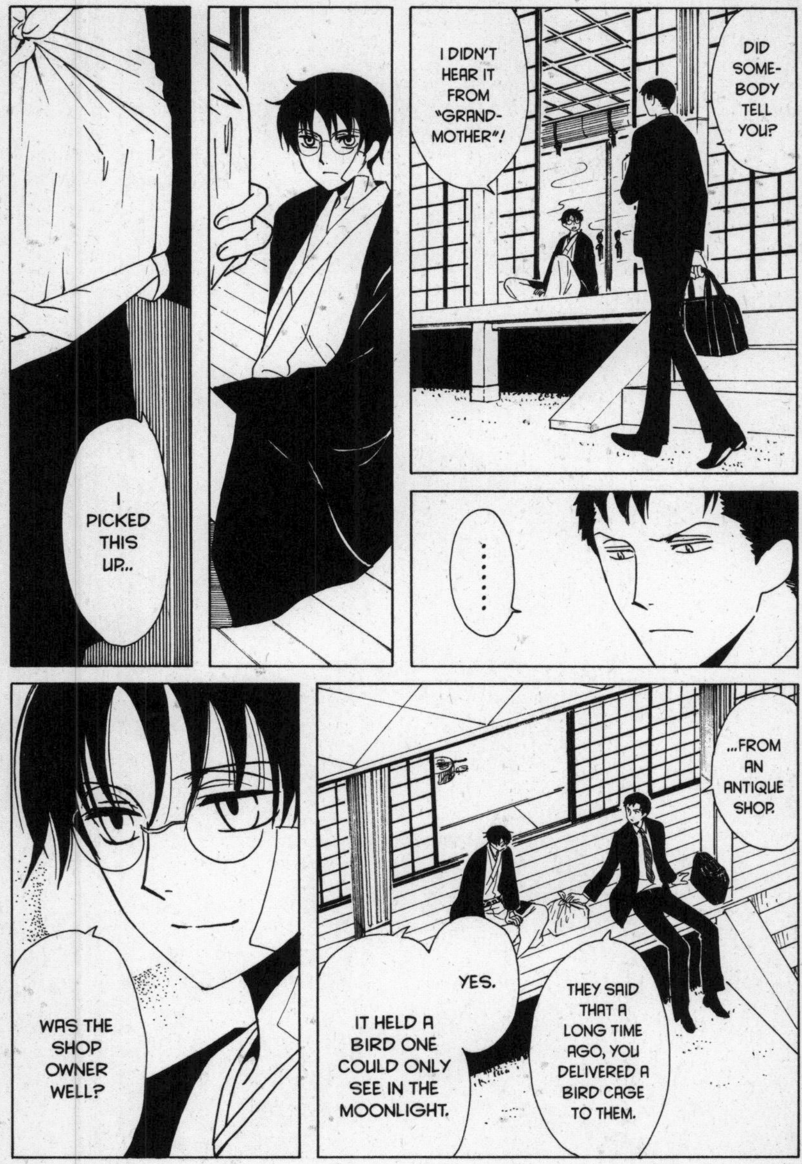
DID SOMEBODY TELL YOU?
I DIDN'T HEAR IT FROM "GRAND-MOTHER"!
......
I PICKED THIS UP...
...FROM AN ANTIQUE SHOP.
THEY SAID THAT A LONG TIME AGO, YOU DELIVERED A BIRD CAGE TO THEM.
YES.
IT HELD A BIRD ONE COULD ONLY SEE IN THE MOONLIGHT.
WAS THE SHOP OWNER WELL?

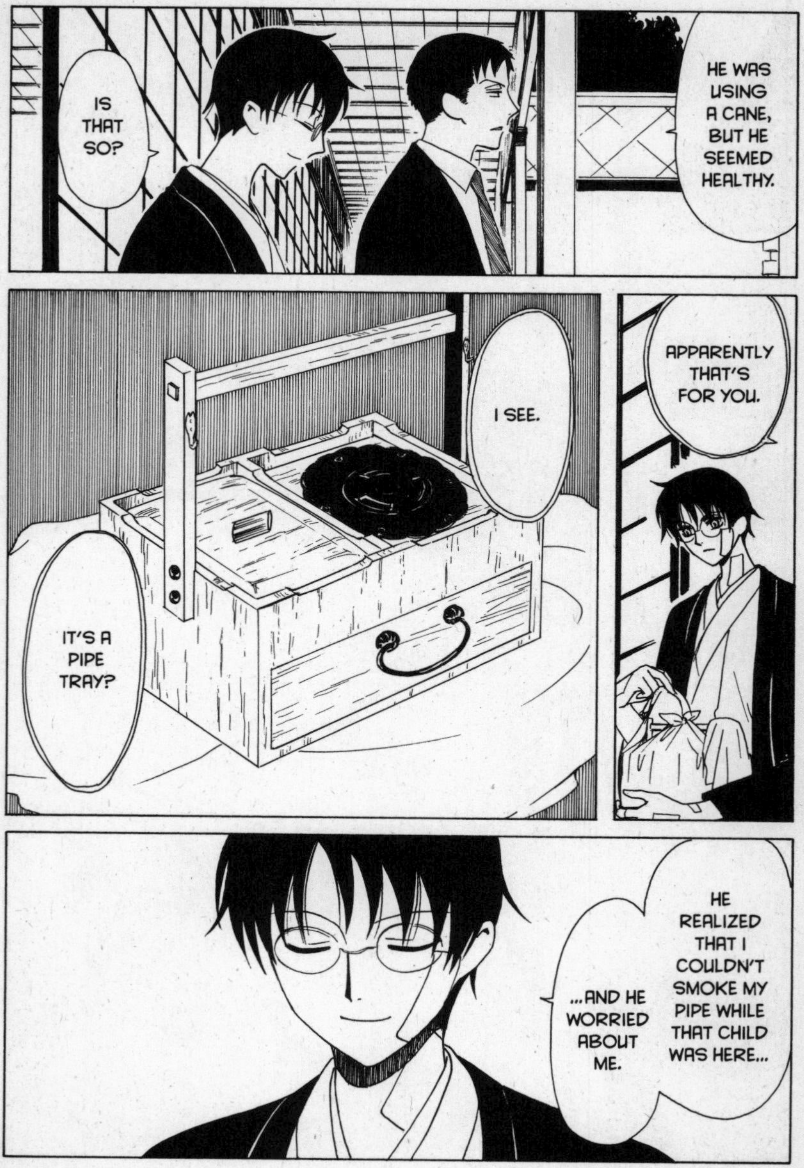
HE WAS USING A CANE, BUT HE SEEMED HEALTHY.
IS THAT SO?
APPARENTLY THAT'S FOR YOU.
I SEE.
IT'S A PIPE TRAY?
HE REALIZED THAT I COULDN'T SMOKE MY PIPE WHILE THAT CHILD WAS HERE...
...AND HE WORRIED ABOUT ME.

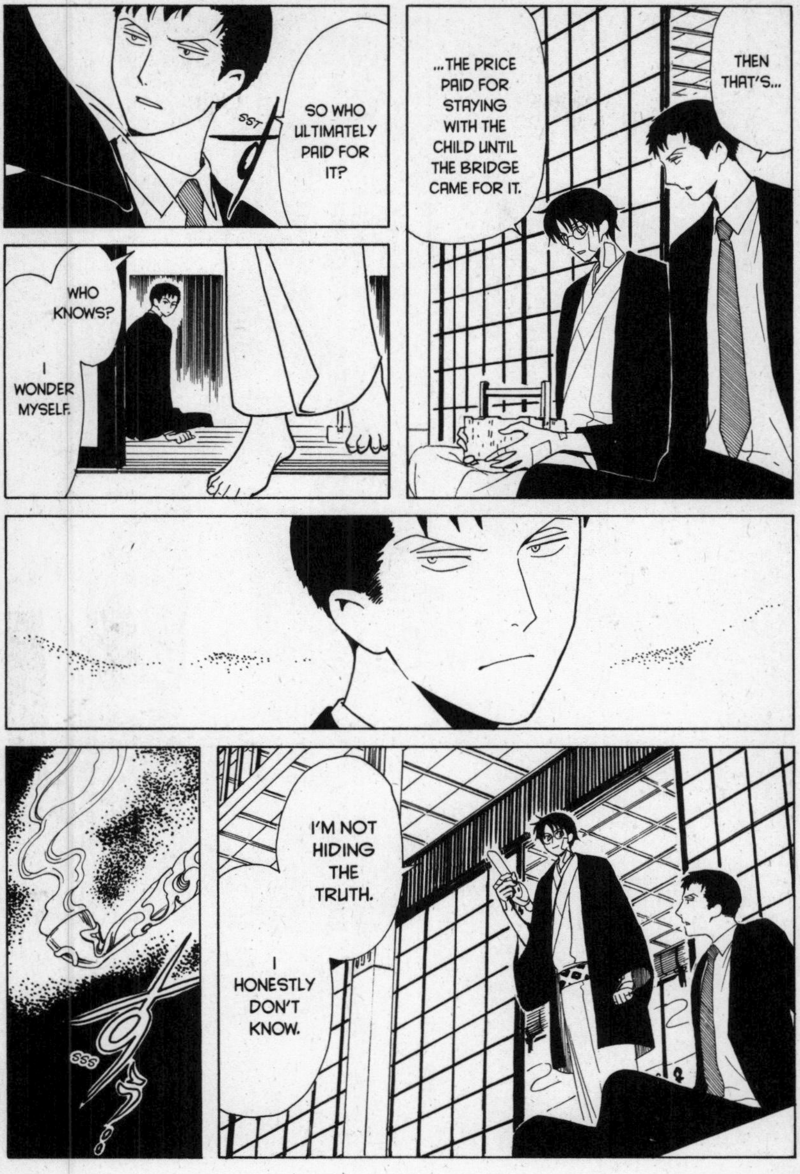
THEN THAT'S...
...THE PRICE PAID FOR STAYING WITH THE CHILD UNTIL THE BRIDGE CAME FOR IT.
SST
SO WHO ULTIMATELY PAID FOR IT?
WHO KNOWS?
I WONDER MYSELF.
I'M NOT HIDING THE TRUTH.
I HONESTLY DON'T KNOW.
SSS

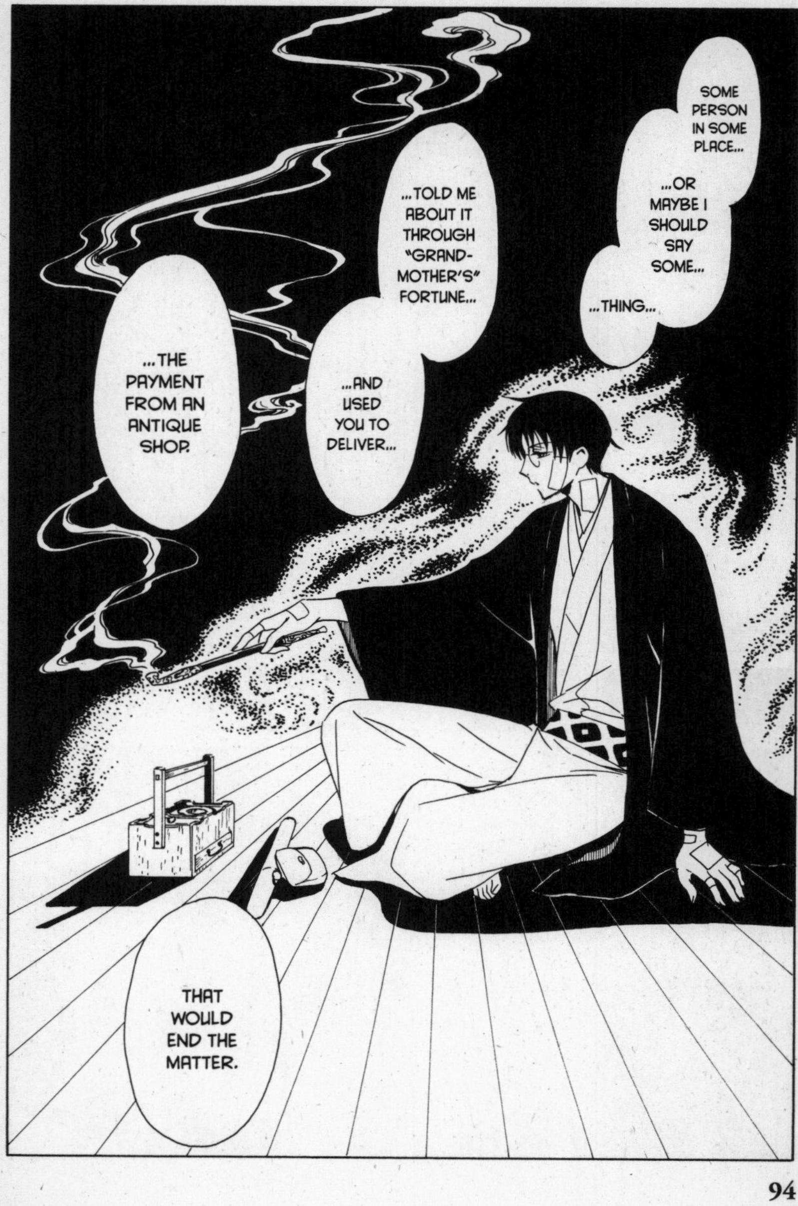
SOME PERSON IN SOME PLACE...
...OR MAYBE I SHOULD SAY SOME...
...THING...
...TOLD ME ABOUT IT THROUGH "GRAND-MOTHER'S" FORTUNE...
...AND USED YOU TO DELIVER...
...THE PAYMENT FROM AN ANTIQUE SHOP.
THAT WOULD END THE MATTER.

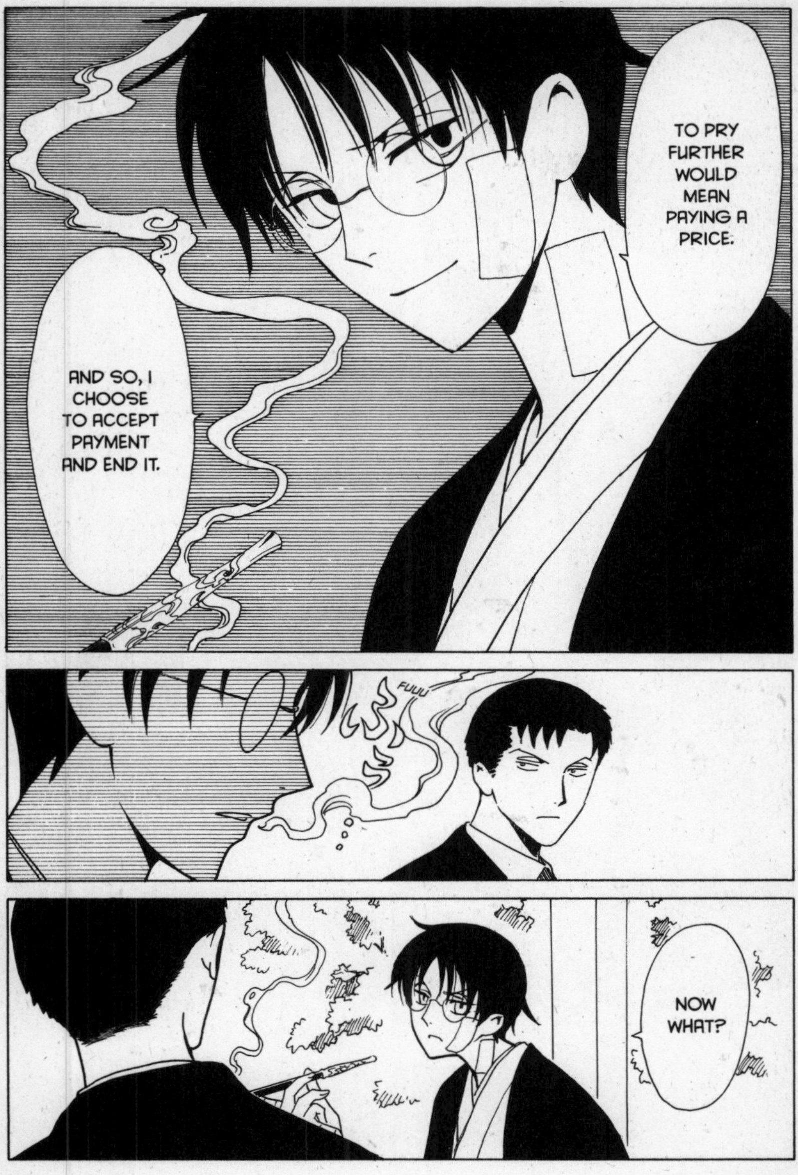
TO PRY FURTHER WOULD MEAN PAYING A PRICE.
AND SO, I CHOOSE TO ACCEPT PAYMENT AND END IT.
FUUU
NOW WHAT?

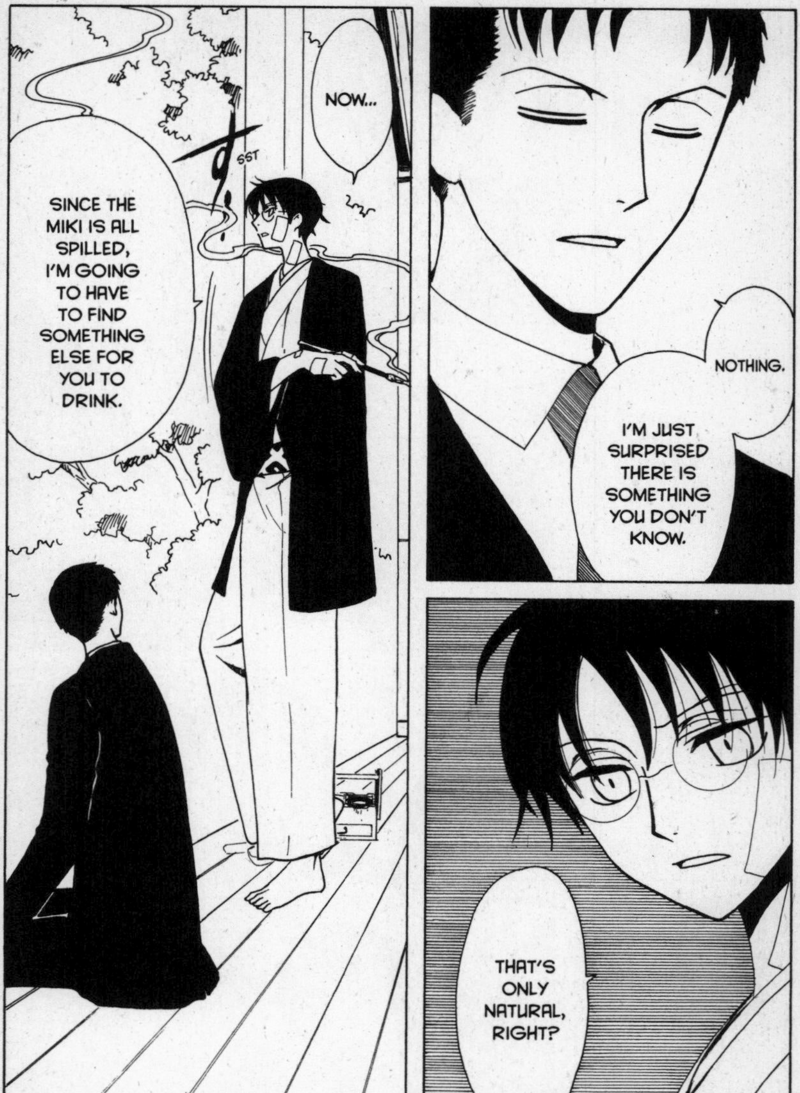
NOTHING.
I'M JUST SURPRISED THERE IS SOMETHING YOU DON'T KNOW.
THAT'S ONLY NATURAL, RIGHT?
NOW...
SST
SINCE THE MIKI IS ALL SPILLED, I'M GOING TO HAVE TO FIND SOMETHING ELSE FOR YOU TO DRINK.

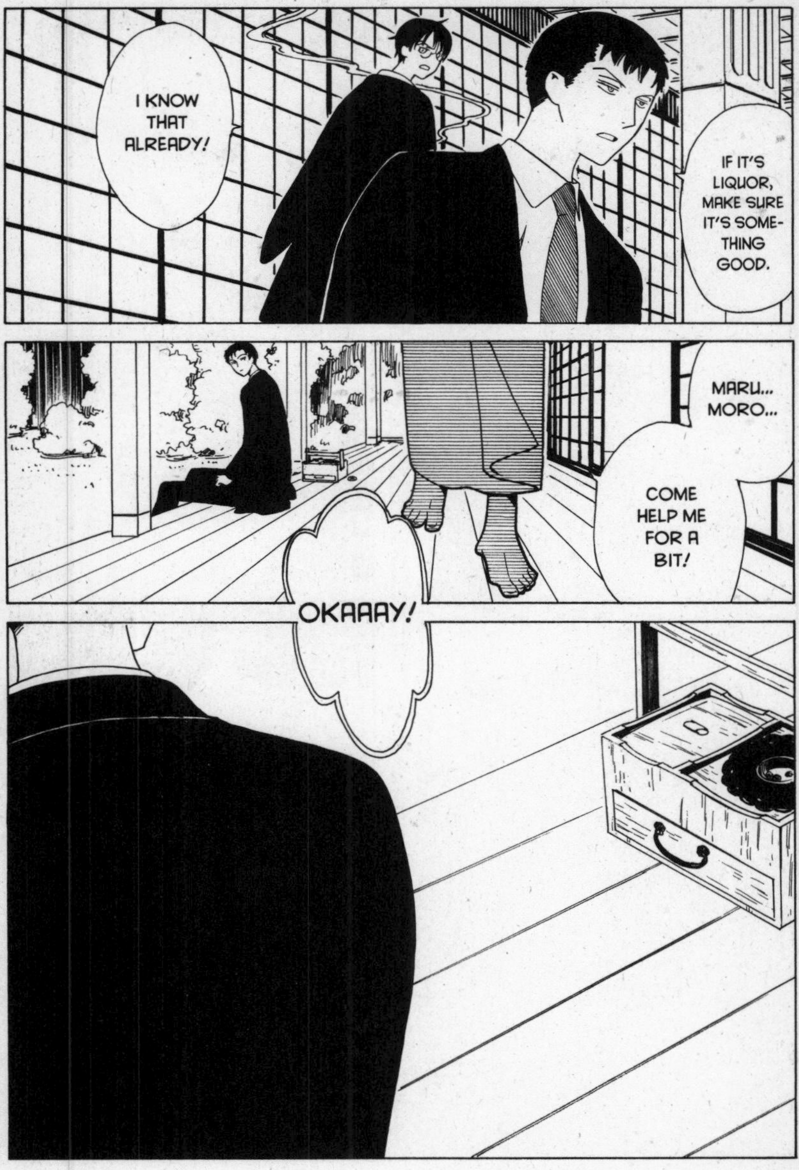
IF IT'S LIQUOR, MAKE SURE IT'S SOME-THING GOOD.
I KNOW THAT ALREADY!
MARU... MORO...
COME HELP ME FOR A BIT!
OKAAAY!

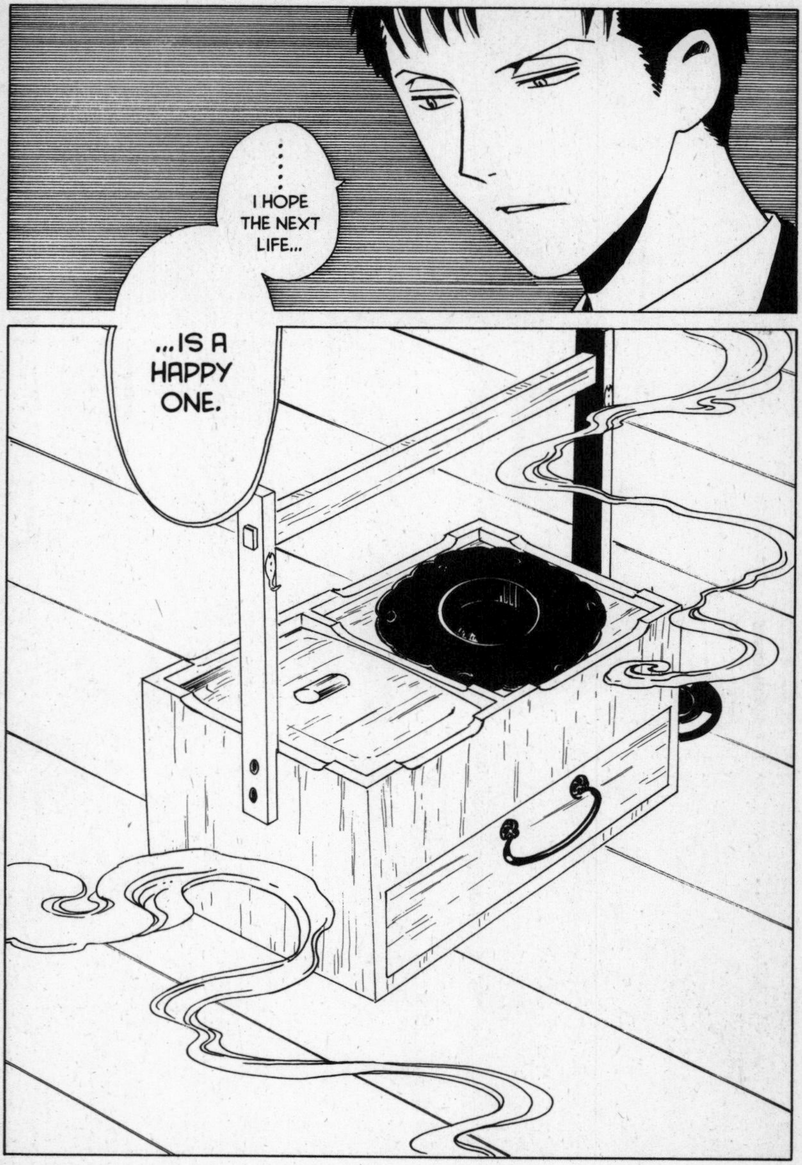
......
I HOPE THE NEXT LIFE...
...IS A HAPPY ONE.

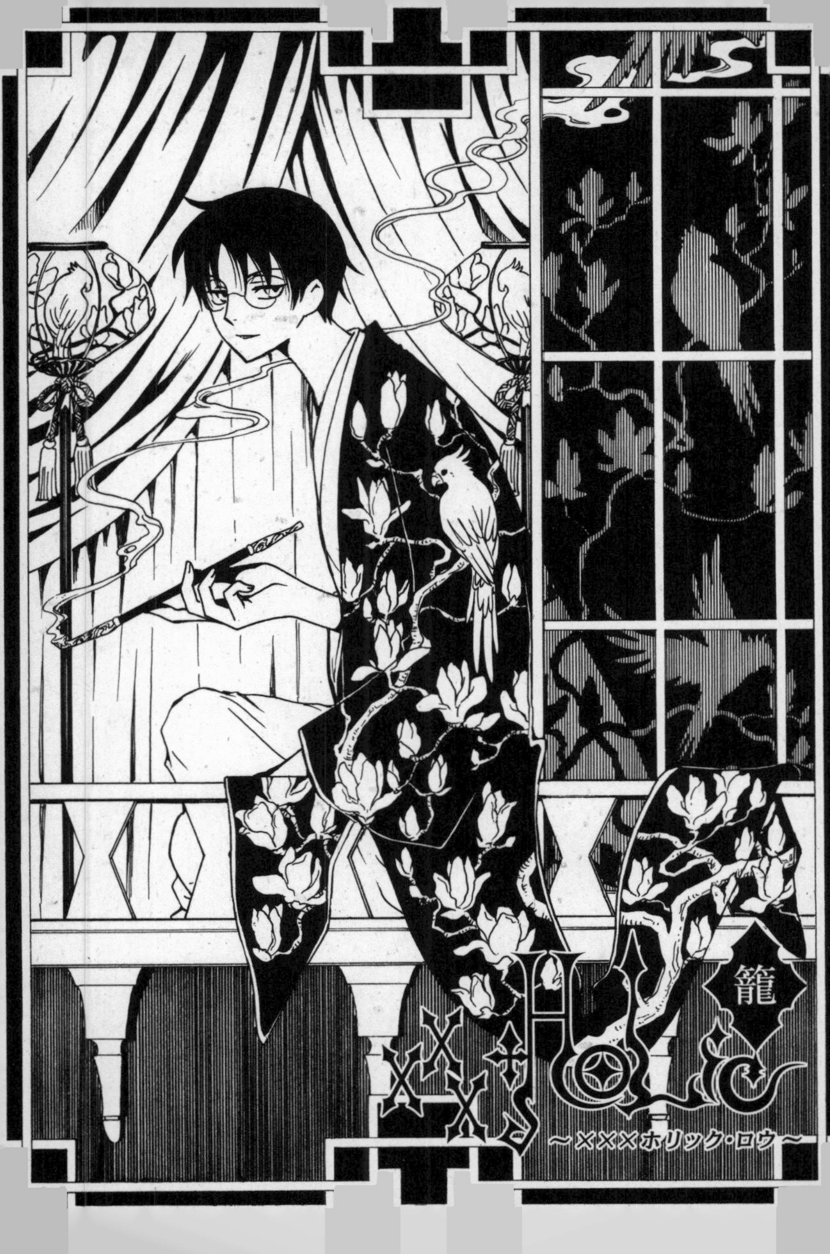

xxxHOLiC
籠
～×××ホリック・ロウ～

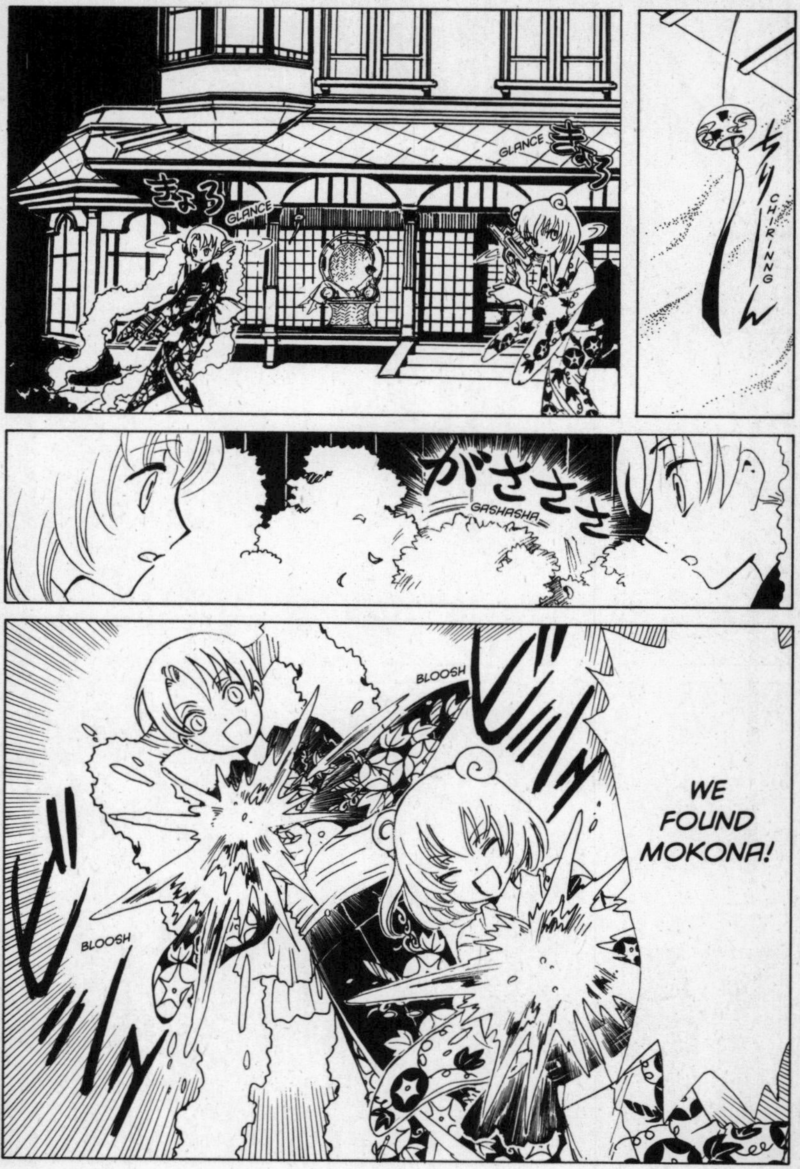
ちりーん
CHIRINNG
きょろ
GLANCE
きょろ
GLANCE
がさささ
GASHASHA
WE FOUND MOKONA!
BLOOSH
BLOOSH

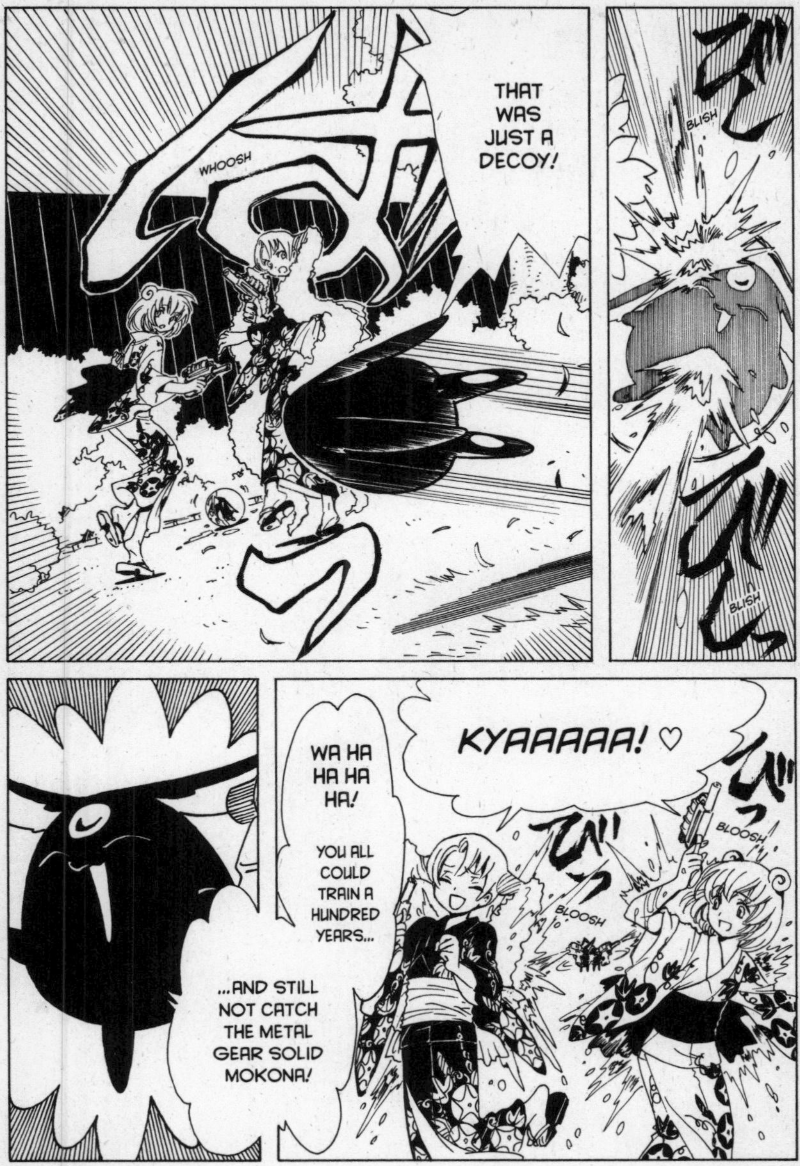
BLISH
BLISH
THAT WAS JUST A DECOY!
WHOOSH
KYAAAAA! ♡
BLOOSH
BLOOSH
WA HA HA HA HA!
YOU ALL COULD TRAIN A HUNDRED YEARS...
...AND STILL NOT CATCH THE METAL GEAR SOLID MOKONA!

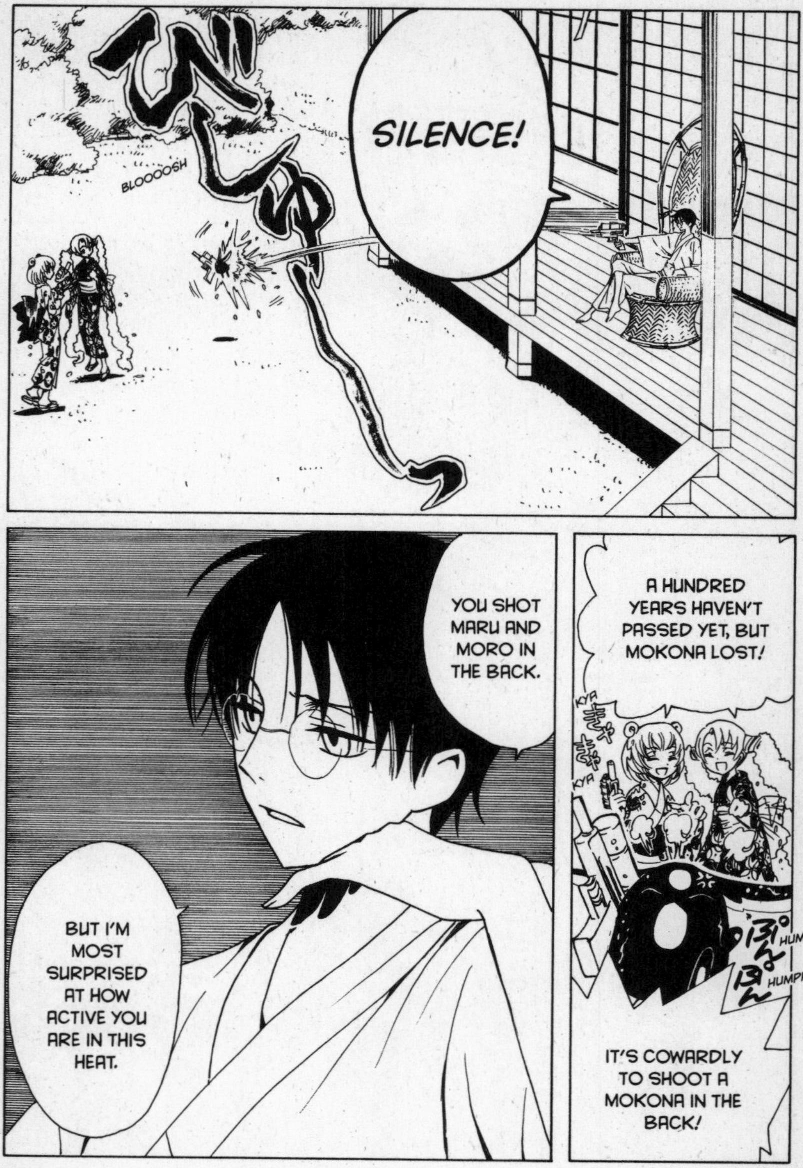
SILENCE!
BLOOOOSH
A HUNDRED YEARS HAVEN'T PASSED YET, BUT MOKONA LOST!
KYA
KYA
HUMPH
HUMPH
IT'S COWARDLY TO SHOOT A MOKONA IN THE BACK!
YOU SHOT MARU AND MORO IN THE BACK.
BUT I'M MOST SURPRISED AT HOW ACTIVE YOU ARE IN THIS HEAT.

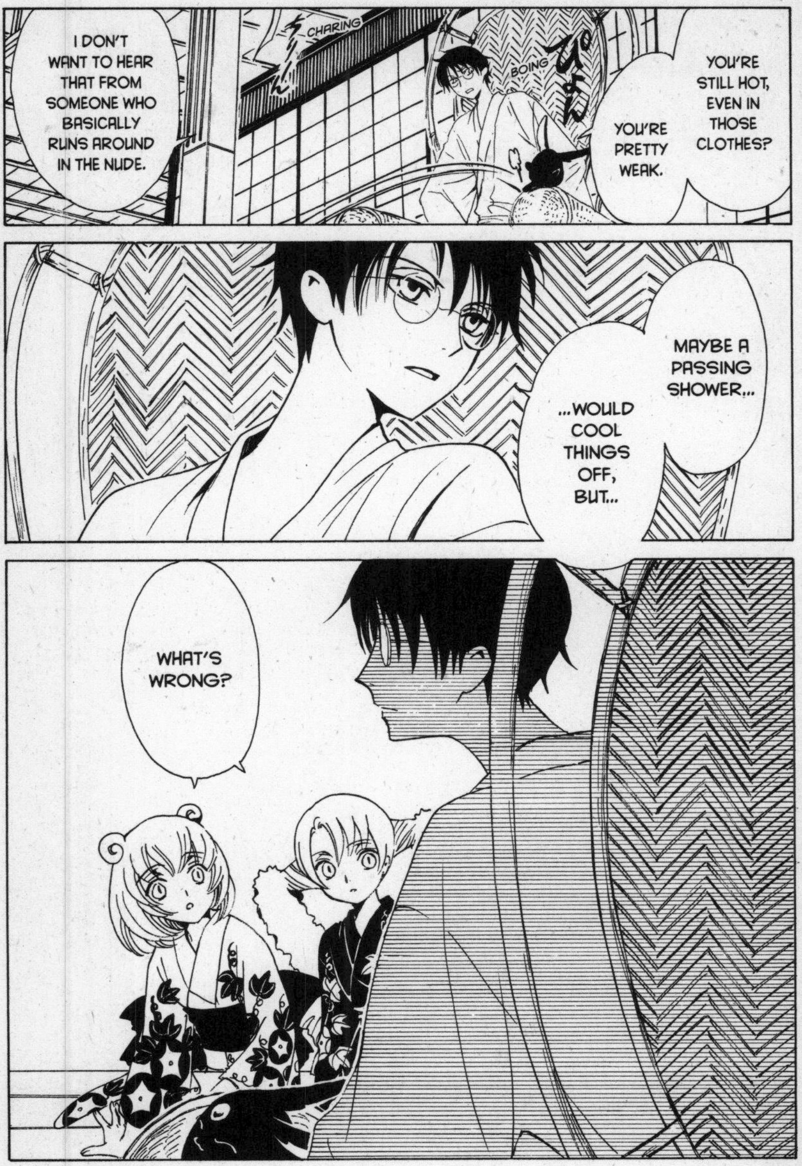
YOU'RE STILL HOT, EVEN IN THOSE CLOTHES?
YOU'RE PRETTY WEAK.
BOING
CHARING
I DON'T WANT TO HEAR THAT FROM SOMEONE WHO BASICALLY RUNS AROUND IN THE NUDE.
MAYBE A PASSING SHOWER...
...WOULD COOL THINGS OFF, BUT...
WHAT'S WRONG?

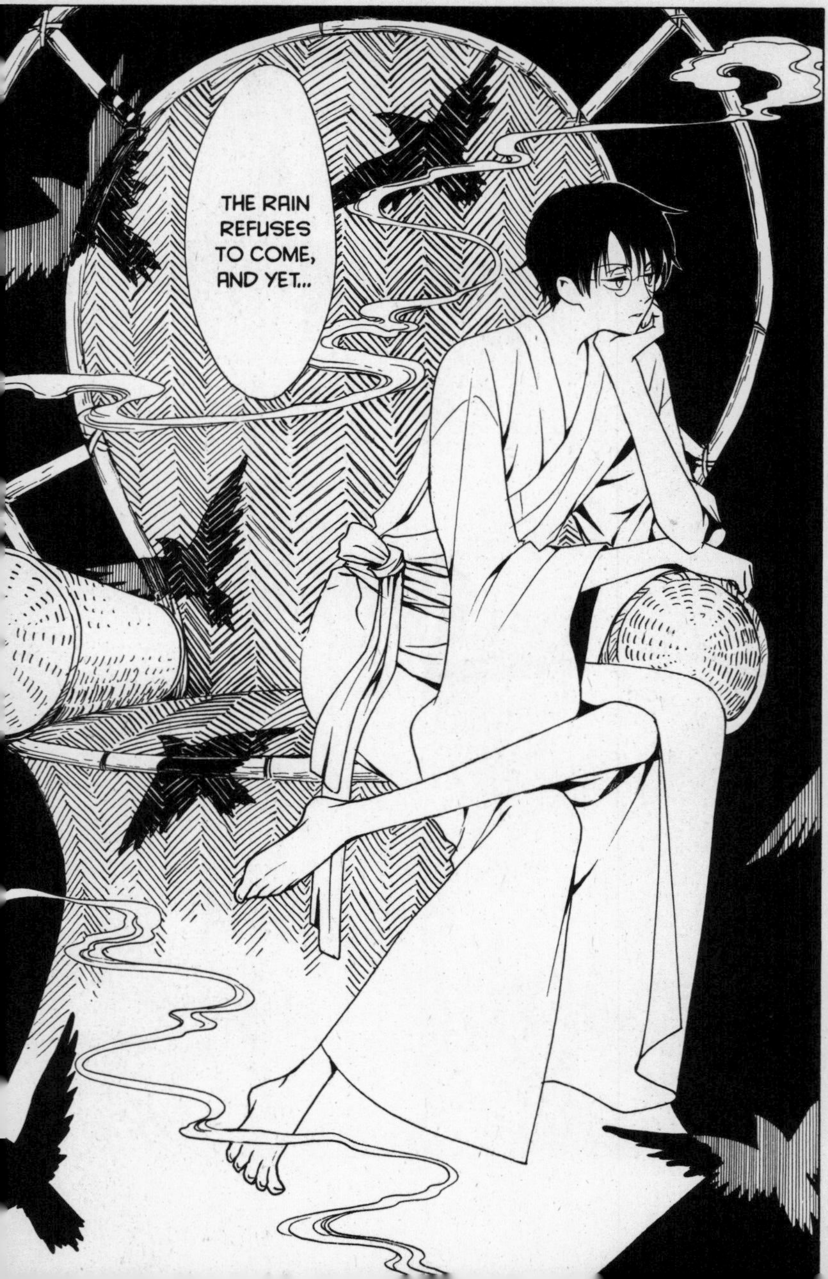
THE RAIN REFUSES TO COME, AND YET...

I'M SORRY TO HAVE KEPT YOU WAITING.

...A CUSTOMER HAS ARRIVED.

I DON'T MIND.

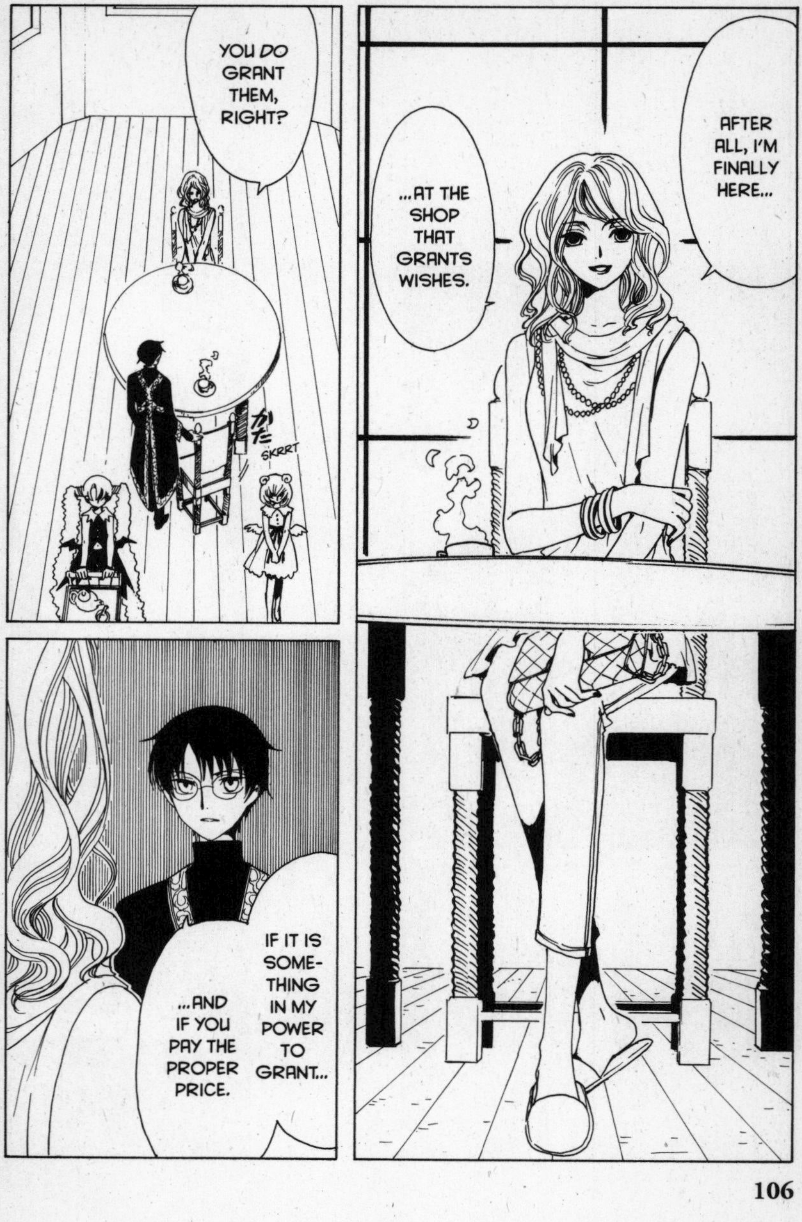
AFTER ALL, I'M FINALLY HERE...
...AT THE SHOP THAT GRANTS WISHES.
YOU DO GRANT THEM, RIGHT?
かた
SKRRT
IF IT IS SOME-THING IN MY POWER TO GRANT...
...AND IF YOU PAY THE PROPER PRICE.

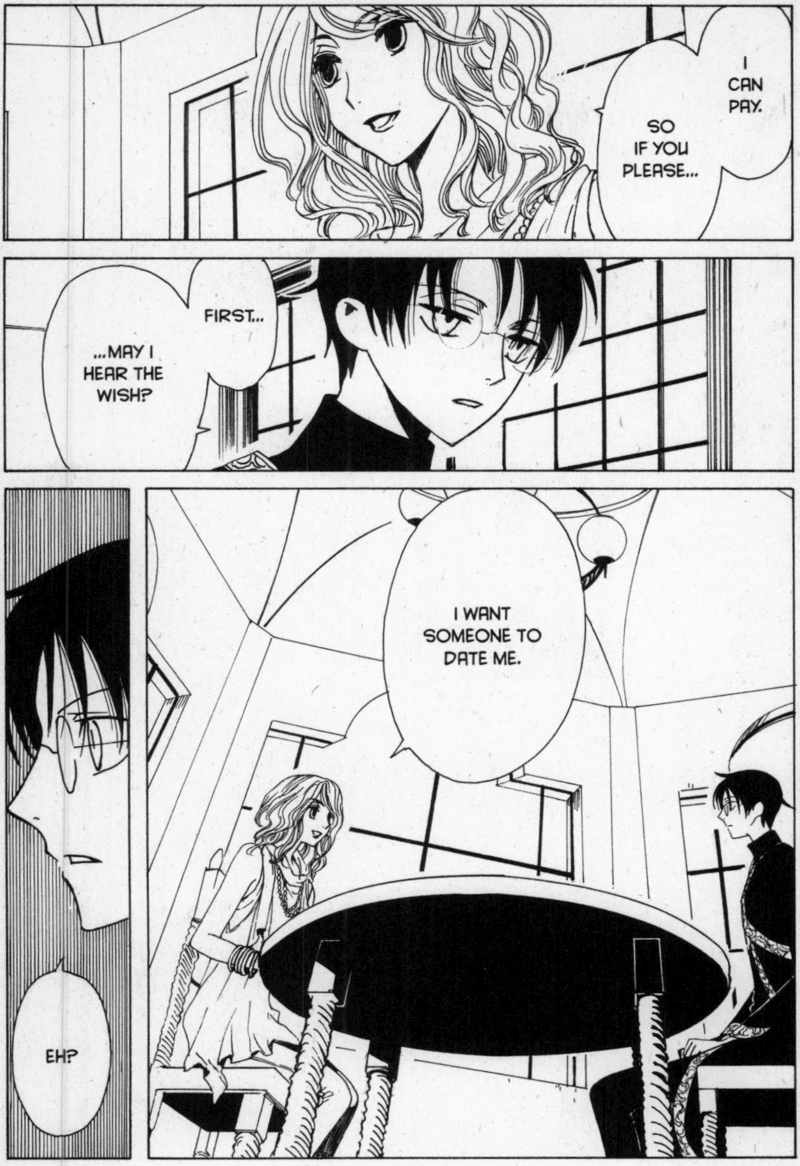
I CAN PAY.
SO IF YOU PLEASE...
FIRST...
...MAY I HEAR THE WISH?
I WANT SOMEONE TO DATE ME.
EH?

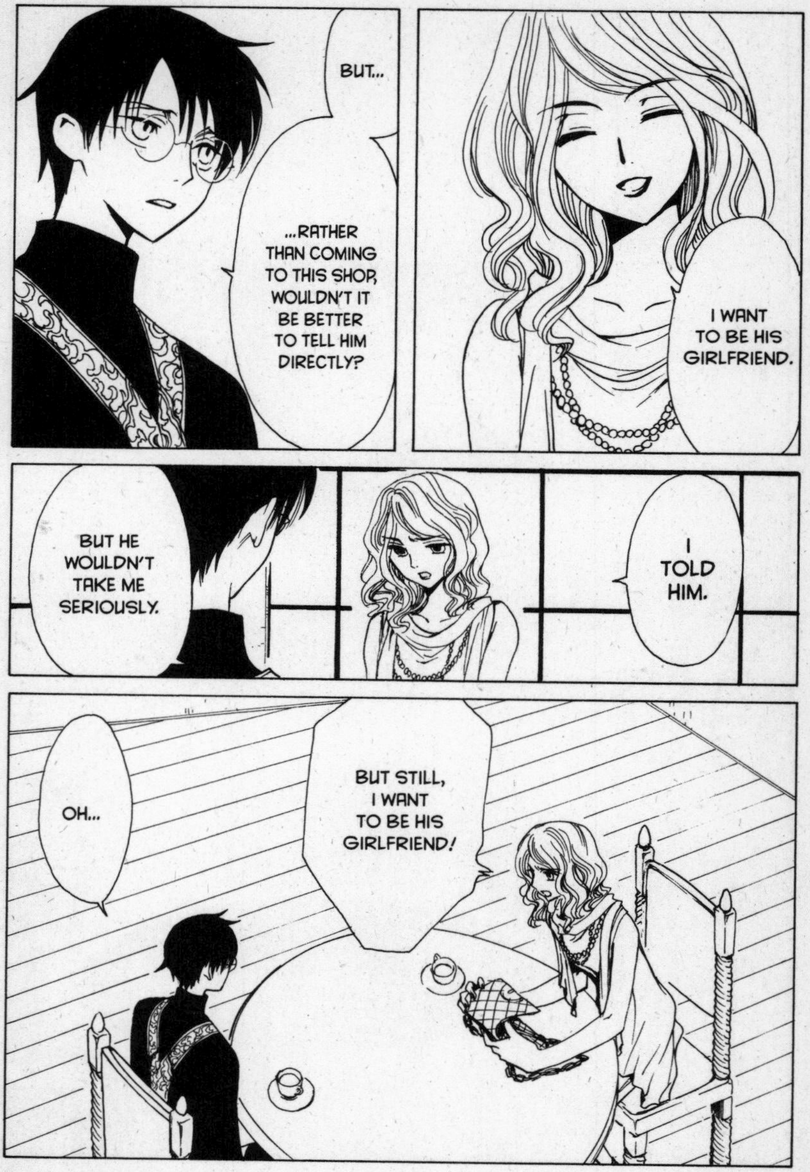
I WANT TO BE HIS GIRLFRIEND.
BUT...
...RATHER THAN COMING TO THIS SHOP, WOULDN'T IT BE BETTER TO TELL HIM DIRECTLY?
I TOLD HIM.
BUT HE WOULDN'T TAKE ME SERIOUSLY.
BUT STILL, I WANT TO BE HIS GIRLFRIEND!
OH...

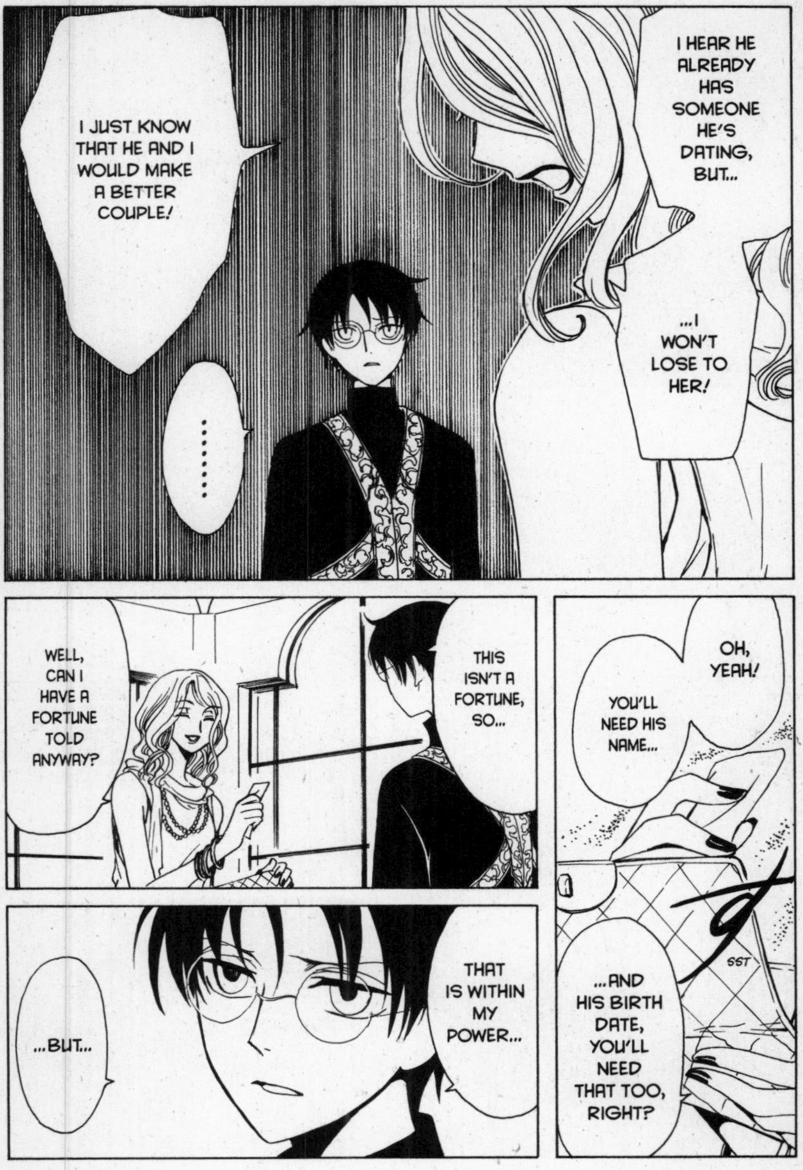
I HEAR HE ALREADY HAS SOMEONE HE'S DATING, BUT...
...I WON'T LOSE TO HER!
I JUST KNOW THAT HE AND I WOULD MAKE A BETTER COUPLE!
......
OH, YEAH!
YOU'LL NEED HIS NAME...
SST
...AND HIS BIRTH DATE, YOU'LL NEED THAT TOO, RIGHT?
THIS ISN'T A FORTUNE, SO...
WELL, CAN I HAVE A FORTUNE TOLD ANYWAY?
THAT IS WITHIN MY POWER...
...BUT...

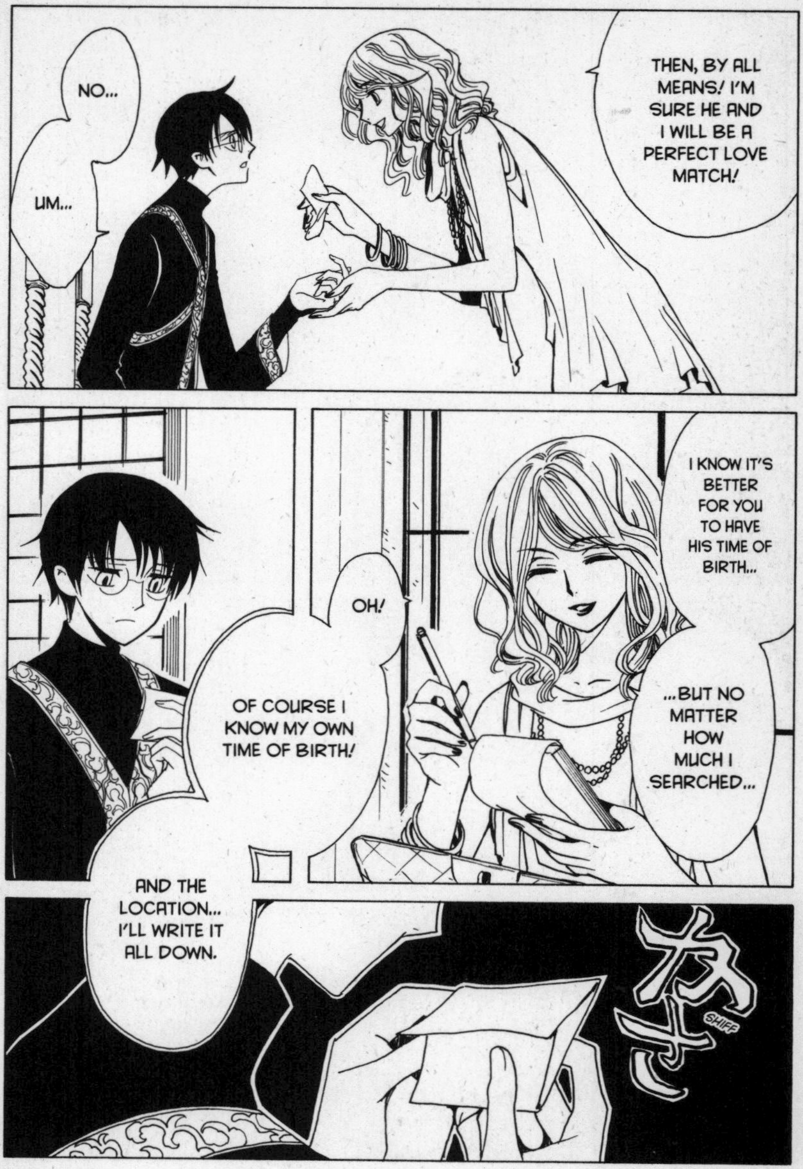
THEN, BY ALL MEANS! I'M SURE HE AND I WILL BE A PERFECT LOVE MATCH!
NO...
UM...
I KNOW IT'S BETTER FOR YOU TO HAVE HIS TIME OF BIRTH...
...BUT NO MATTER HOW MUCH I SEARCHED...
OH!
OF COURSE I KNOW MY OWN TIME OF BIRTH!
AND THE LOCATION... I'LL WRITE IT ALL DOWN.
かさ
SHIFF

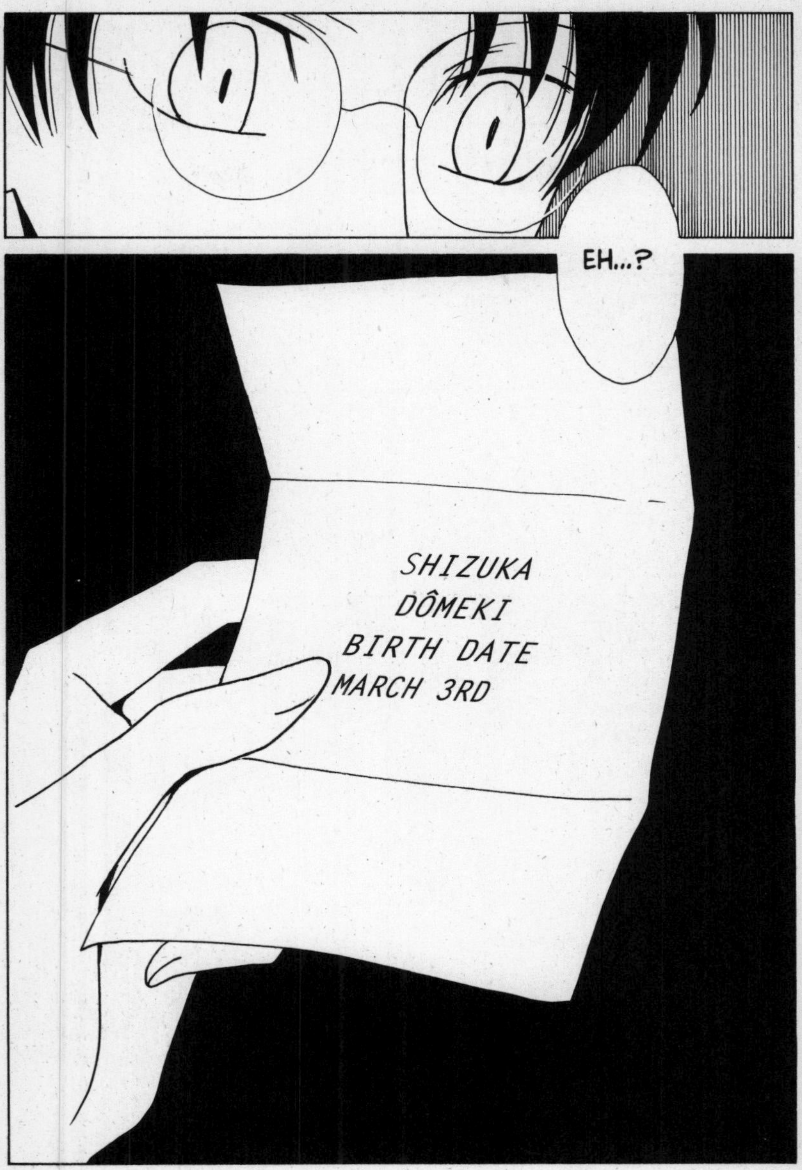
EH...?
SHIZUKA DÔMEKI BIRTH DATE MARCH 3RD

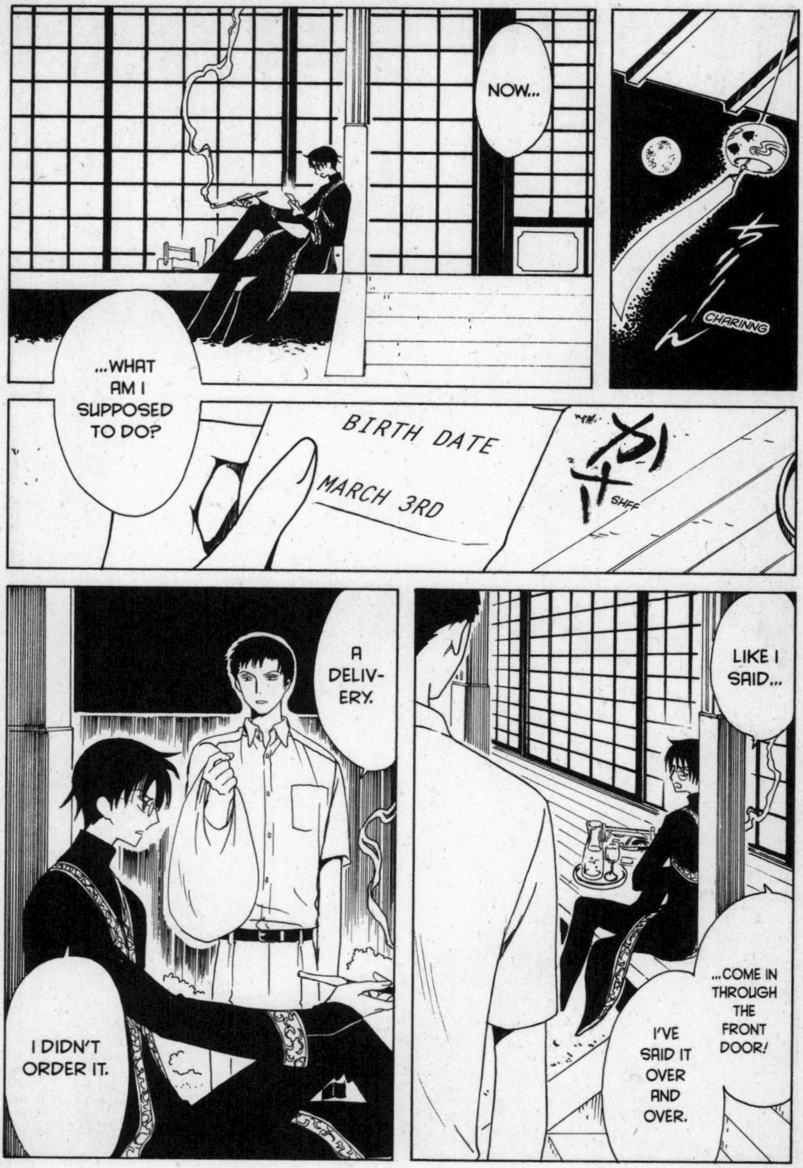

CHARINNG
NOW...
...WHAT AM I SUPPOSED TO DO?
SHFF
BIRTH DATE
MARCH 3RD
LIKE I SAID...
...COME IN THROUGH THE FRONT DOOR!
I'VE SAID IT OVER AND OVER.
A DELIVERY.
I DIDN'T ORDER IT.

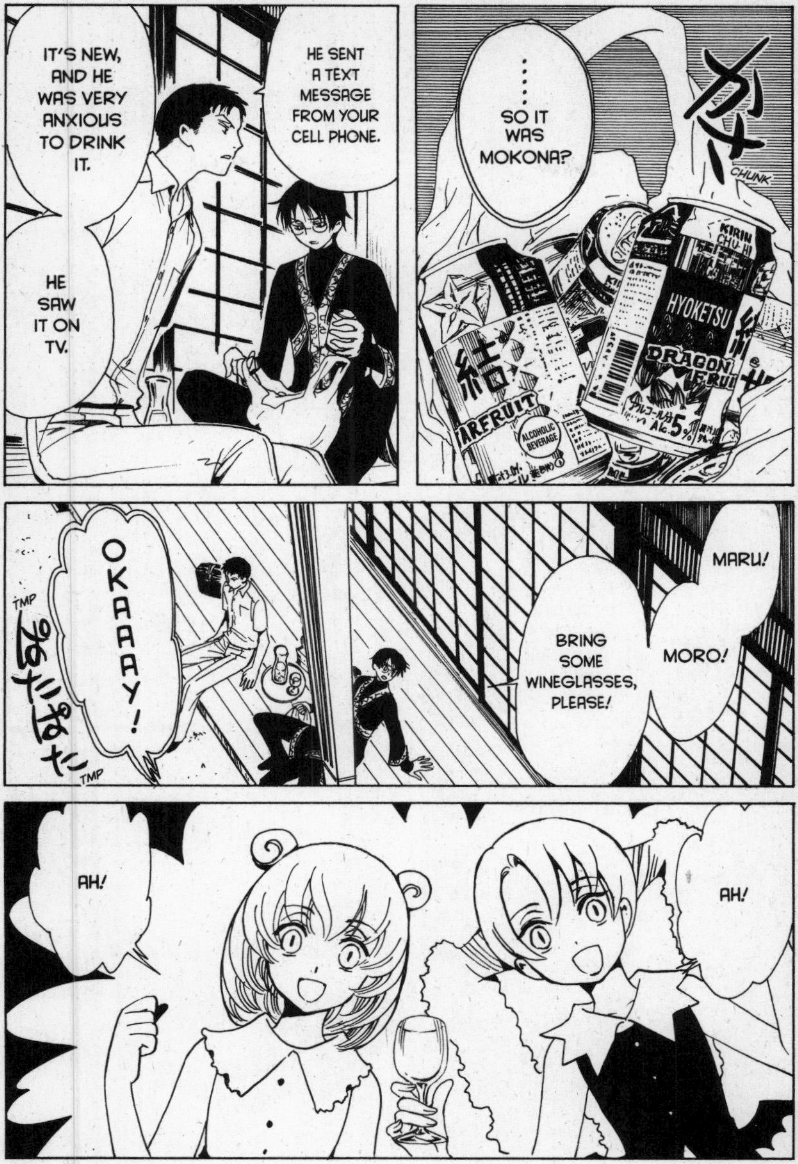
......
SO IT WAS MOKONA?
CHUNK
KIRIN CHU-HI
HYOKETSU
DRAGON FRUIT
ALCOHOLIC BEVERAGE
Alc. 5%
HE SENT A TEXT MESSAGE FROM YOUR CELL PHONE.
IT'S NEW, AND HE WAS VERY ANXIOUS TO DRINK IT.
HE SAW IT ON TV.
MARU!
MORO!
BRING SOME WINEGLASSES, PLEASE!
OKAAAY!
TMP
TMP
AH!
AH!

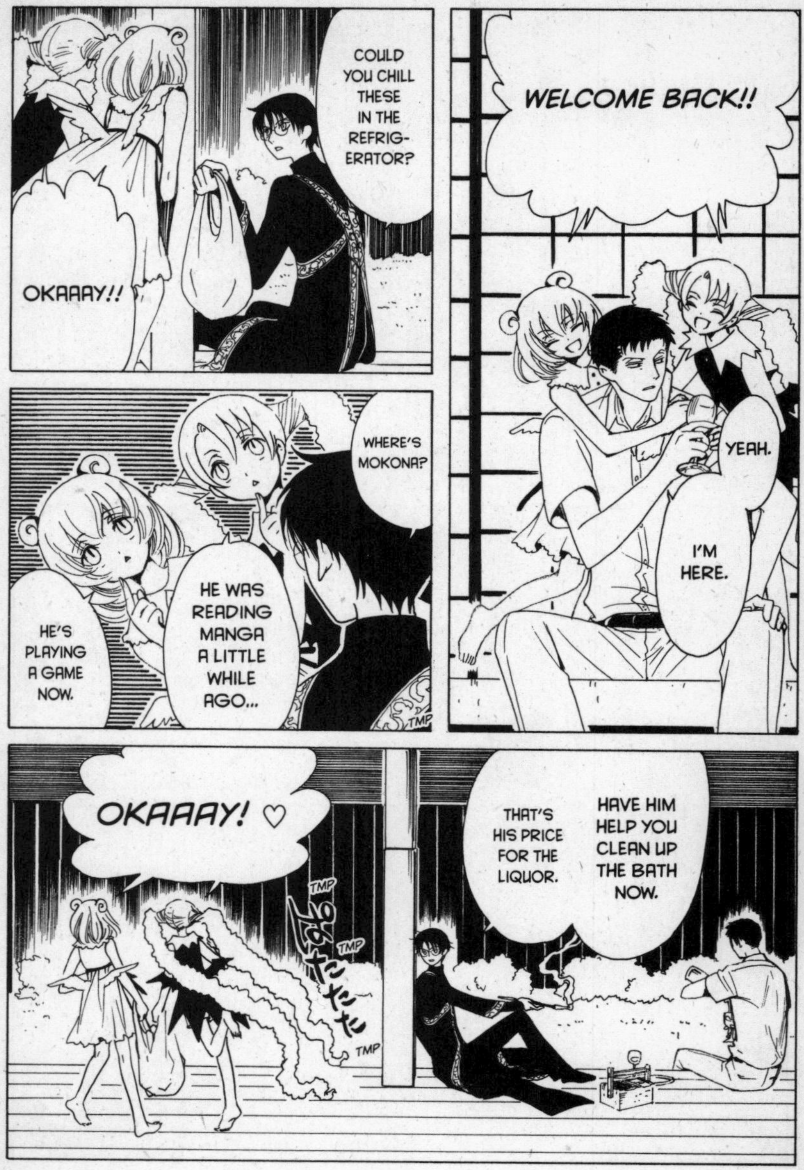
WELCOME BACK!!
YEAH.
I'M HERE.
COULD YOU CHILL THESE IN THE REFRIG-ERATOR?
OKAAAY!!
WHERE'S MOKONA?
HE WAS READING MANGA A LITTLE WHILE AGO...
HE'S PLAYING A GAME NOW.
TMP
HAVE HIM HELP YOU CLEAN UP THE BATH NOW.
THAT'S HIS PRICE FOR THE LIQUOR.
OKAAAY! ♡
TMP
TMP
TMP

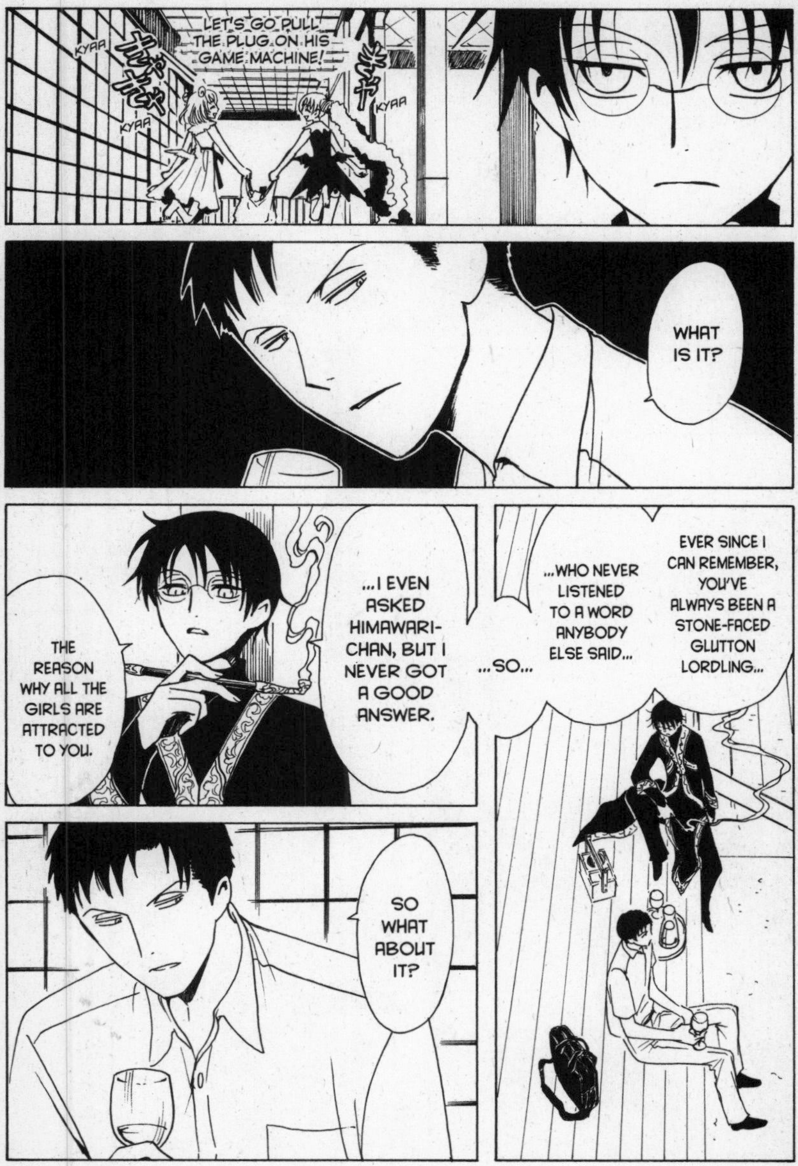
LET'S GO PULL THE PLUG ON HIS GAME MACHINE!
KYAA
KYAA
KYAA
WHAT IS IT?
EVER SINCE I CAN REMEMBER, YOU'VE ALWAYS BEEN A STONE-FACED GLUTTON LORDLING...
...WHO NEVER LISTENED TO A WORD ANYBODY ELSE SAID...
...SO...
...I EVEN ASKED HIMAWARI-CHAN, BUT I NEVER GOT A GOOD ANSWER.
THE REASON WHY ALL THE GIRLS ARE ATTRACTED TO YOU.
SO WHAT ABOUT IT?

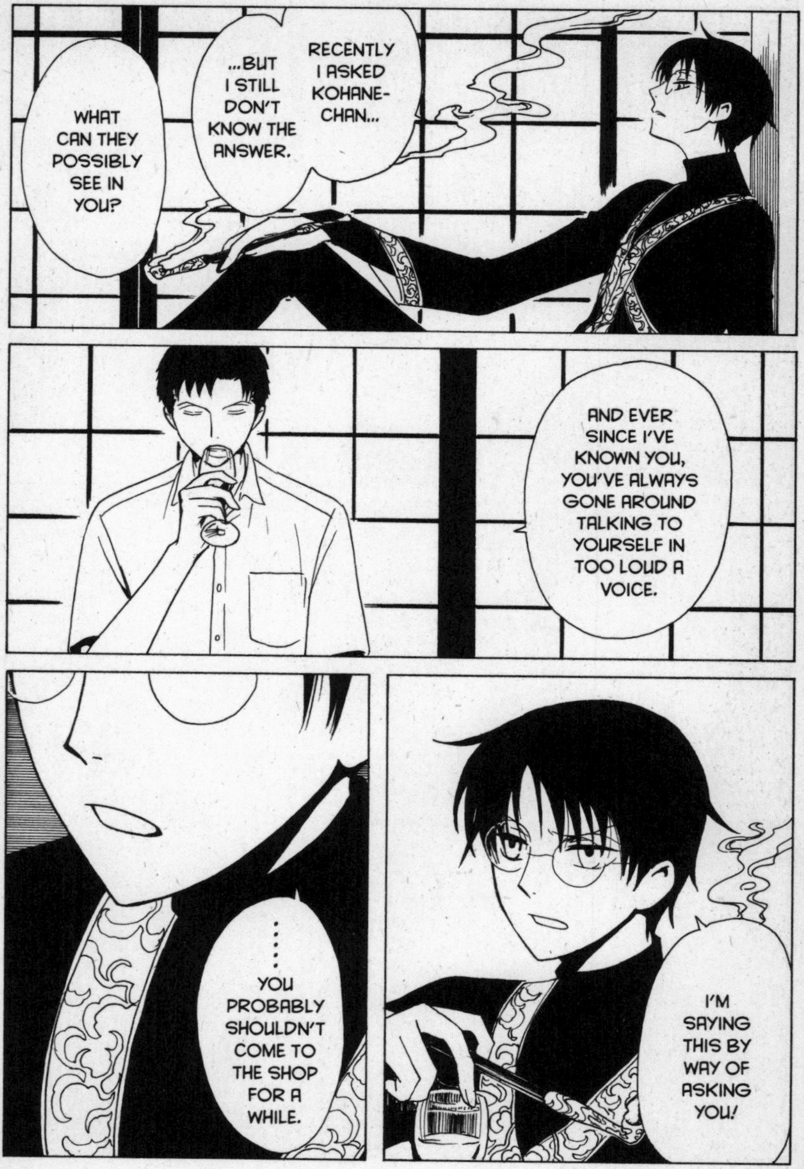
RECENTLY I ASKED KOHANE-CHAN...
...BUT I STILL DON'T KNOW THE ANSWER.
WHAT CAN THEY POSSIBLY SEE IN YOU?
AND EVER SINCE I'VE KNOWN YOU, YOU'VE ALWAYS GONE AROUND TALKING TO YOURSELF IN TOO LOUD A VOICE.
I'M SAYING THIS BY WAY OF ASKING YOU!
...... YOU PROBABLY SHOULDN'T COME TO THE SHOP FOR A WHILE.

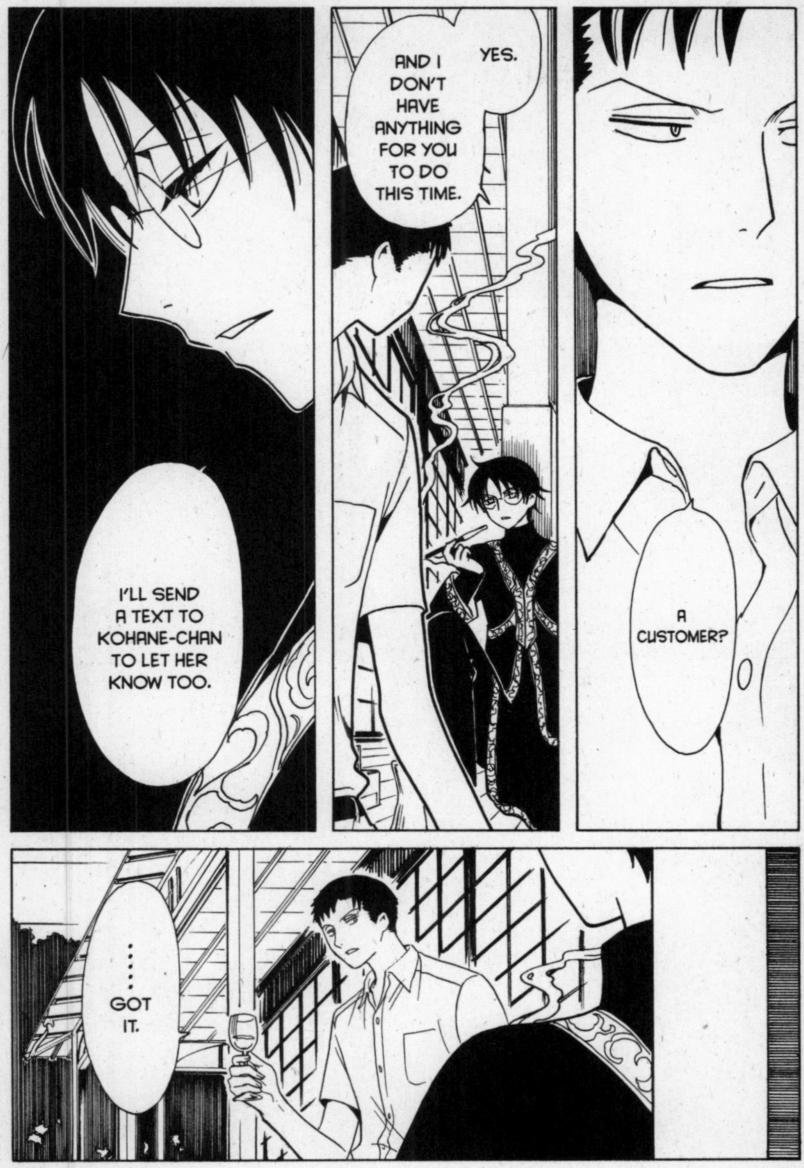
A CUSTOMER?
YES.
AND I DON'T HAVE ANYTHING FOR YOU TO DO THIS TIME.
I'LL SEND A TEXT TO KOHANE-CHAN TO LET HER KNOW TOO.
...... GOT IT.

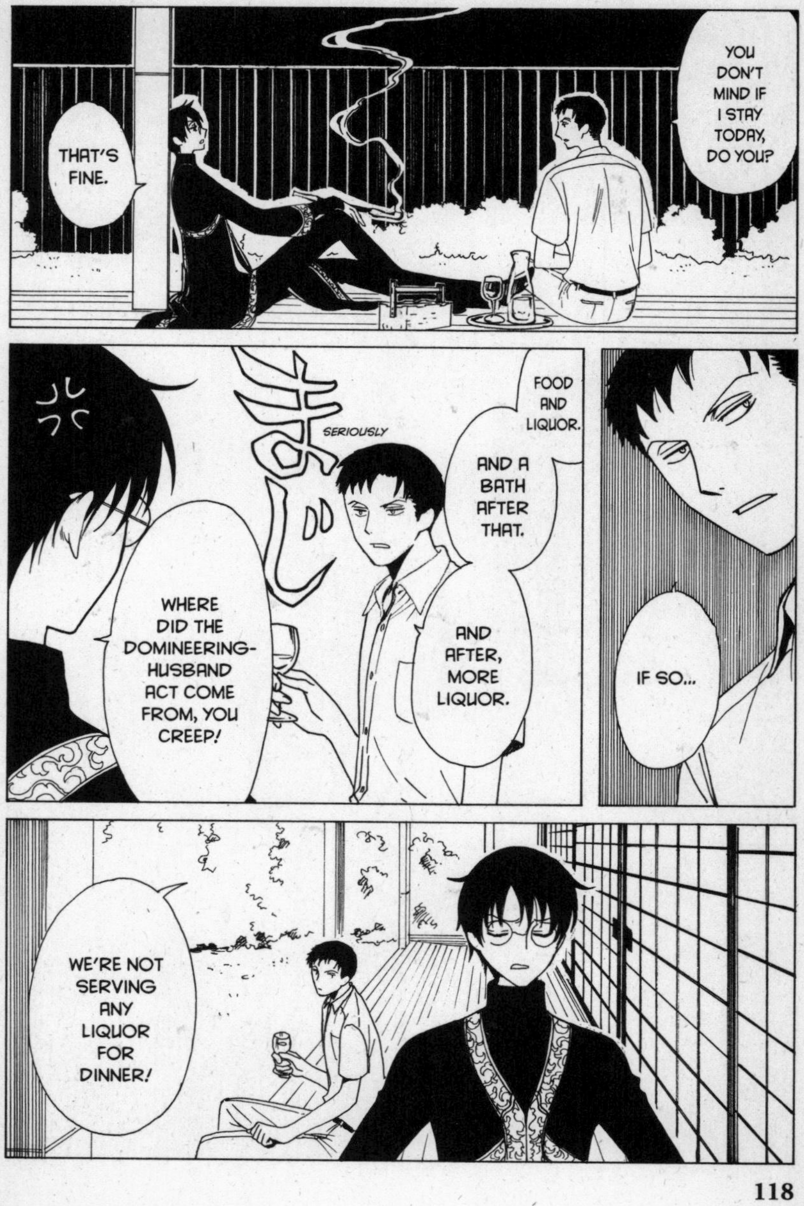
YOU DON'T MIND IF I STAY TODAY, DO YOU?
THAT'S FINE.
IF SO...
FOOD AND LIQUOR.
AND A BATH AFTER THAT.
AND AFTER, MORE LIQUOR.
SERIOUSLY
WHERE DID THE DOMINEERING-HUSBAND ACT COME FROM, YOU CREEP!
WE'RE NOT SERVING ANY LIQUOR FOR DINNER!

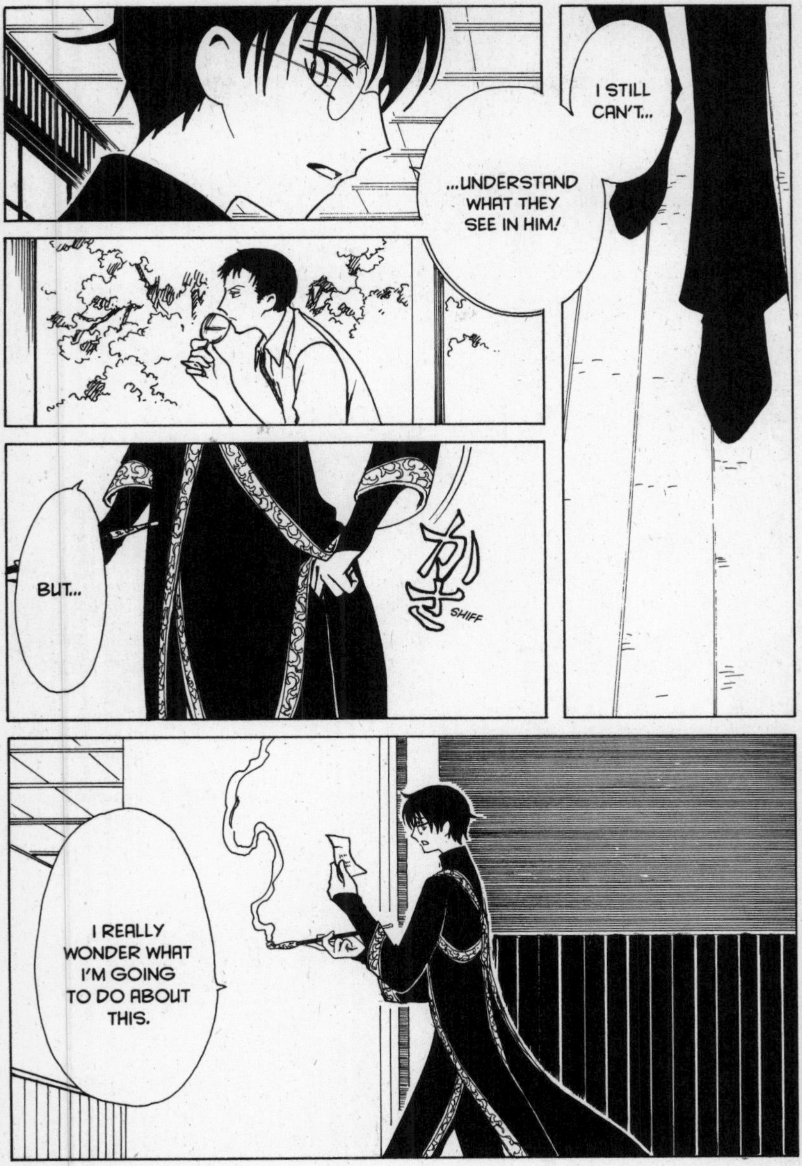

I STILL CAN'T...
...UNDERSTAND WHAT THEY SEE IN HIM!
BUT...
SHIFF
I REALLY WONDER WHAT I'M GOING TO DO ABOUT THIS.

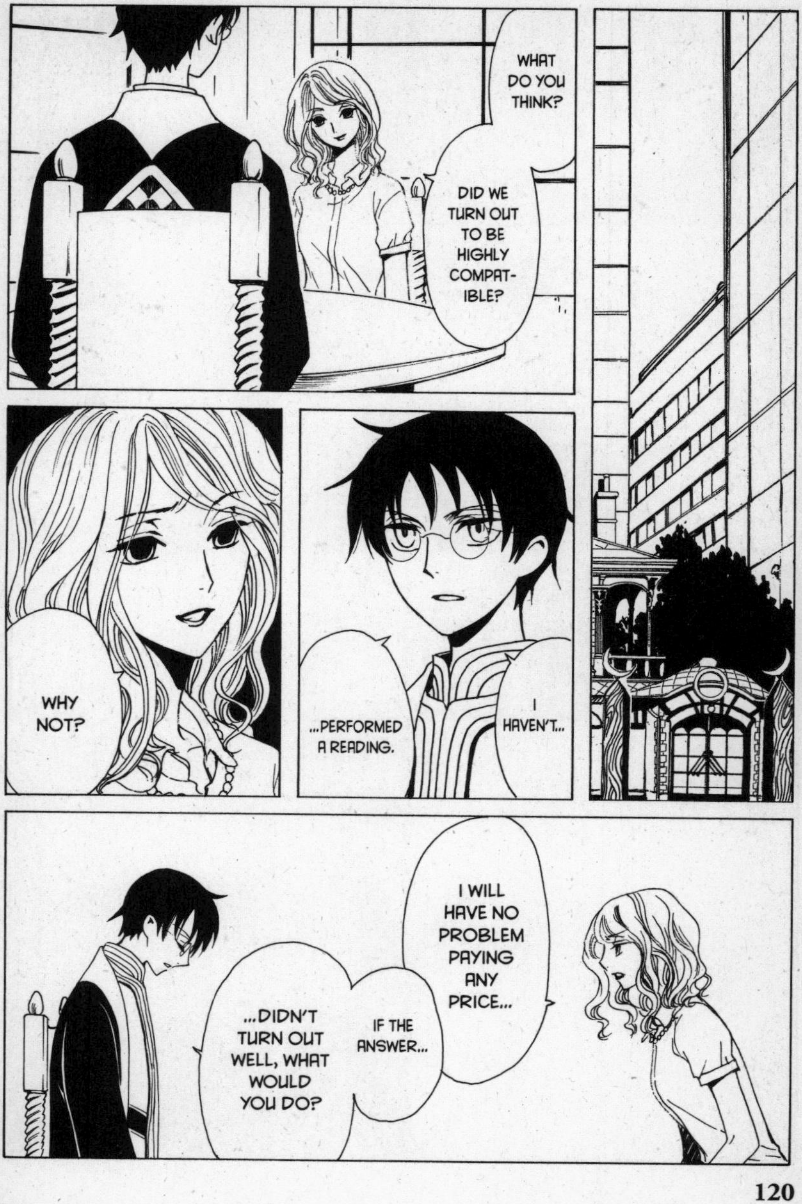
WHAT DO YOU THINK?
DID WE TURN OUT TO BE HIGHLY COMPAT-IBLE?
I HAVEN'T...
...PERFORMED A READING.
WHY NOT?
I WILL HAVE NO PROBLEM PAYING ANY PRICE...
IF THE ANSWER...
...DIDN'T TURN OUT WELL, WHAT WOULD YOU DO?

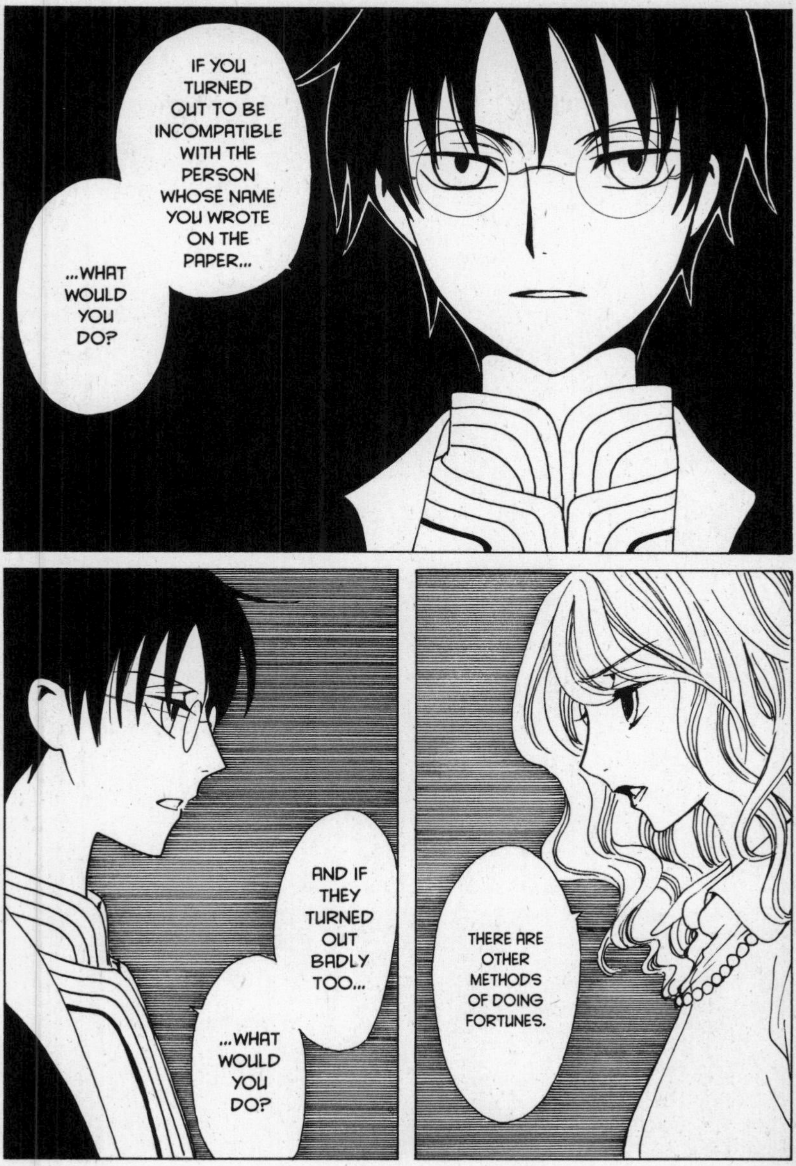
IF YOU TURNED OUT TO BE INCOMPATIBLE WITH THE PERSON WHOSE NAME YOU WROTE ON THE PAPER...
...WHAT WOULD YOU DO?
THERE ARE OTHER METHODS OF DOING FORTUNES.
AND IF THEY TURNED OUT BADLY TOO...
...WHAT WOULD YOU DO?

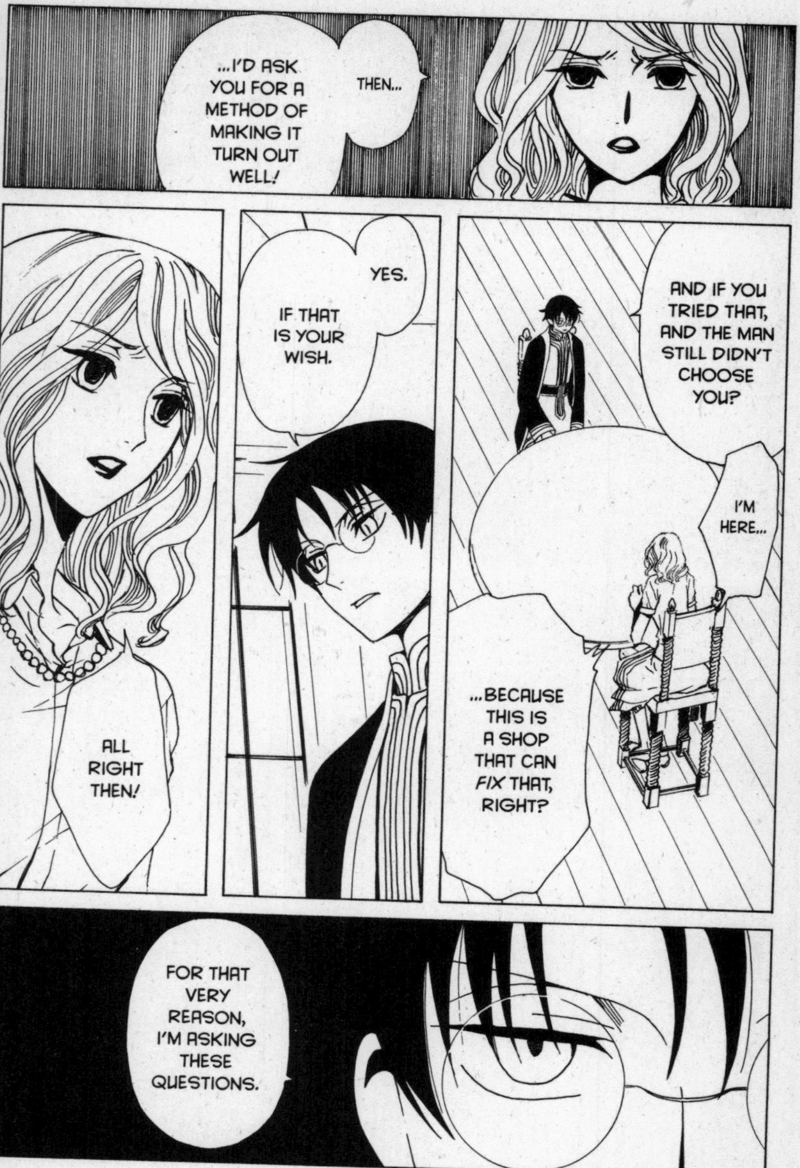
THEN...
...I'D ASK YOU FOR A METHOD OF MAKING IT TURN OUT WELL!
AND IF YOU TRIED THAT, AND THE MAN STILL DIDN'T CHOOSE YOU?
I'M HERE...
...BECAUSE THIS IS A SHOP THAT CAN *FIX* THAT, RIGHT?
YES.
IF THAT IS YOUR WISH.
ALL RIGHT THEN!
FOR THAT VERY REASON, I'M ASKING THESE QUESTIONS.

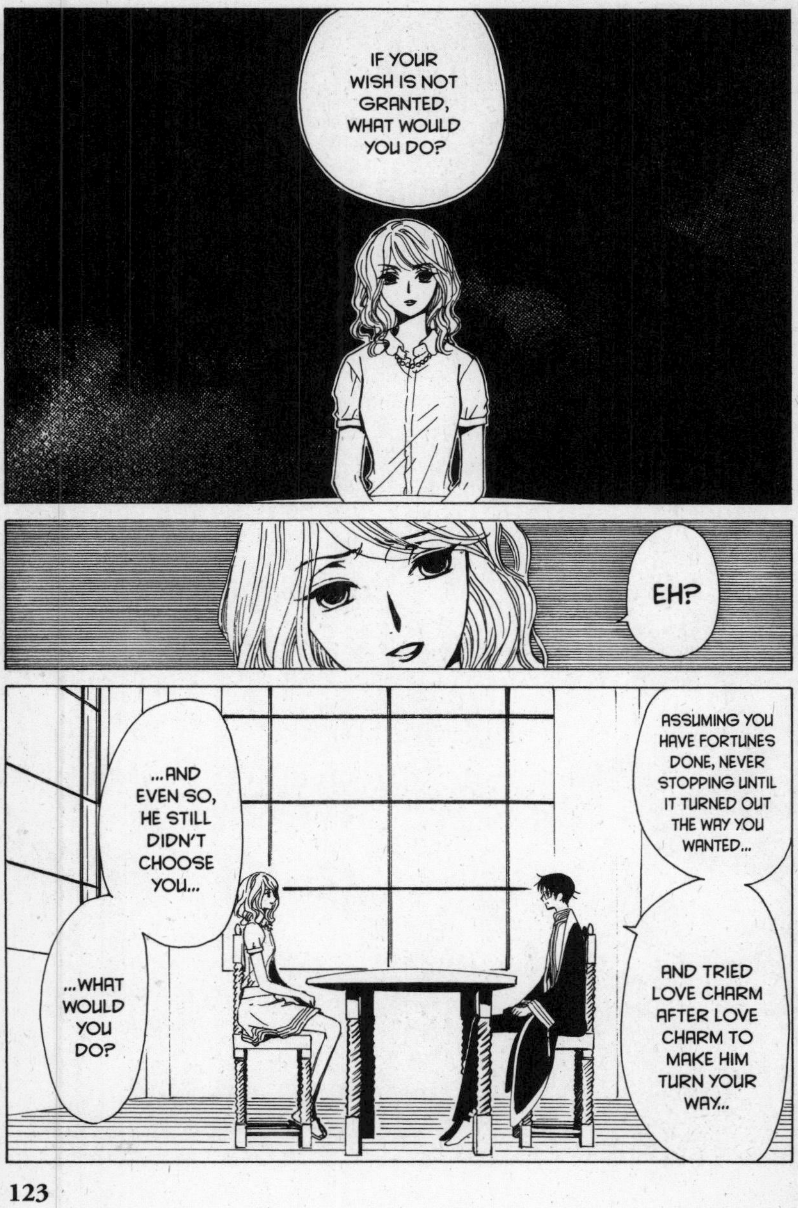
IF YOUR WISH IS NOT GRANTED, WHAT WOULD YOU DO?
EH?
ASSUMING YOU HAVE FORTUNES DONE, NEVER STOPPING UNTIL IT TURNED OUT THE WAY YOU WANTED...
AND TRIED LOVE CHARM AFTER LOVE CHARM TO MAKE HIM TURN YOUR WAY...
...AND EVEN SO, HE STILL DIDN'T CHOOSE YOU...
...WHAT WOULD YOU DO?

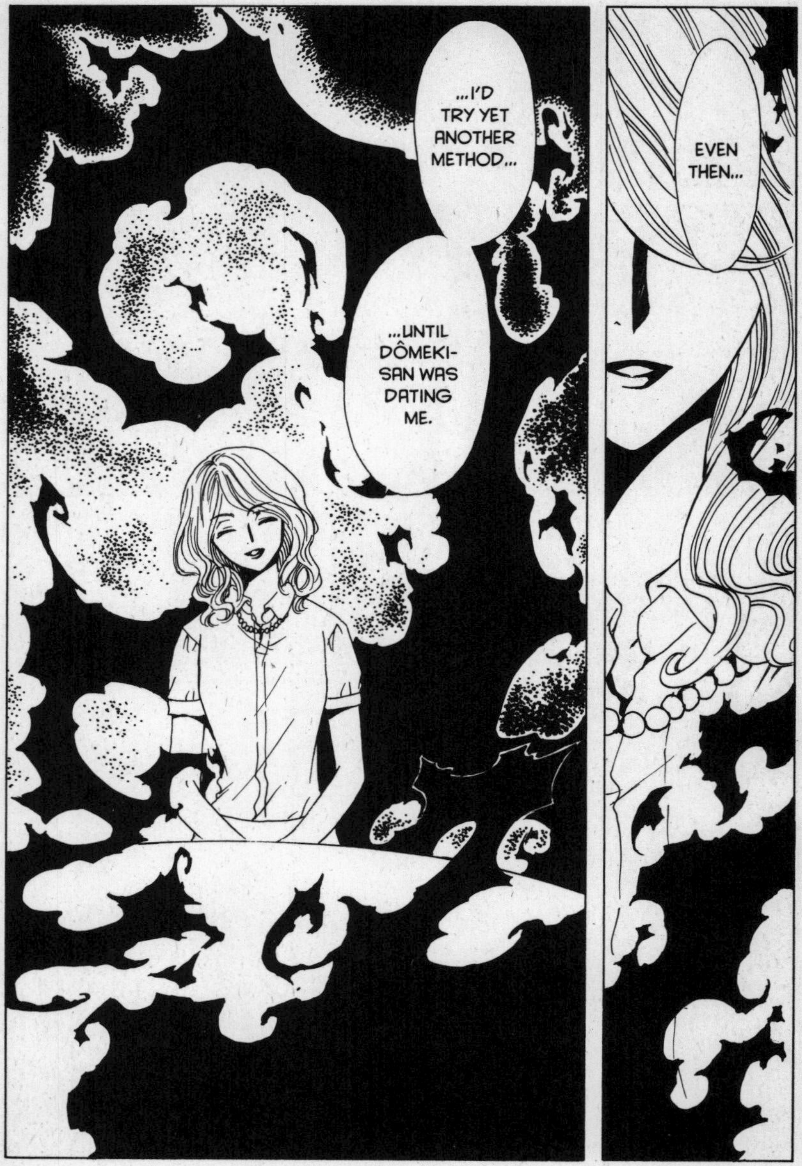
EVEN THEN...
...I'D TRY YET ANOTHER METHOD...
...UNTIL DÔMEKI-SAN WAS DATING ME.

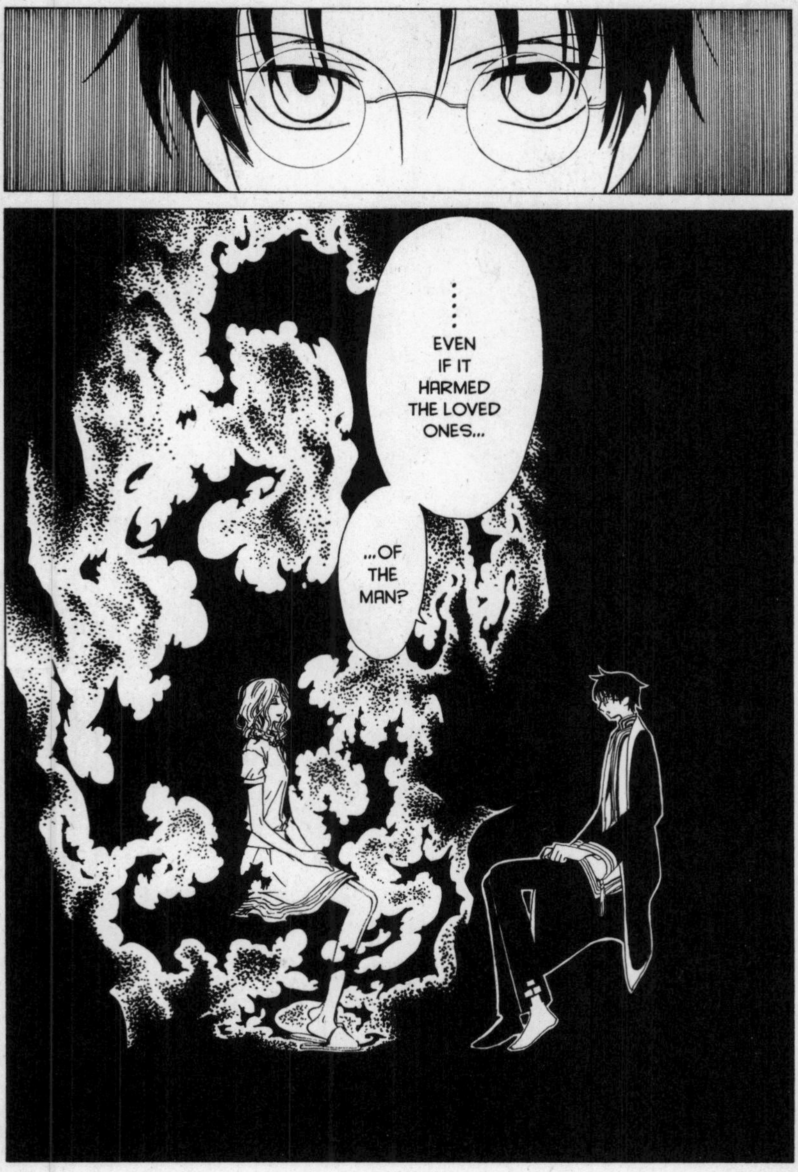
......
EVEN IF IT HARMED THE LOVED ONES...
...OF THE MAN?

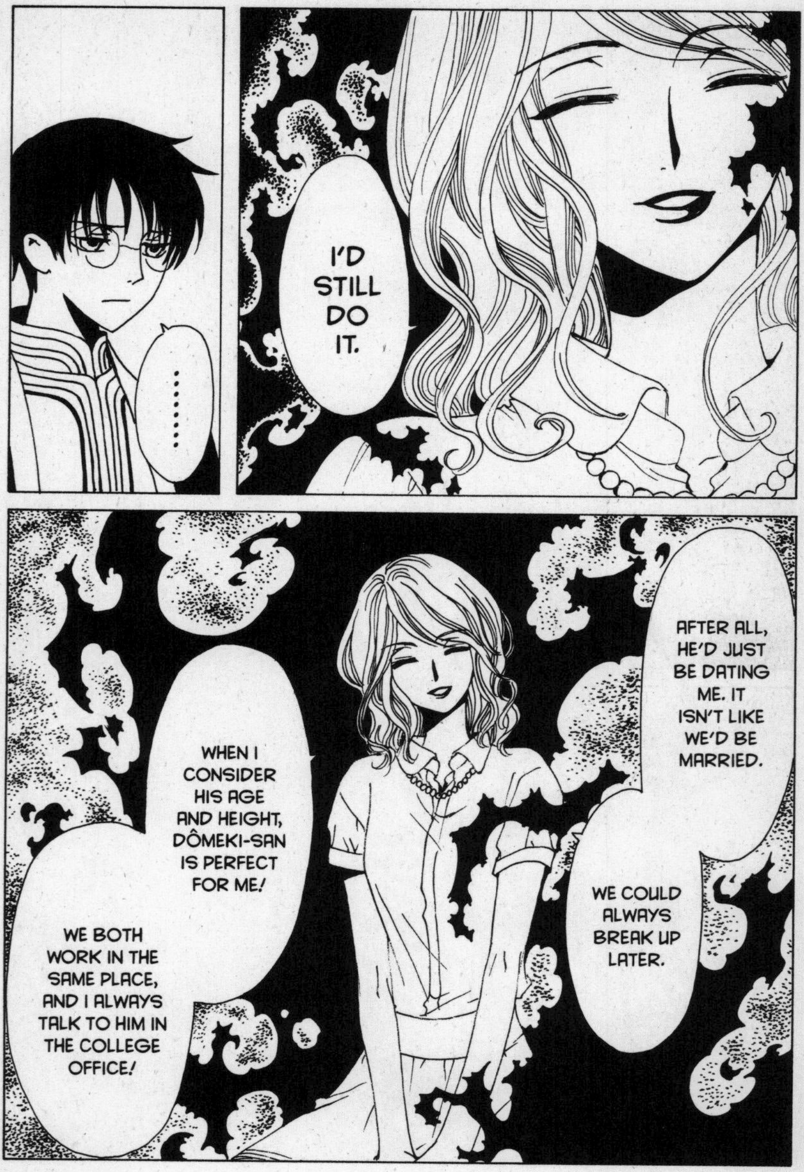
I'D STILL DO IT.
......
AFTER ALL, HE'D JUST BE DATING ME. IT ISN'T LIKE WE'D BE MARRIED.
WE COULD ALWAYS BREAK UP LATER.
WHEN I CONSIDER HIS AGE AND HEIGHT, DÔMEKI-SAN IS PERFECT FOR ME!
WE BOTH WORK IN THE SAME PLACE, AND I ALWAYS TALK TO HIM IN THE COLLEGE OFFICE!

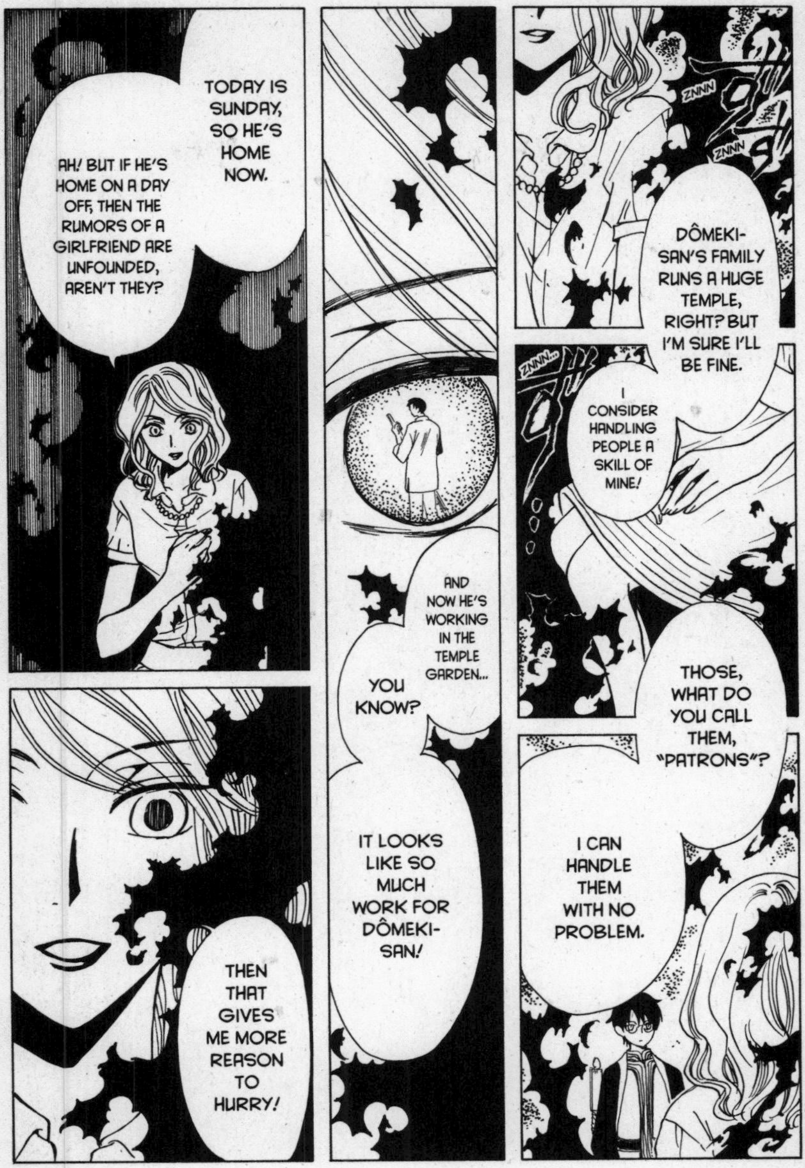
ZNNN
ZNNN
DÔMEKI-SAN'S FAMILY RUNS A HUGE TEMPLE, RIGHT? BUT I'M SURE I'LL BE FINE.
ZNNN...
I CONSIDER HANDLING PEOPLE A SKILL OF MINE!
THOSE, WHAT DO YOU CALL THEM, "PATRONS"?
I CAN HANDLE THEM WITH NO PROBLEM.
AND NOW HE'S WORKING IN THE TEMPLE GARDEN...
YOU KNOW?
IT LOOKS LIKE SO MUCH WORK FOR DÔMEKI-SAN!
TODAY IS SUNDAY, SO HE'S HOME NOW.
AH! BUT IF HE'S HOME ON A DAY OFF, THEN THE RUMORS OF A GIRLFRIEND ARE UNFOUNDED, AREN'T THEY?
THEN THAT GIVES ME MORE REASON TO HURRY!

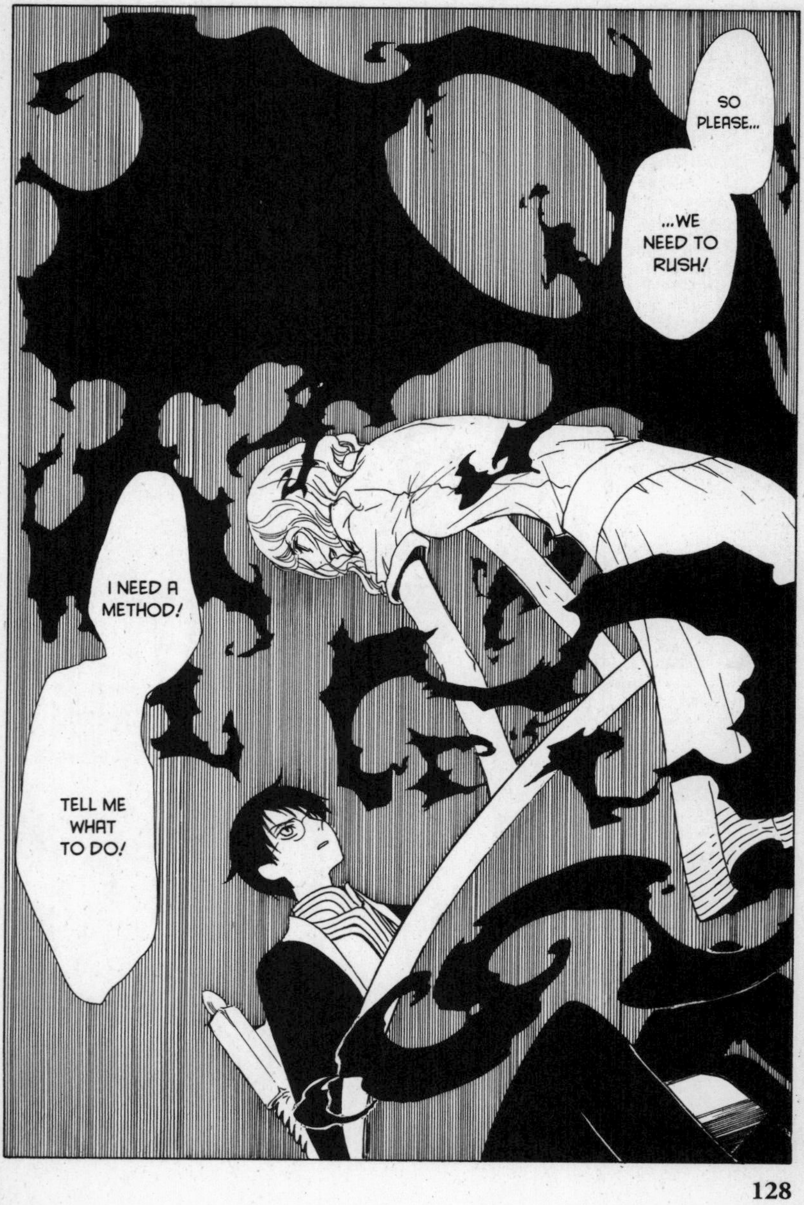
SO PLEASE...
...WE NEED TO RUSH!
I NEED A METHOD!
TELL ME WHAT TO DO!

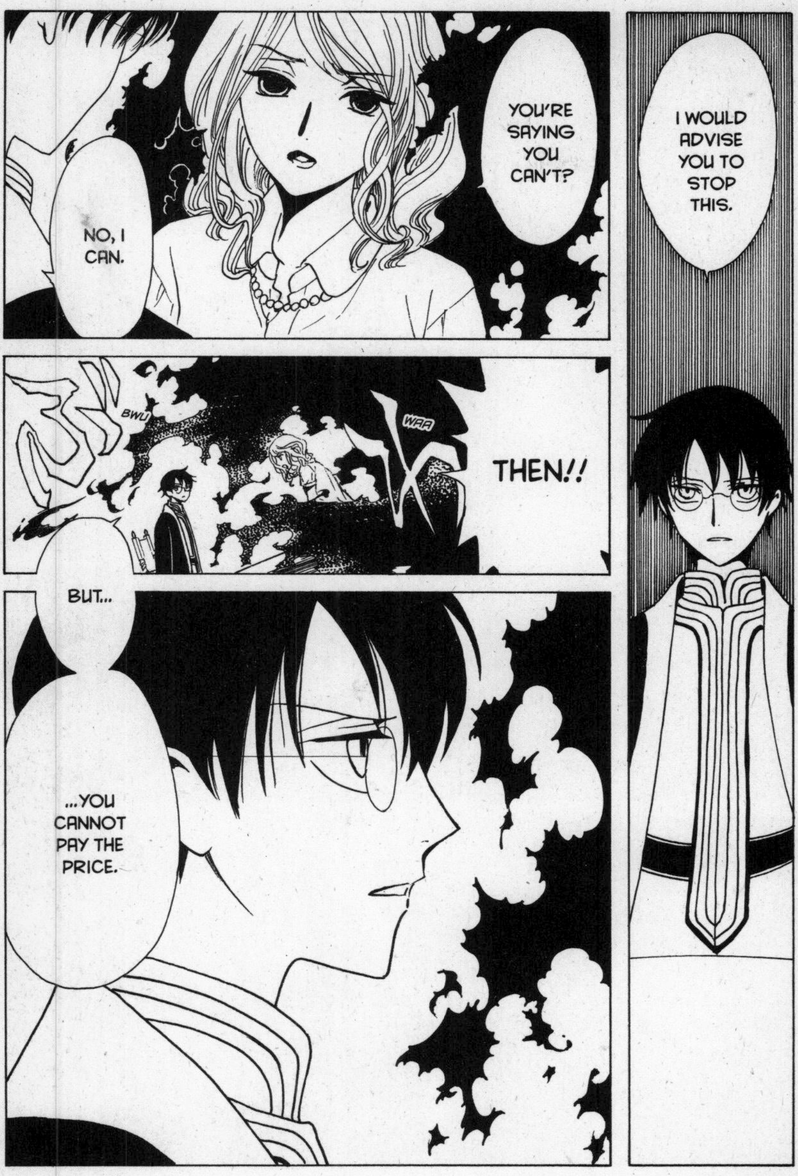
I WOULD ADVISE YOU TO STOP THIS.
YOU'RE SAYING YOU CAN'T?
NO, I CAN.
THEN!!
WAA
BWU
BUT...
...YOU CANNOT PAY THE PRICE.

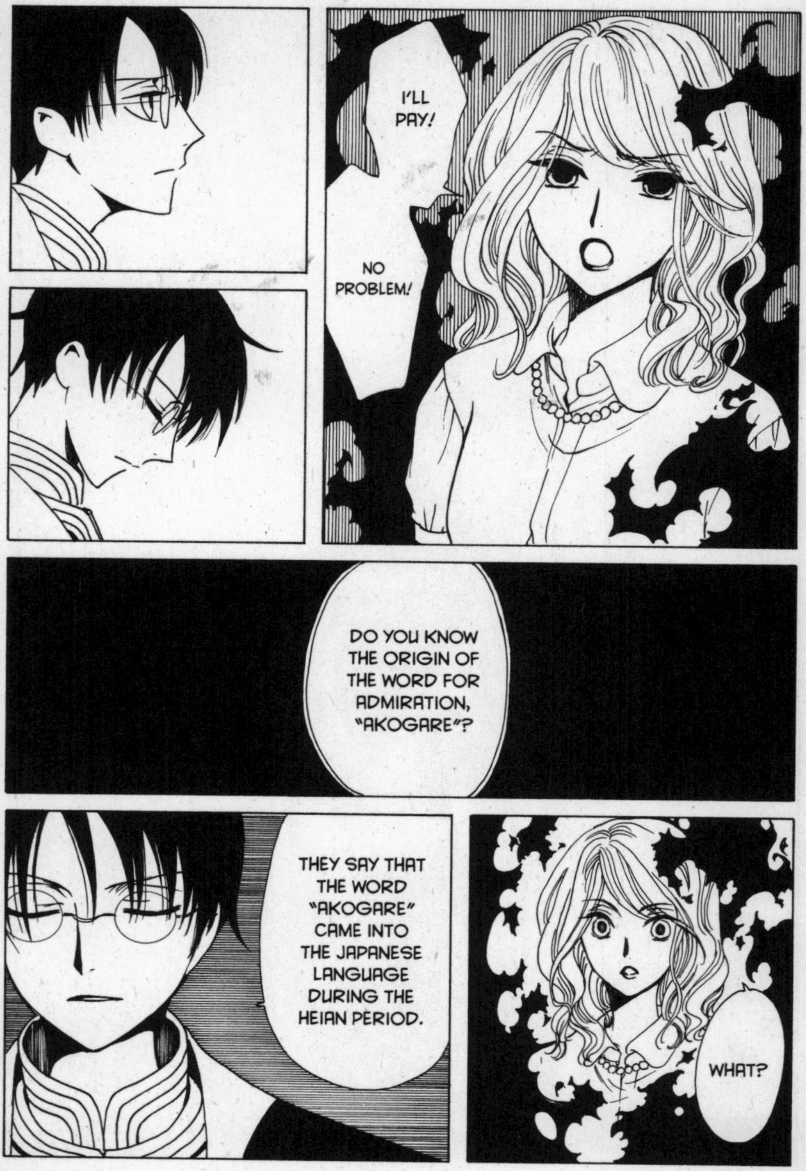
I'LL PAY!
NO PROBLEM!
DO YOU KNOW THE ORIGIN OF THE WORD FOR ADMIRATION, "AKOGARE"?
WHAT?
THEY SAY THAT THE WORD "AKOGARE" CAME INTO THE JAPANESE LANGUAGE DURING THE HEIAN PERIOD.

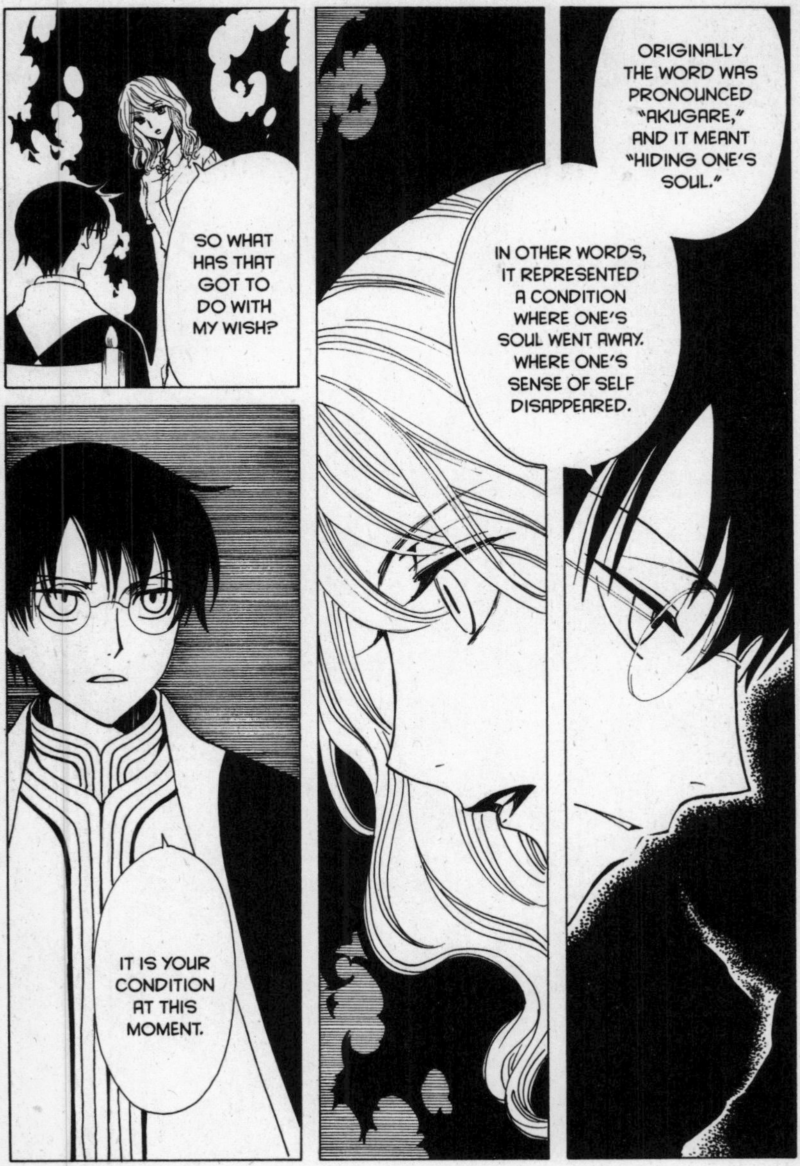
ORIGINALLY THE WORD WAS PRONOUNCED "AKUGARE," AND IT MEANT "HIDING ONE'S SOUL."
IN OTHER WORDS, IT REPRESENTED A CONDITION WHERE ONE'S SOUL WENT AWAY. WHERE ONE'S SENSE OF SELF DISAPPEARED.
SO WHAT HAS THAT GOT TO DO WITH MY WISH?
IT IS YOUR CONDITION AT THIS MOMENT.

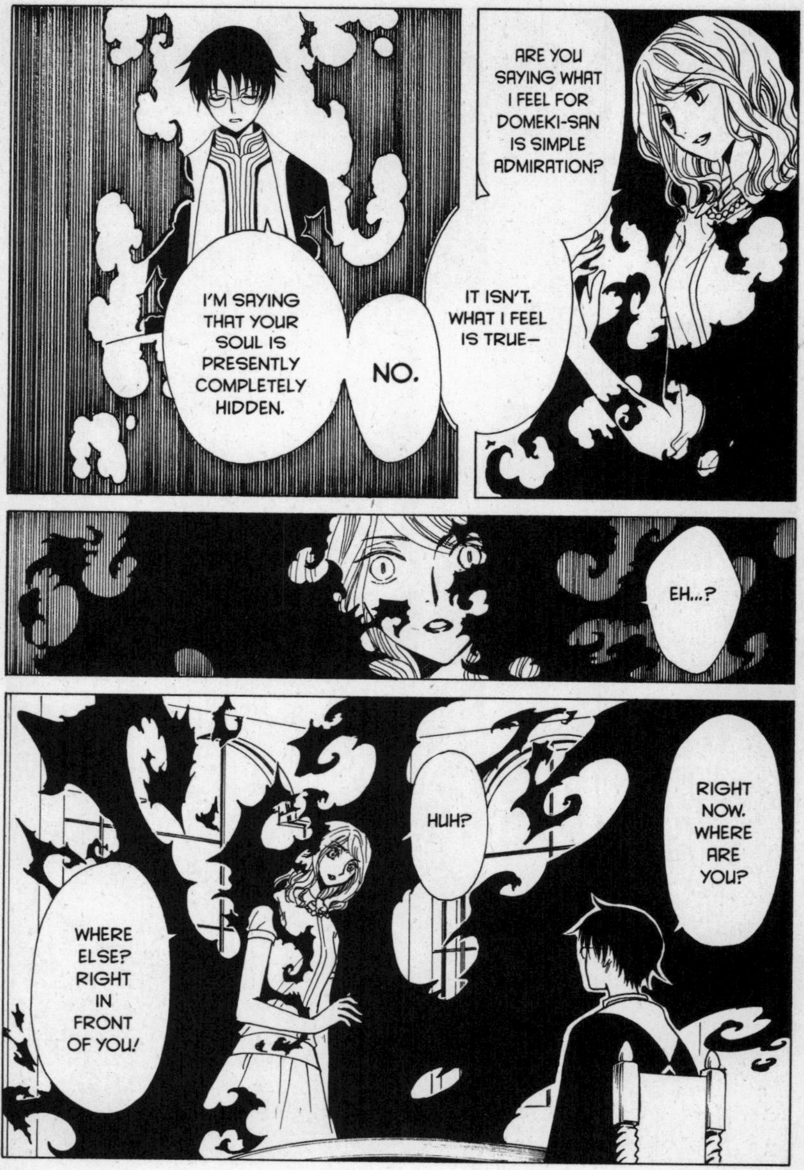
ARE YOU SAYING WHAT I FEEL FOR DOMEKI-SAN IS SIMPLE ADMIRATION?
IT ISN'T. WHAT I FEEL IS TRUE–
NO.
I'M SAYING THAT YOUR SOUL IS PRESENTLY COMPLETELY HIDDEN.
EH...?
RIGHT NOW. WHERE ARE YOU?
HUH?
WHERE ELSE? RIGHT IN FRONT OF YOU!

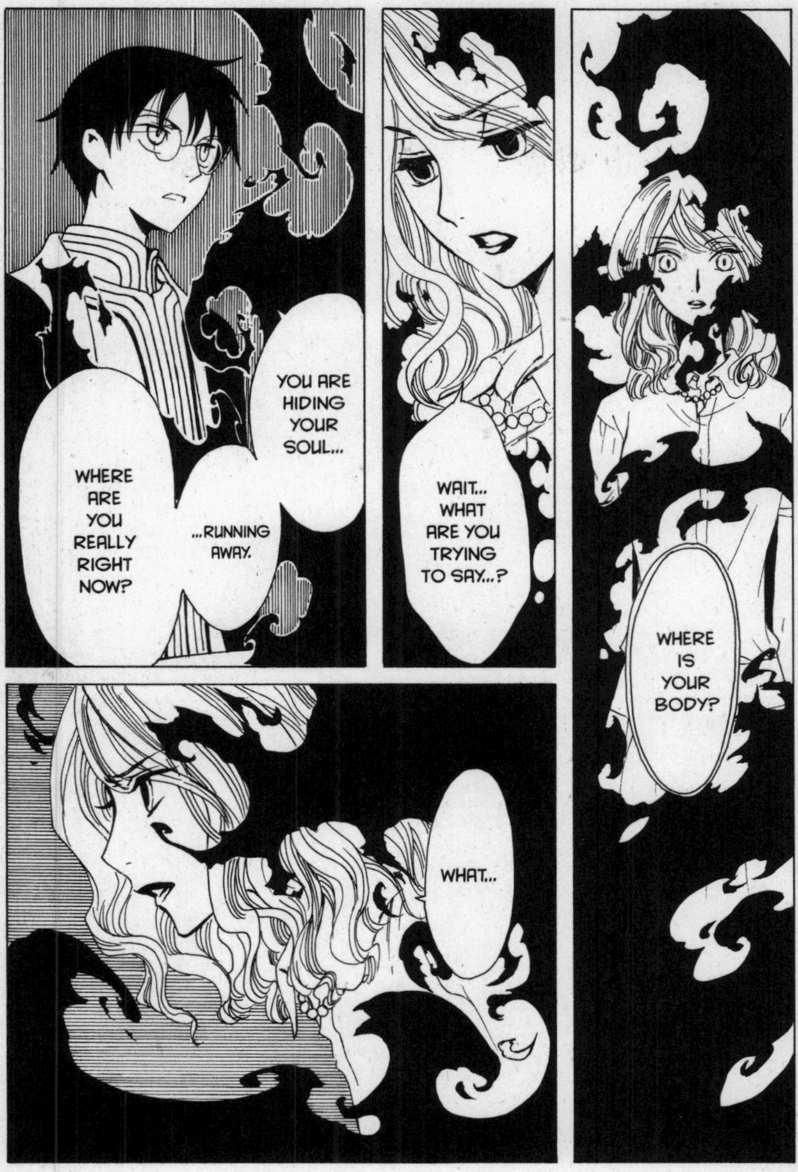
WHERE IS YOUR BODY?
WAIT... WHAT ARE YOU TRYING TO SAY...?
YOU ARE HIDING YOUR SOUL...
...RUNNING AWAY.
WHERE ARE YOU REALLY RIGHT NOW?
WHAT...

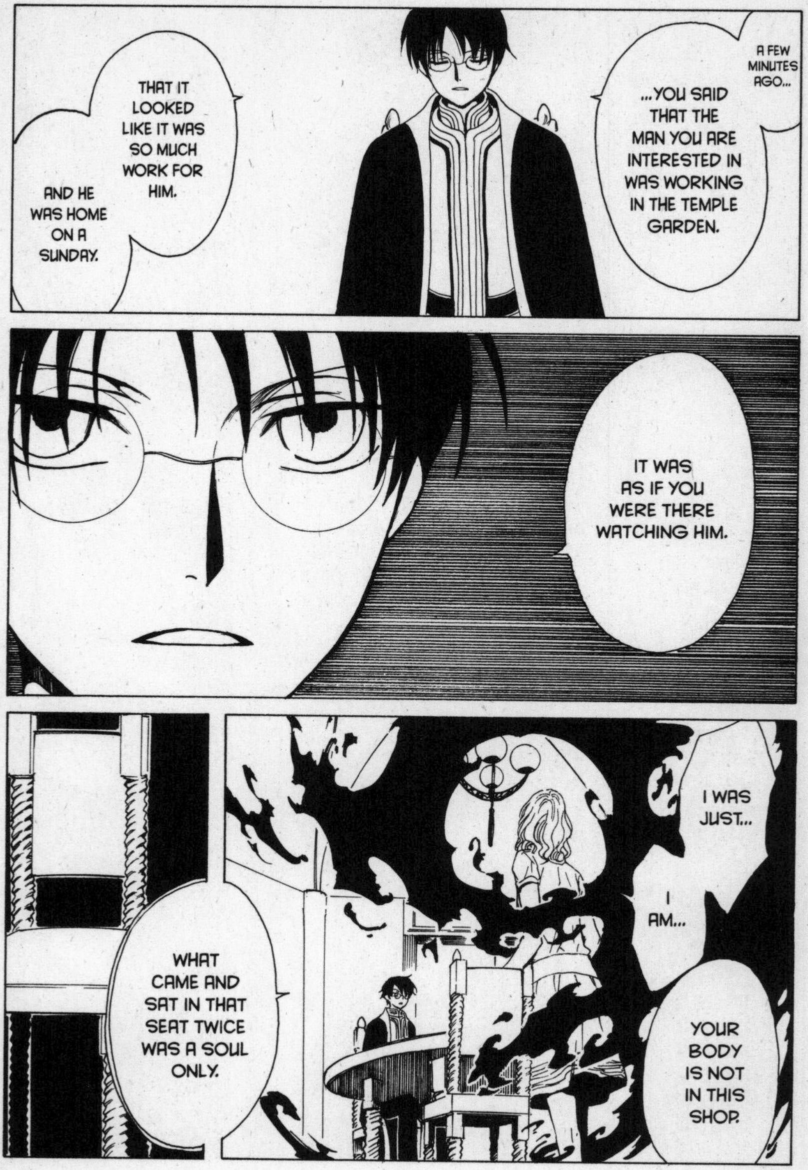
A FEW MINUTES AGO...
...YOU SAID THAT THE MAN YOU ARE INTERESTED IN WAS WORKING IN THE TEMPLE GARDEN.
THAT IT LOOKED LIKE IT WAS SO MUCH WORK FOR HIM.
AND HE WAS HOME ON A SUNDAY.
IT WAS AS IF YOU WERE THERE WATCHING HIM.
I WAS JUST...
I AM...
YOUR BODY IS NOT IN THIS SHOP.
WHAT CAME AND SAT IN THAT SEAT TWICE WAS A SOUL ONLY.

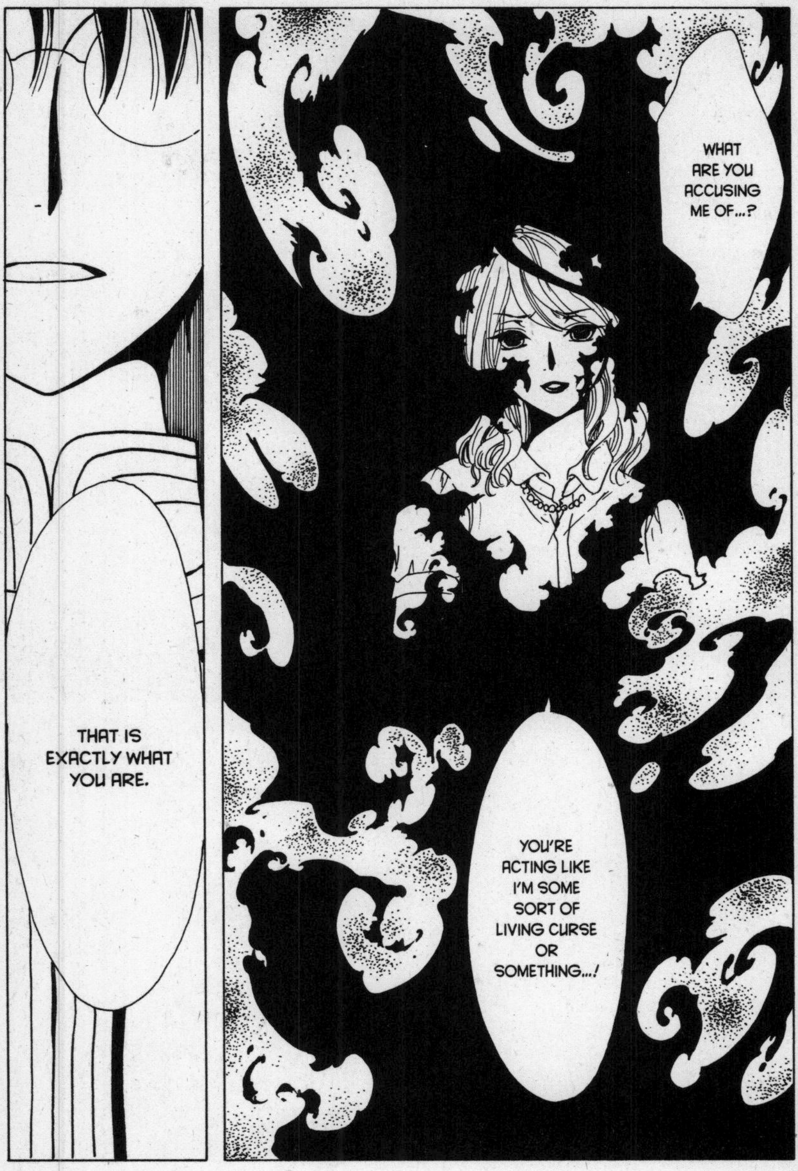
WHAT ARE YOU ACCUSING ME OF...?
YOU'RE ACTING LIKE I'M SOME SORT OF LIVING CURSE OR SOMETHING...!
THAT IS EXACTLY WHAT YOU ARE.

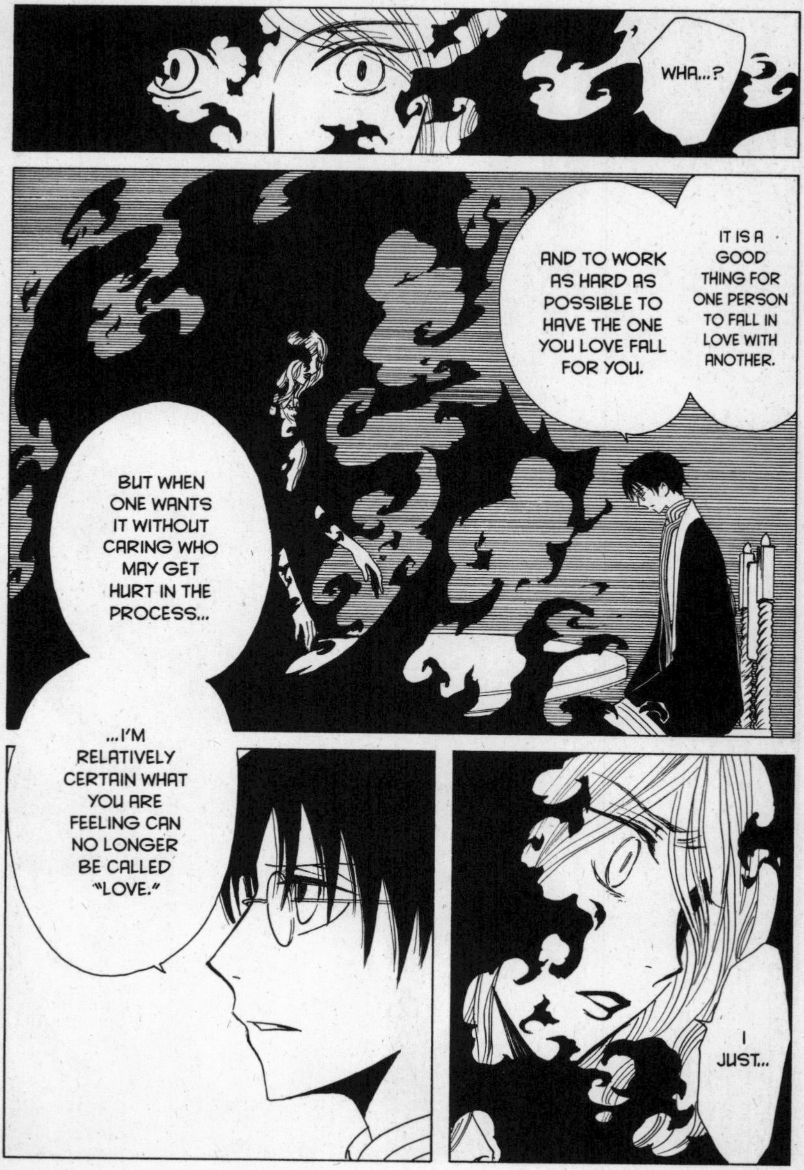
WHA...?
IT IS A GOOD THING FOR ONE PERSON TO FALL IN LOVE WITH ANOTHER.
AND TO WORK AS HARD AS POSSIBLE TO HAVE THE ONE YOU LOVE FALL FOR YOU.
BUT WHEN ONE WANTS IT WITHOUT CARING WHO MAY GET HURT IN THE PROCESS...
I JUST...
...I'M RELATIVELY CERTAIN WHAT YOU ARE FEELING CAN NO LONGER BE CALLED "LOVE."

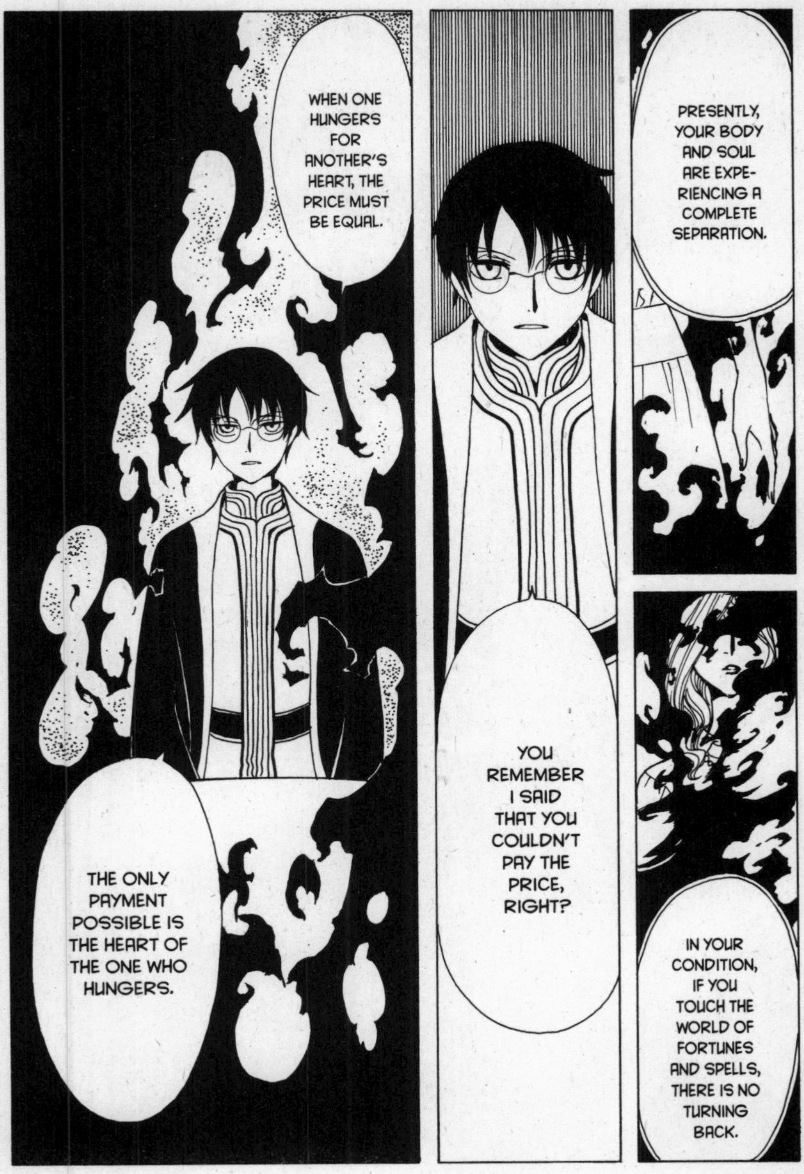
PRESENTLY, YOUR BODY AND SOUL ARE EXPE- RIENCING A COMPLETE SEPARATION.
IN YOUR CONDITION, IF YOU TOUCH THE WORLD OF FORTUNES AND SPELLS, THERE IS NO TURNING BACK.
YOU REMEMBER I SAID THAT YOU COULDN'T PAY THE PRICE, RIGHT?
WHEN ONE HUNGERS FOR ANOTHER'S HEART, THE PRICE MUST BE EQUAL.
THE ONLY PAYMENT POSSIBLE IS THE HEART OF THE ONE WHO HUNGERS.

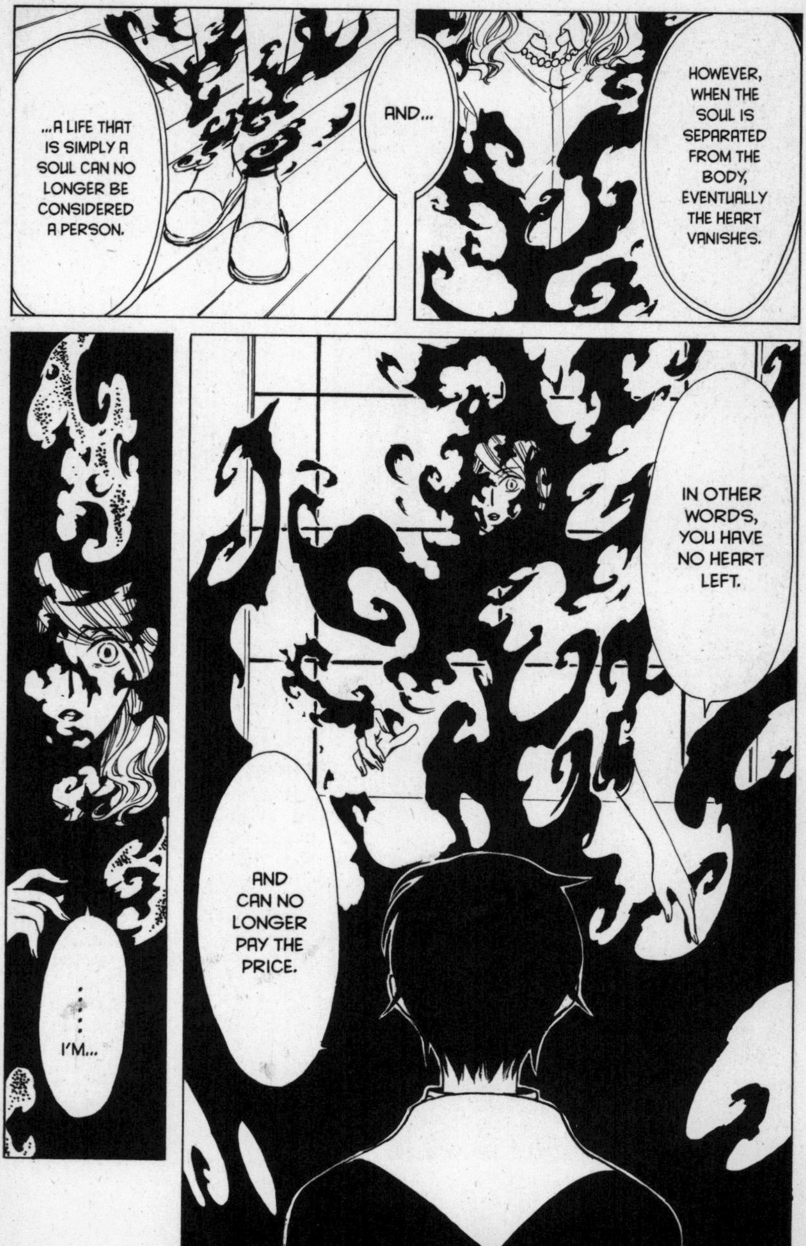
HOWEVER, WHEN THE SOUL IS SEPARATED FROM THE BODY, EVENTUALLY THE HEART VANISHES.
AND...
...A LIFE THAT IS SIMPLY A SOUL CAN NO LONGER BE CONSIDERED A PERSON.
IN OTHER WORDS, YOU HAVE NO HEART LEFT.
AND CAN NO LONGER PAY THE PRICE.
... I'M...

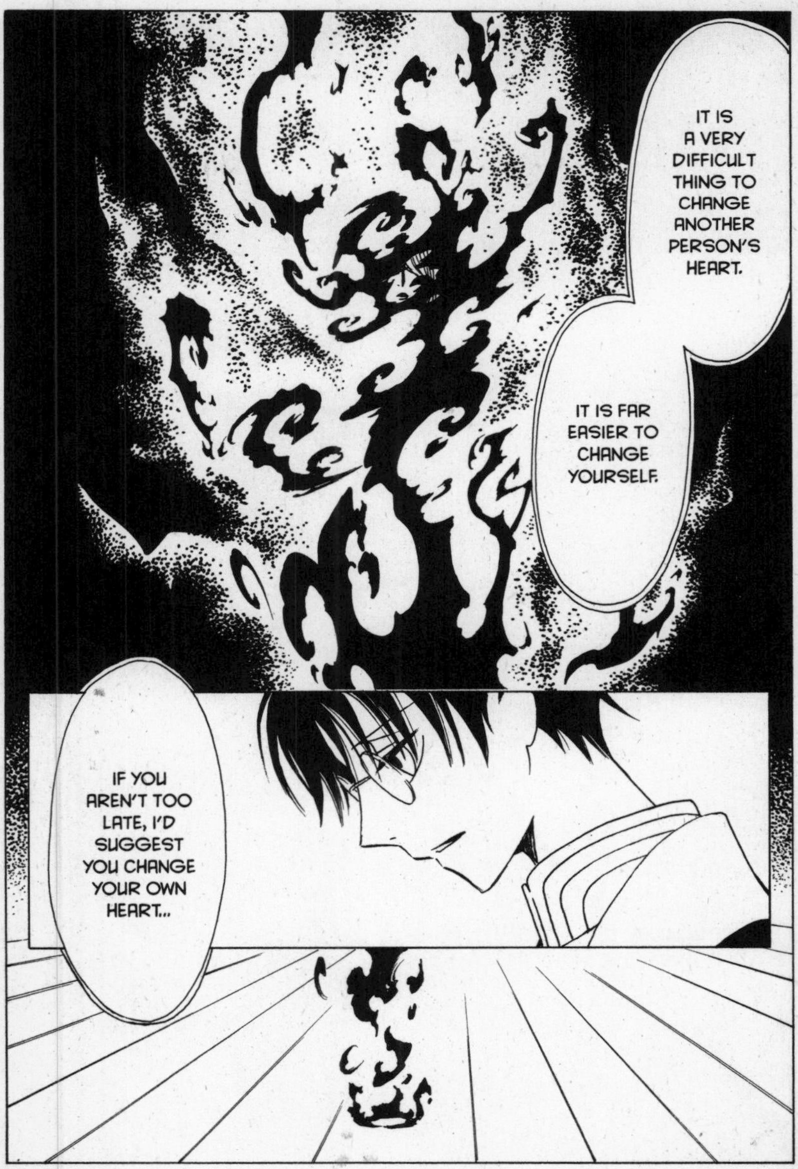
IT IS A VERY DIFFICULT THING TO CHANGE ANOTHER PERSON'S HEART.
IT IS FAR EASIER TO CHANGE YOURSELF.
IF YOU AREN'T TOO LATE, I'D SUGGEST YOU CHANGE YOUR OWN HEART...

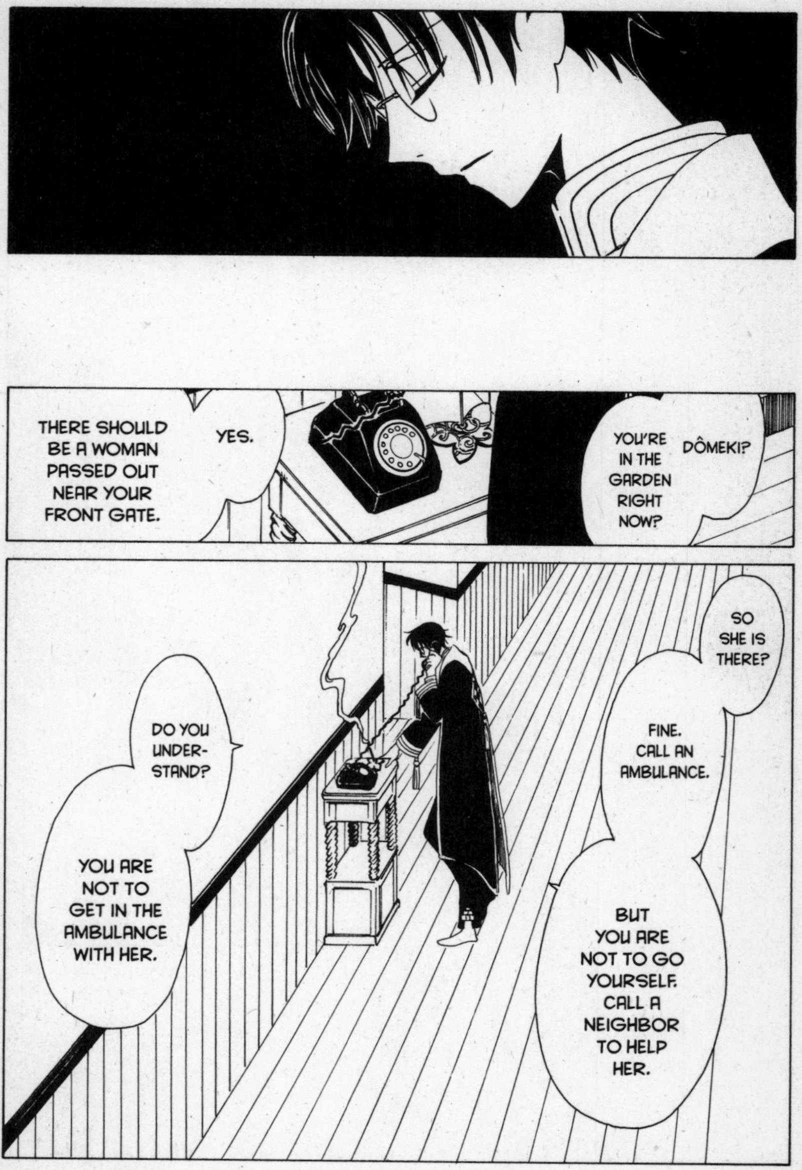
DÔMEKI?
YOU'RE IN THE GARDEN RIGHT NOW?
YES.
THERE SHOULD BE A WOMAN PASSED OUT NEAR YOUR FRONT GATE.
SO SHE IS THERE?
FINE. CALL AN AMBULANCE.
BUT YOU ARE NOT TO GO YOURSELF. CALL A NEIGHBOR TO HELP HER.
DO YOU UNDER-STAND?
YOU ARE NOT TO GET IN THE AMBULANCE WITH HER.

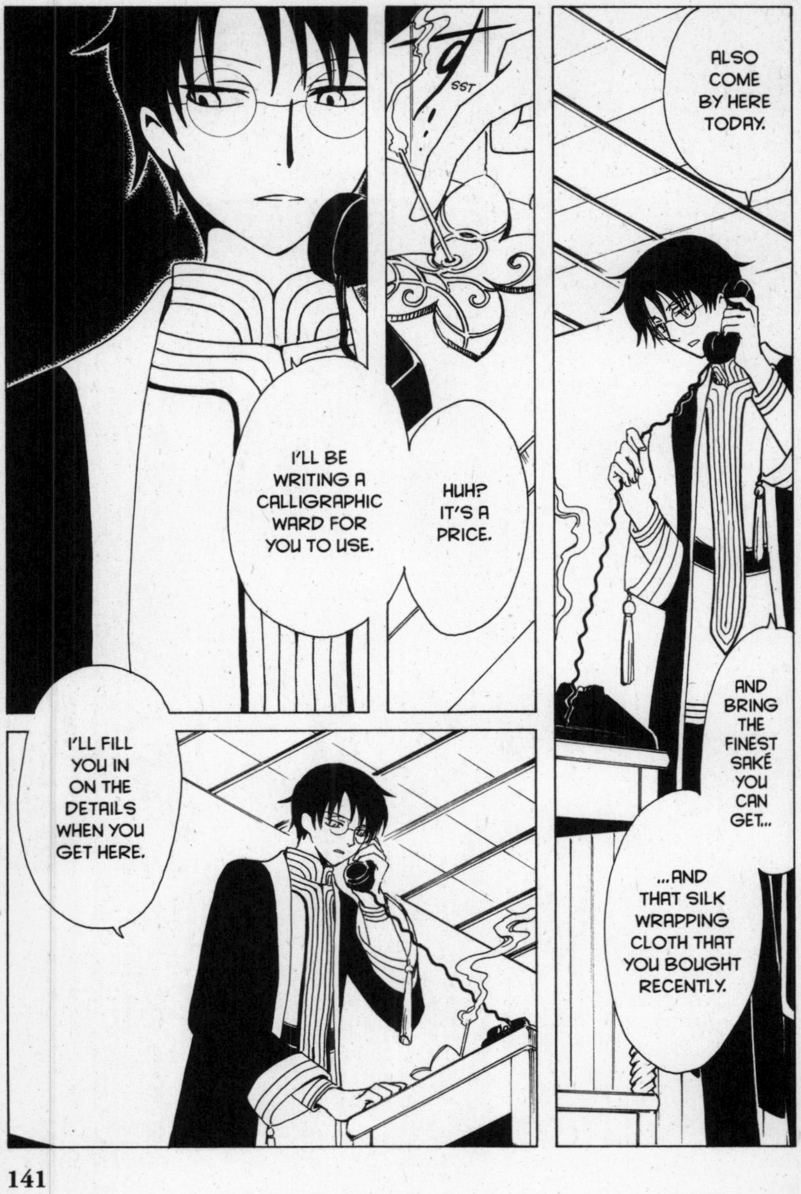
ALSO COME BY HERE TODAY.
AND BRING THE FINEST SAKÉ YOU CAN GET...
...AND THAT SILK WRAPPING CLOTH THAT YOU BOUGHT RECENTLY.
SST
HUH? IT'S A PRICE.
I'LL BE WRITING A CALLIGRAPHIC WARD FOR YOU TO USE.
I'LL FILL YOU IN ON THE DETAILS WHEN YOU GET HERE.

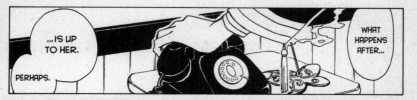

WHAT HAPPENS AFTER...
...IS UP TO HER.
PERHAPS.
UP UNTIL NOW, I COULDN'T SAY HOW MANY WISHES I'VE GRANTED, BUT...
...THE VERY HARDEST OF THEM ALL...
...IS THE DESIRE FOR SOMEONE ELSE.
ALTHOUGH I'M NO DIFFERENT...I SUPPOSE.

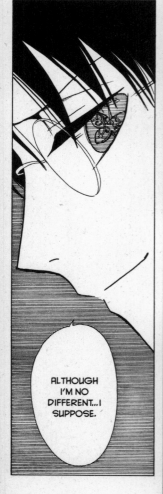

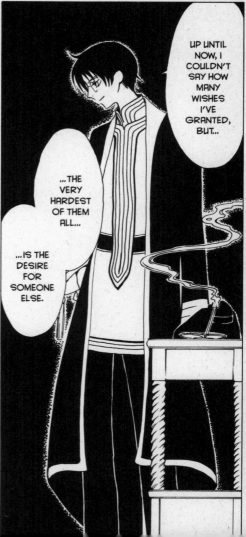

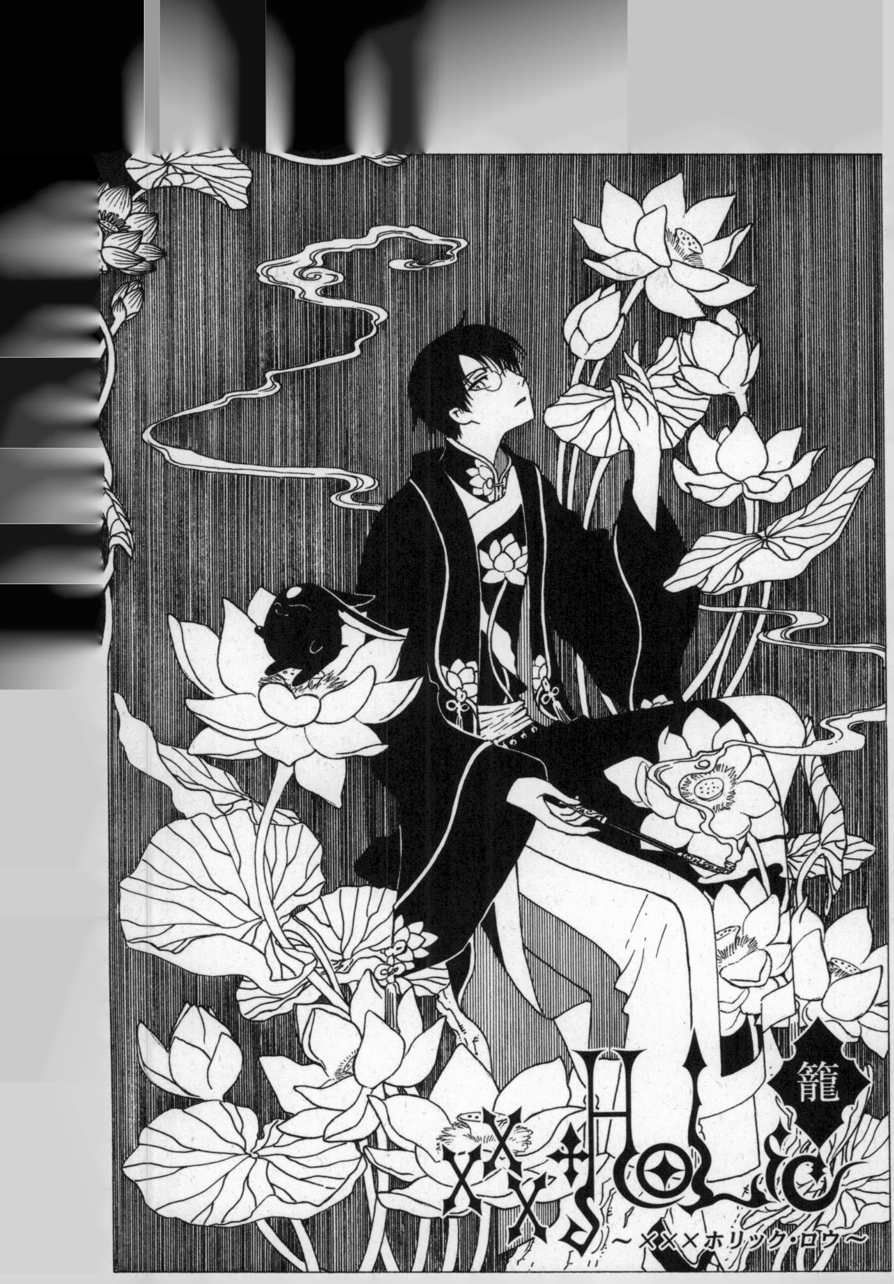

籠
xxxHOLiC
~×××ホリック・ロウ~

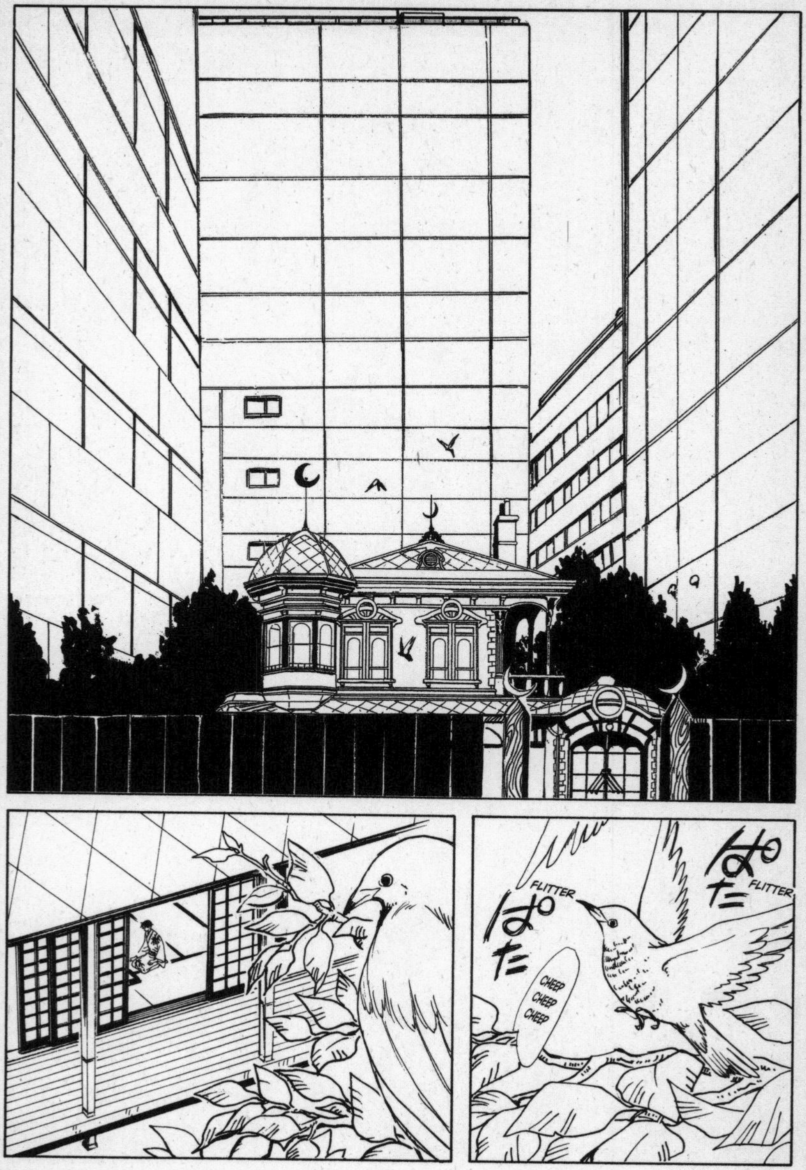
ぱた
FLITTER
ぱた
FLITTER
CHEEP
CHEEP
CHEEP

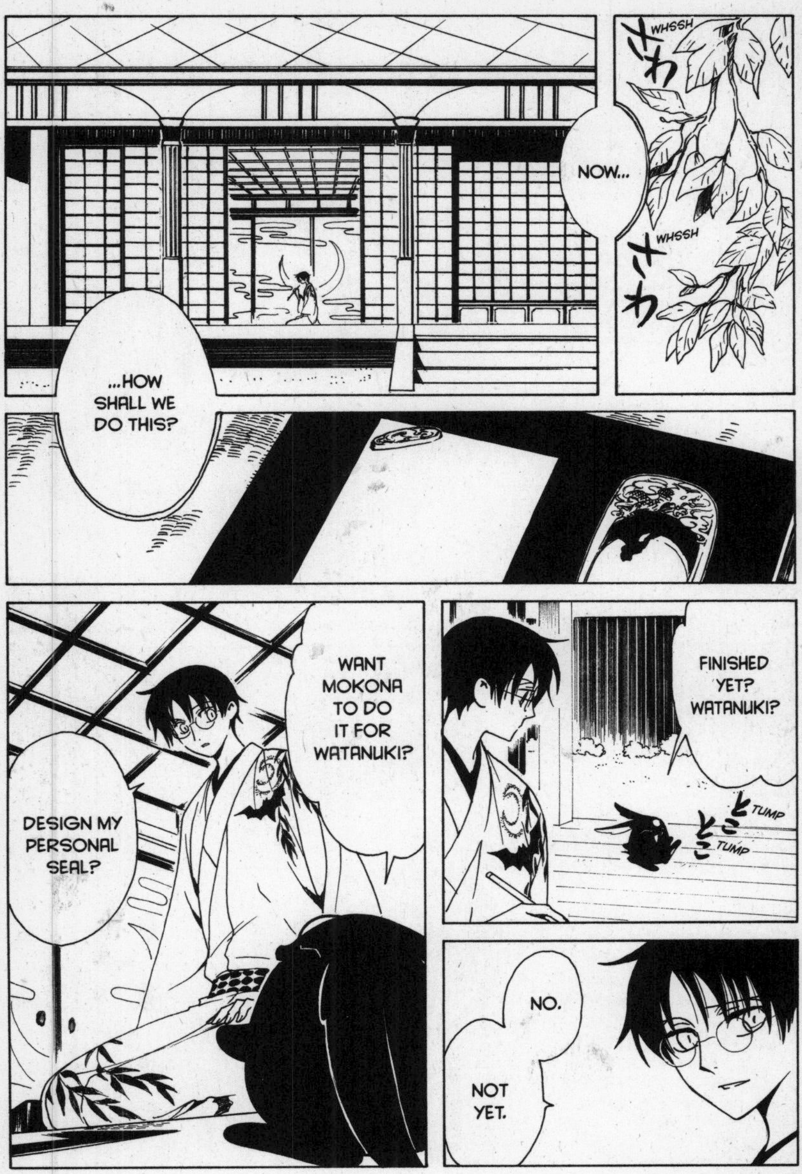
さわ
WHSSH
NOW...
さわ
WHSSH
...HOW SHALL WE DO THIS?
FINISHED YET? WATANUKI?
とこ
TUMP
とこ
TUMP
NO.
NOT YET.
WANT MOKONA TO DO IT FOR WATANUKI?
DESIGN MY PERSONAL SEAL?

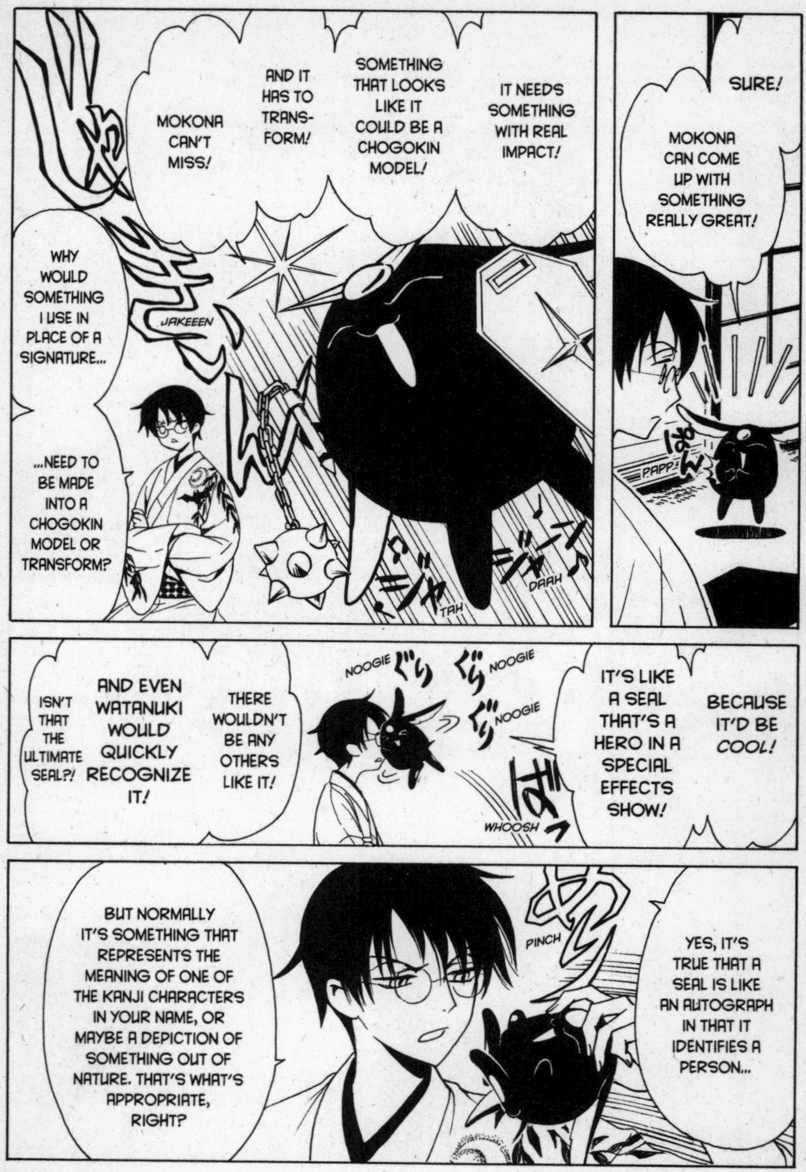
SURE!
MOKONA CAN COME UP WITH SOMETHING REALLY GREAT!
PAPP
IT NEEDS SOMETHING WITH REAL IMPACT!
SOMETHING THAT LOOKS LIKE IT COULD BE A CHOGOKIN MODEL!
AND IT HAS TO TRANSFORM!
MOKONA CAN'T MISS!
JAKEEN
DAAH
TAH
WHY WOULD SOMETHING I USE IN PLACE OF A SIGNATURE...
...NEED TO BE MADE INTO A CHOGOKIN MODEL OR TRANSFORM?
BECAUSE IT'D BE *COOL!*
IT'S LIKE A SEAL THAT'S A HERO IN A SPECIAL EFFECTS SHOW!
WHOOSH
NOOGIE
NOOGIE
NOOGIE
THERE WOULDN'T BE ANY OTHERS LIKE IT!
AND EVEN WATANUKI WOULD QUICKLY RECOGNIZE IT!
ISN'T THAT THE ULTIMATE SEAL?!
YES, IT'S TRUE THAT A SEAL IS LIKE AN AUTOGRAPH IN THAT IT IDENTIFIES A PERSON...
PINCH
BUT NORMALLY IT'S SOMETHING THAT REPRESENTS THE MEANING OF ONE OF THE KANJI CHARACTERS IN YOUR NAME, OR MAYBE A DEPICTION OF SOMETHING OUT OF NATURE. THAT'S WHAT'S APPROPRIATE, RIGHT?

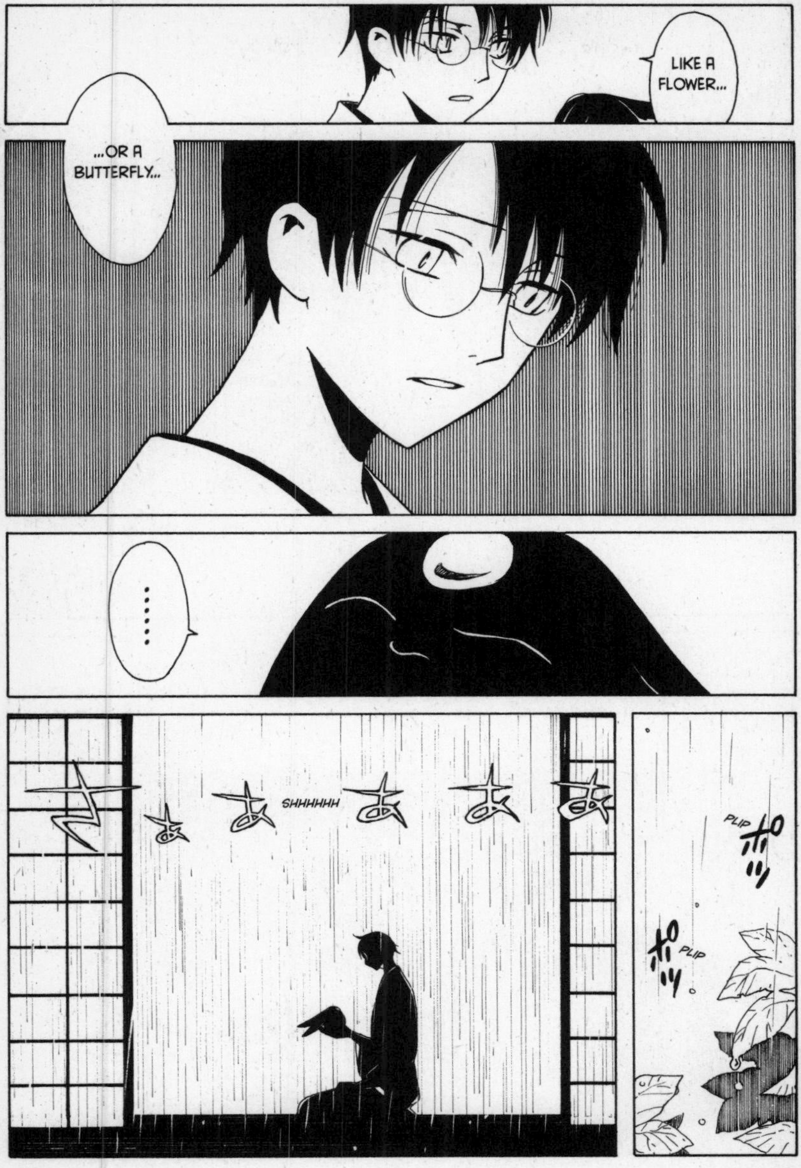
LIKE A FLOWER...
...OR A BUTTERFLY...
......
PLIP
PLIP
SHHHHHH

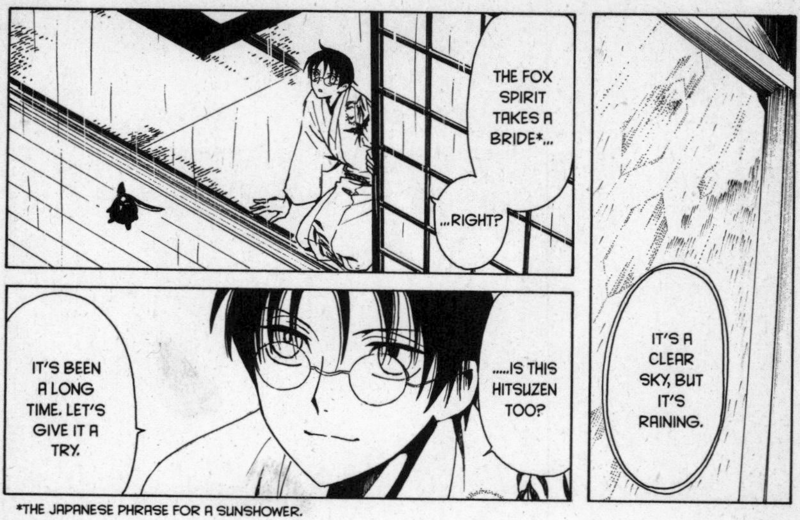
IT'S A CLEAR SKY, BUT IT'S RAINING.
THE FOX SPIRIT TAKES A BRIDE*...
...RIGHT?
.....IS THIS HITSUZEN TOO?
IT'S BEEN A LONG TIME. LET'S GIVE IT A TRY.

*THE JAPANESE PHRASE FOR A SUNSHOWER.

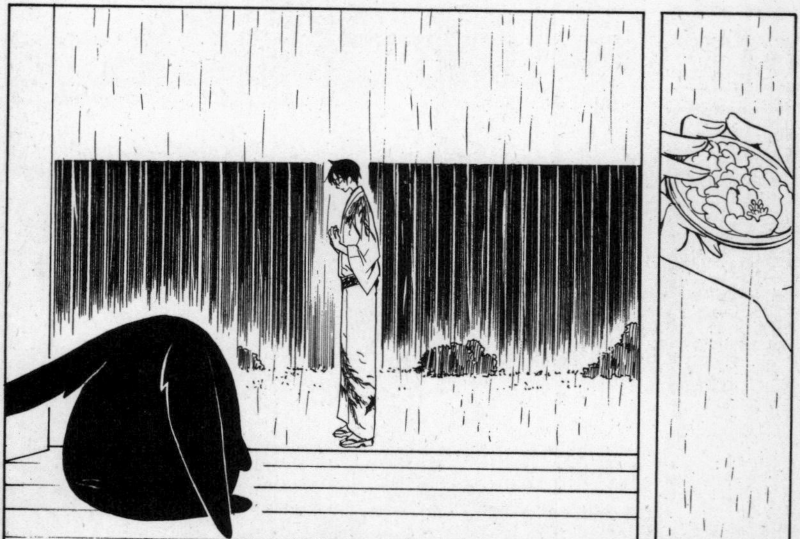

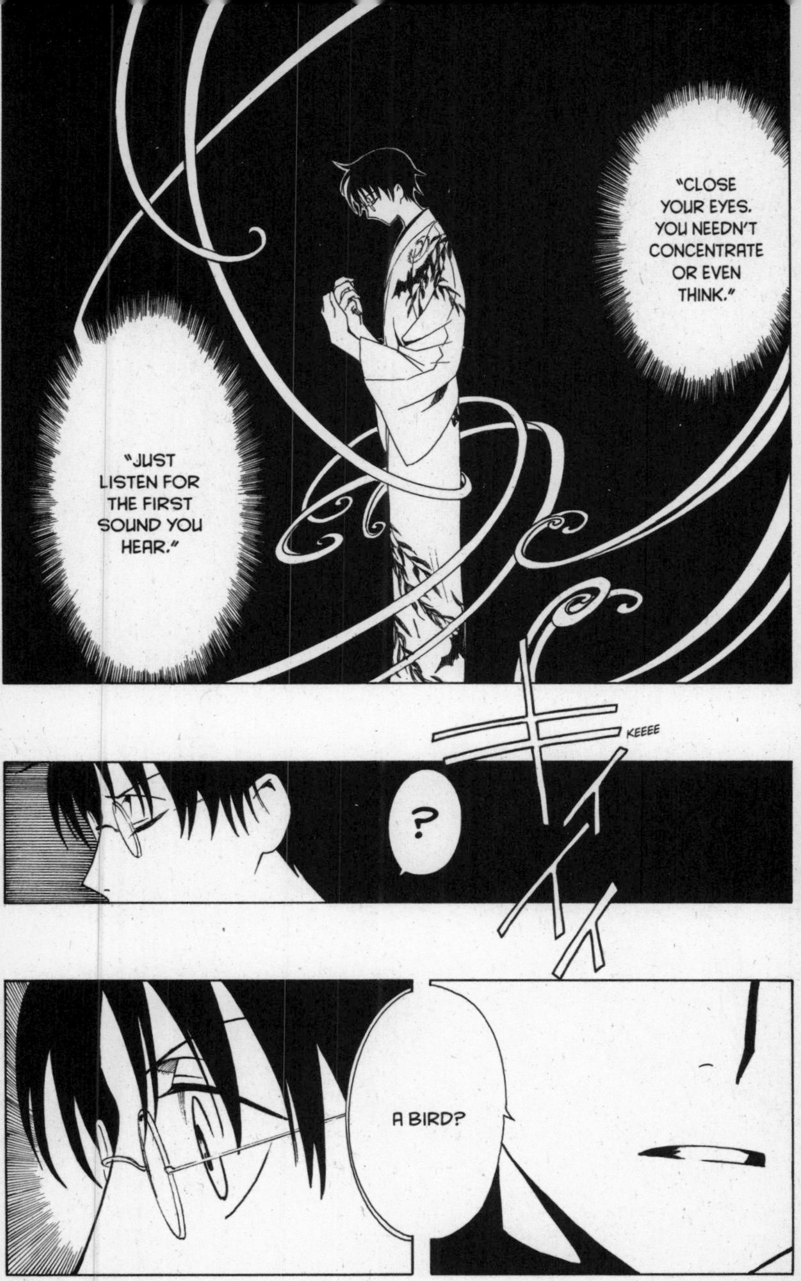
"CLOSE YOUR EYES. YOU NEEDN'T CONCENTRATE OR EVEN THINK."
"JUST LISTEN FOR THE FIRST SOUND YOU HEAR."
KEEEE
?
A BIRD?

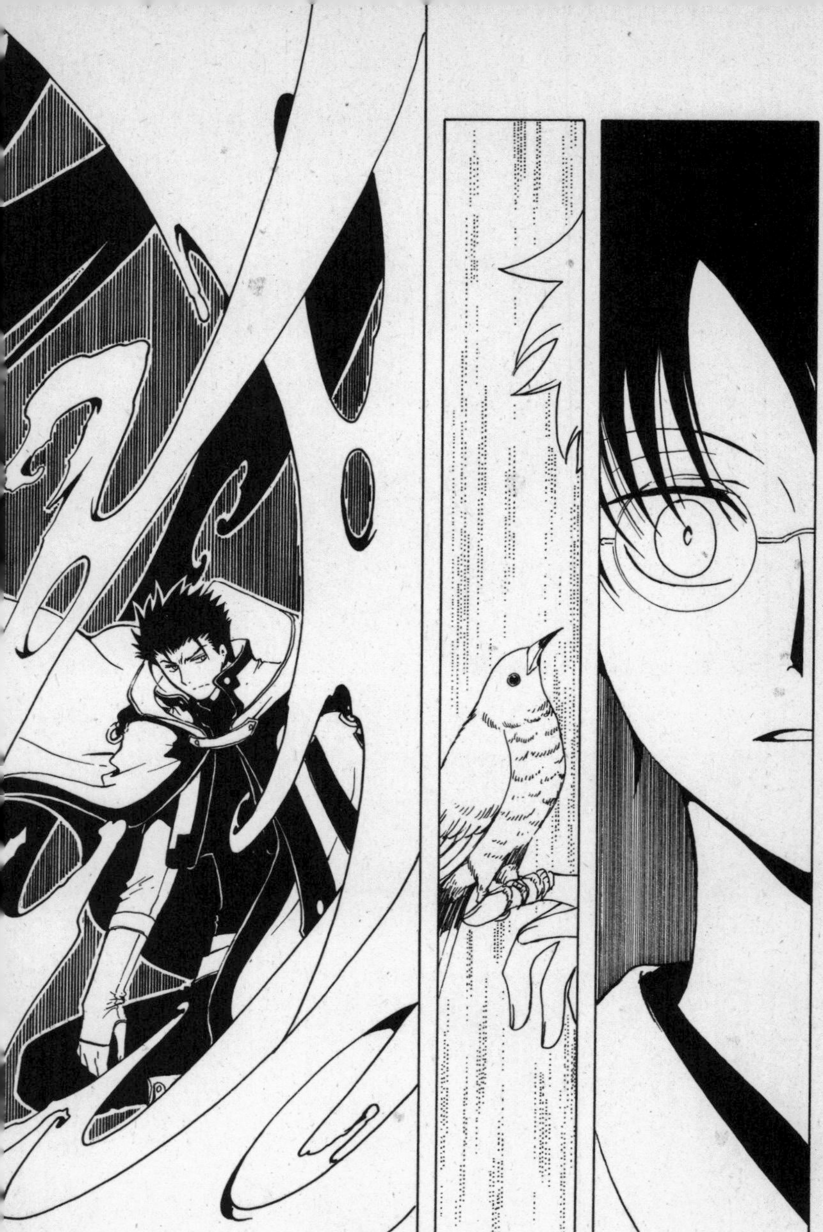

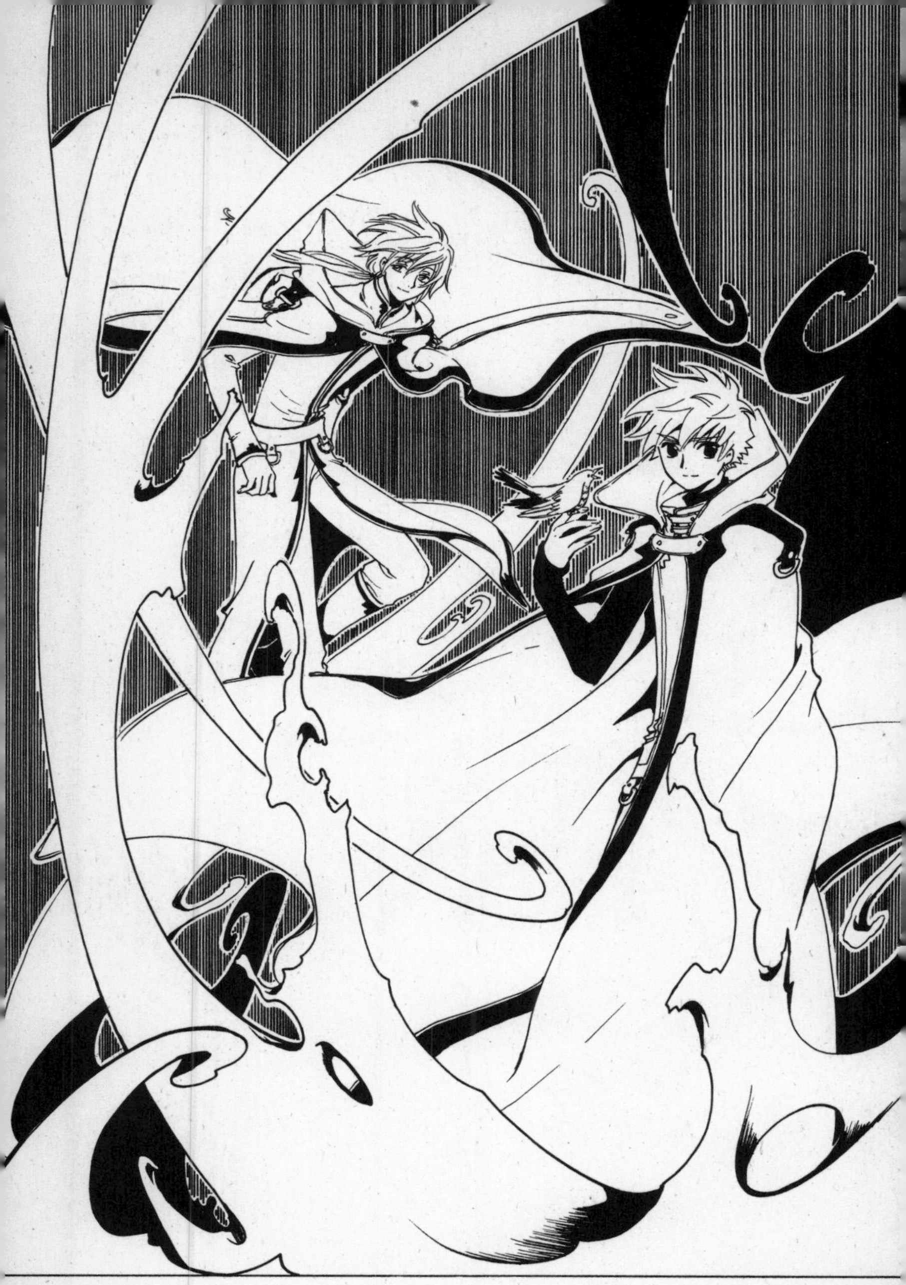

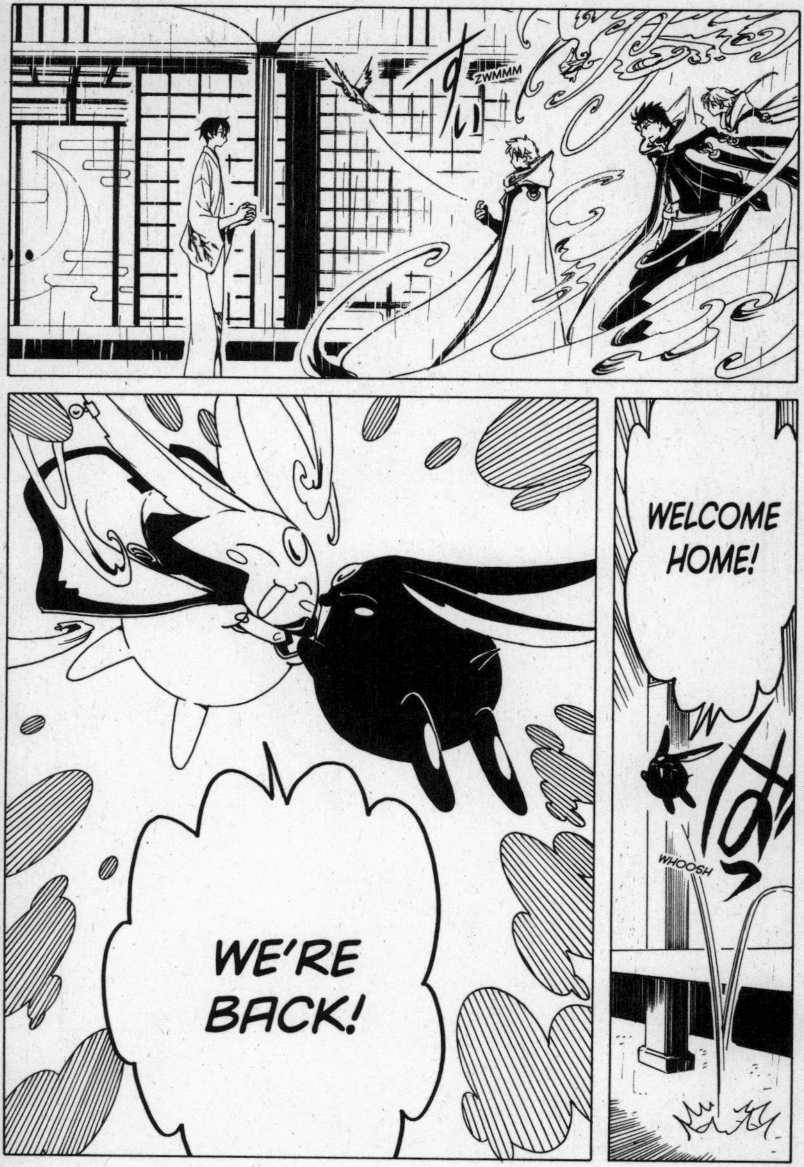
すい
ZWMMM
WELCOME HOME!
はっ
WHOOSH
WE'RE BACK!

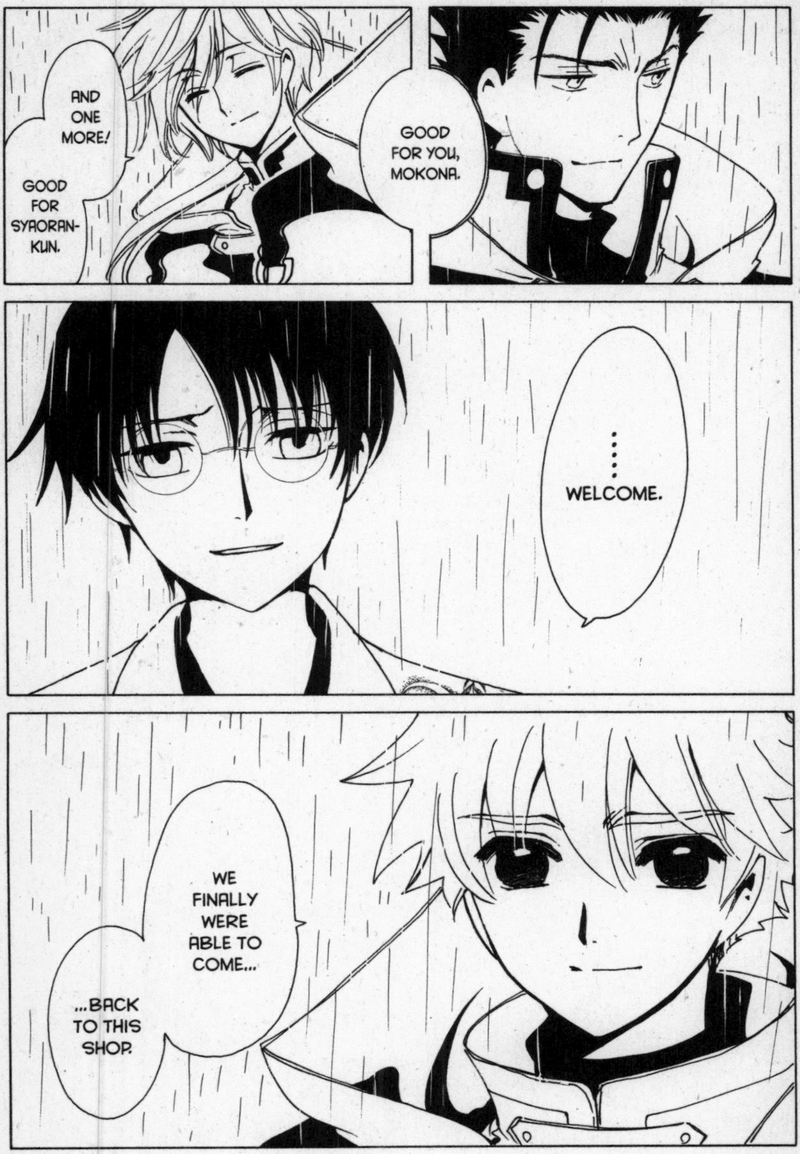
GOOD FOR YOU, MOKONA.
AND ONE MORE!
GOOD FOR SYAORAN-KUN.
..... WELCOME.
WE FINALLY WERE ABLE TO COME...
...BACK TO THIS SHOP.

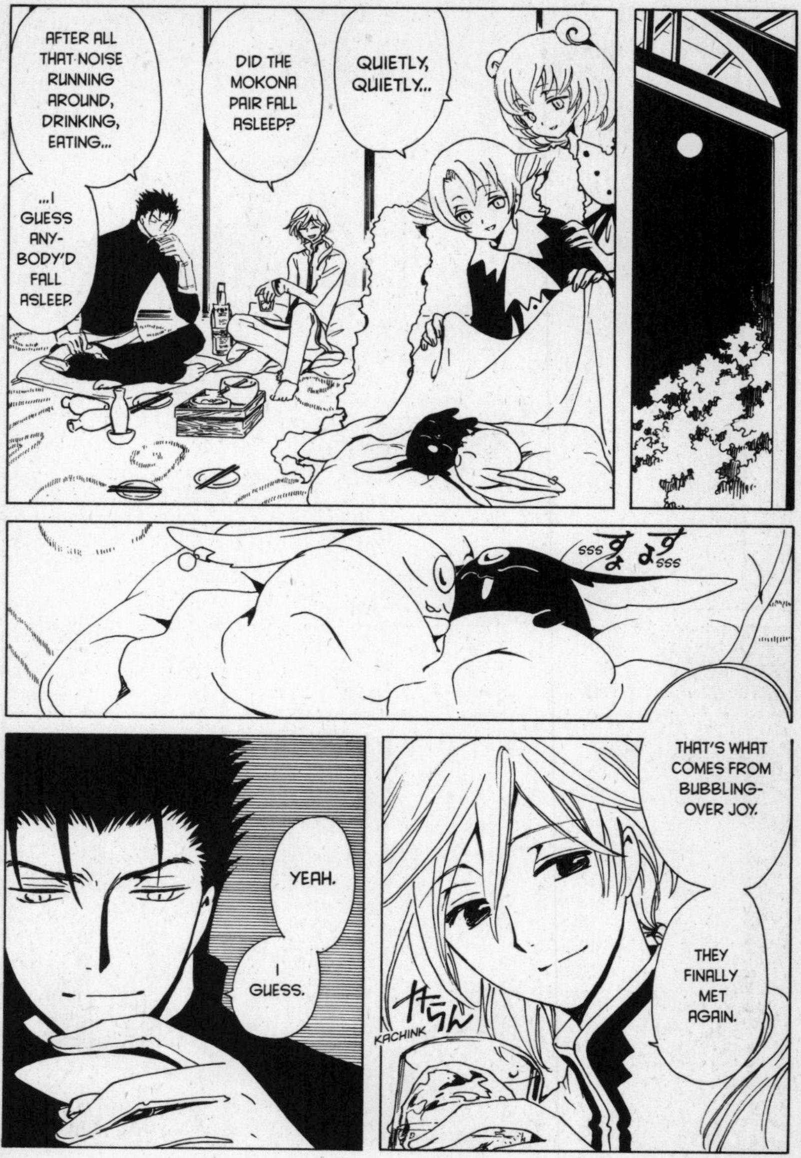
QUIETLY, QUIETLY...
DID THE MOKONA PAIR FALL ASLEEP?
AFTER ALL THAT NOISE RUNNING AROUND, DRINKING, EATING...
...I GUESS ANYBODY'D FALL ASLEEP.
SSS
SSS
THAT'S WHAT COMES FROM BUBBLING-OVER JOY.
THEY FINALLY MET AGAIN.
KACHINK
YEAH.
I GUESS.

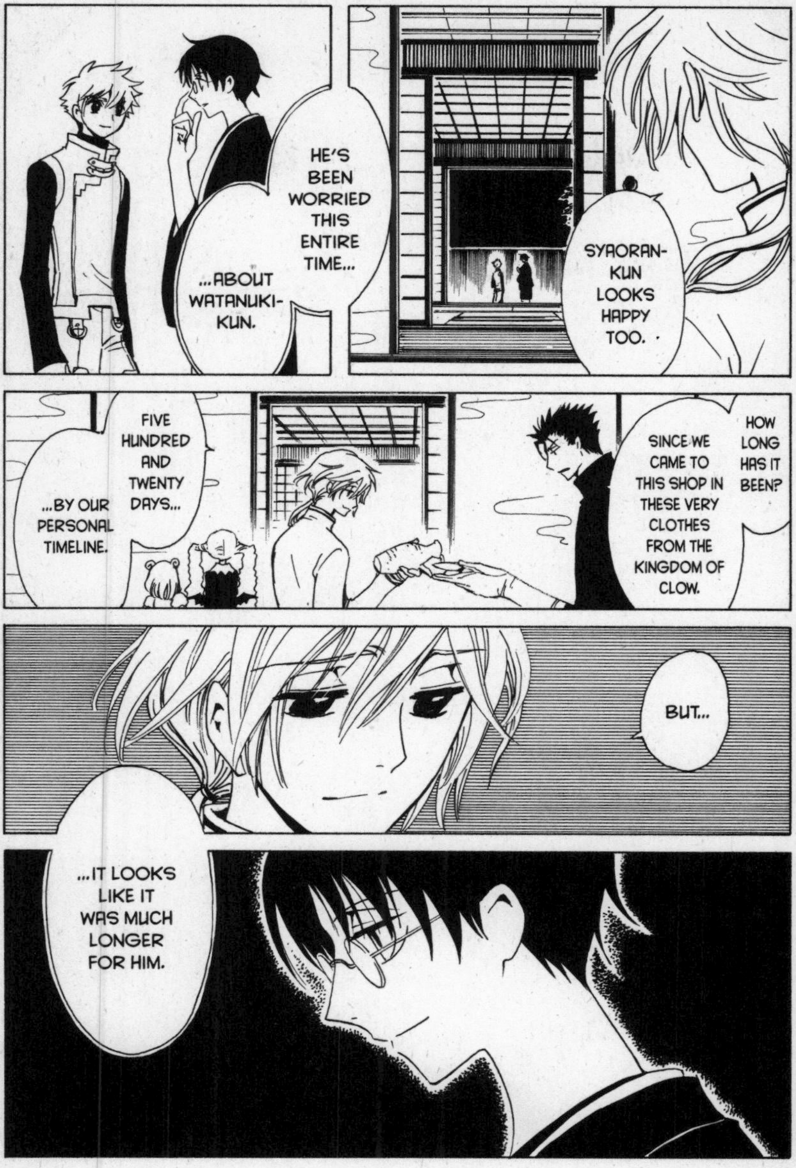
SYAORAN-KUN LOOKS HAPPY TOO.
HE'S BEEN WORRIED THIS ENTIRE TIME...
...ABOUT WATANUKI-KUN.
HOW LONG HAS IT BEEN?
SINCE WE CAME TO THIS SHOP IN THESE VERY CLOTHES FROM THE KINGDOM OF CLOW.
FIVE HUNDRED AND TWENTY DAYS...
...BY OUR PERSONAL TIMELINE.
BUT...
...IT LOOKS LIKE IT WAS MUCH LONGER FOR HIM.

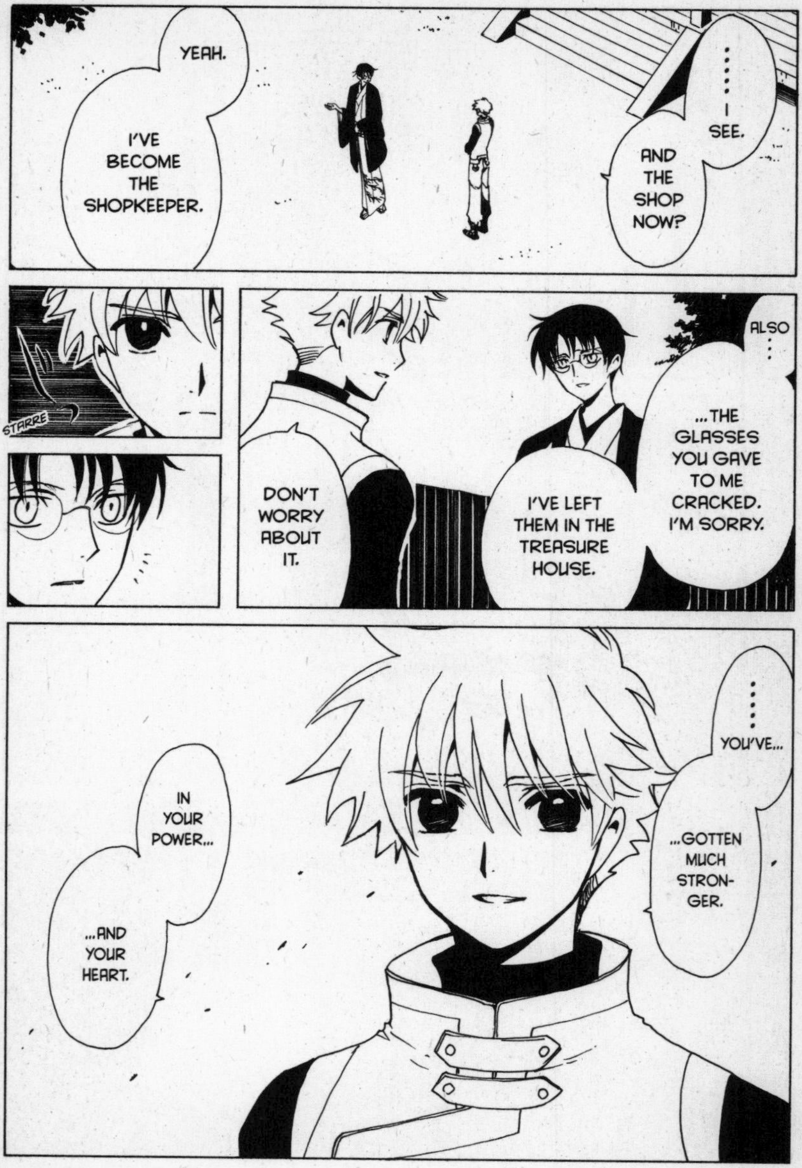
......I SEE.
AND THE SHOP NOW?
YEAH.
I'VE BECOME THE SHOPKEEPER.
ALSO...
...THE GLASSES YOU GAVE TO ME CRACKED. I'M SORRY.
I'VE LEFT THEM IN THE TREASURE HOUSE.
DON'T WORRY ABOUT IT.
STARRE
......YOU'VE...
...GOTTEN MUCH STRONGER.
IN YOUR POWER...
...AND YOUR HEART.

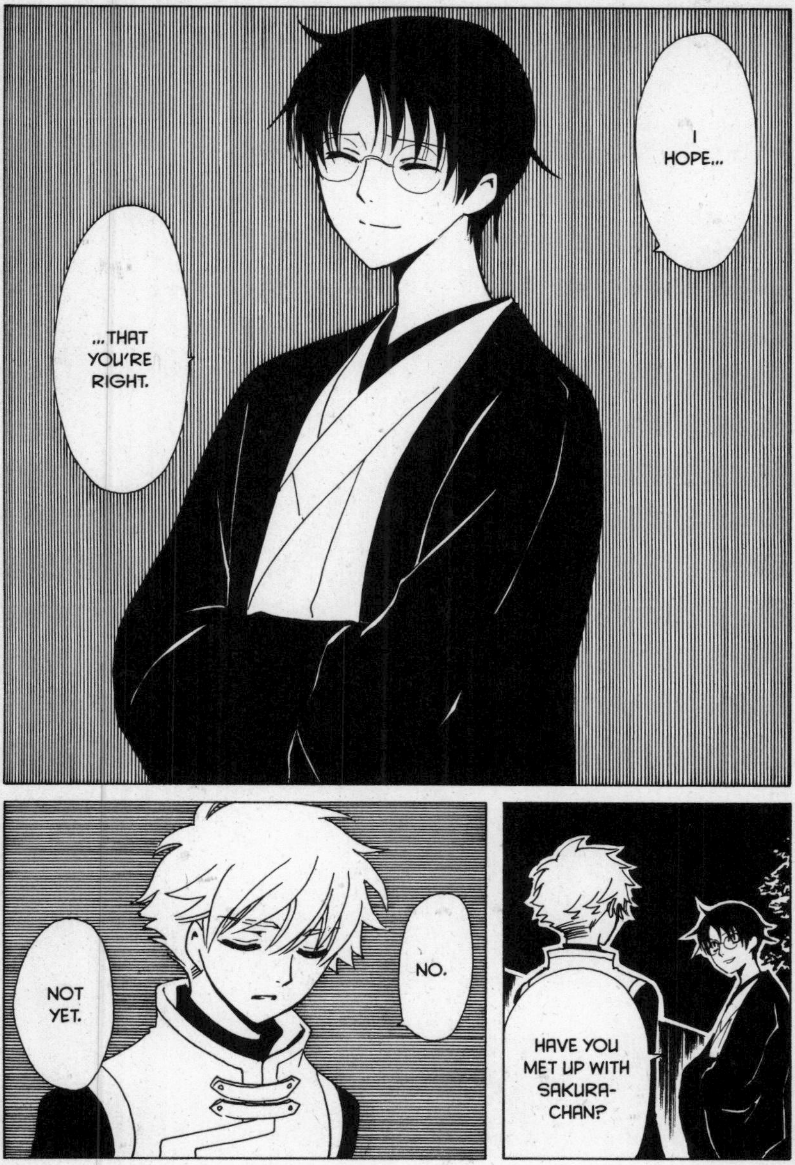
I HOPE...
...THAT YOU'RE RIGHT.
HAVE YOU MET UP WITH SAKURA-CHAN?
NO.
NOT YET.

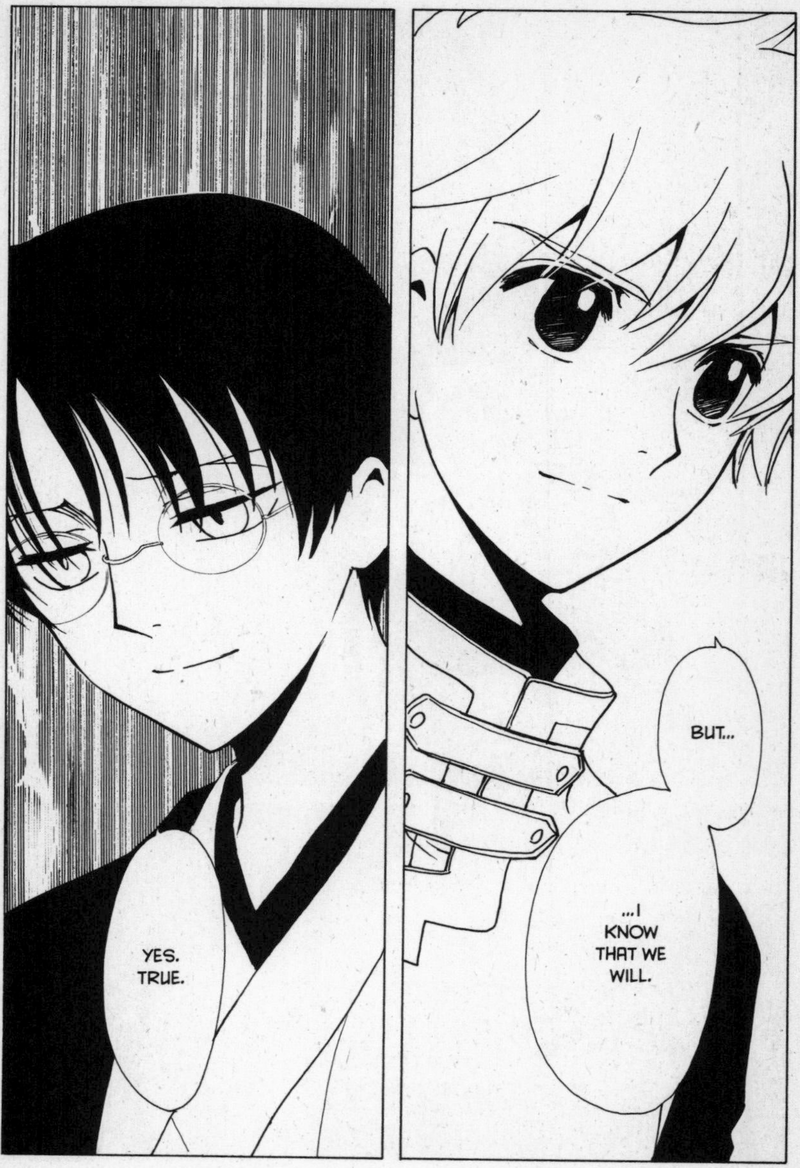
BUT...
...I KNOW THAT WE WILL.
YES. TRUE.

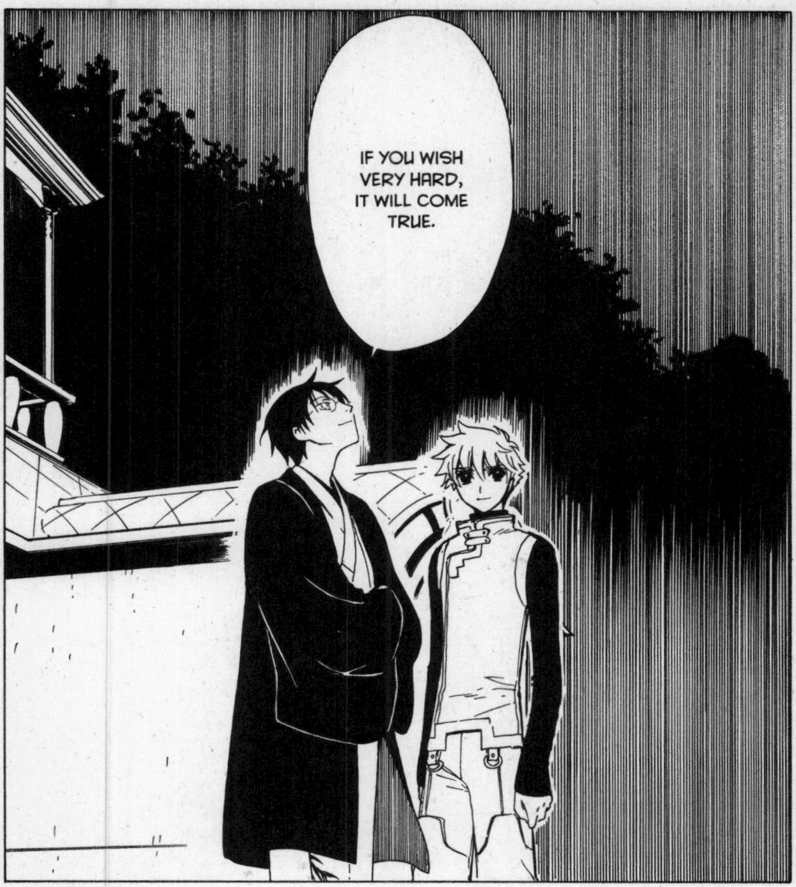
IF YOU WISH VERY HARD, IT WILL COME TRUE.
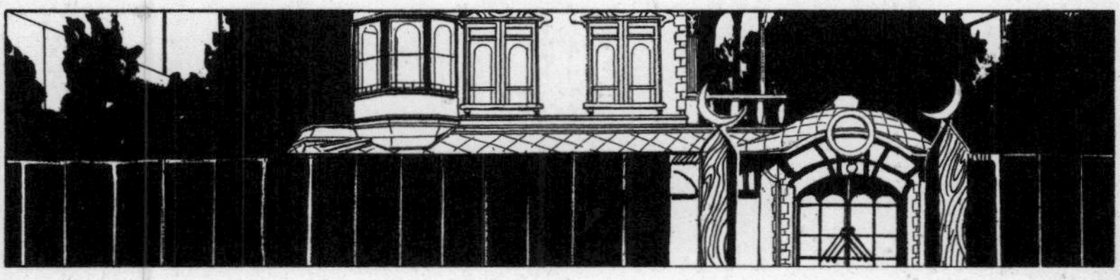

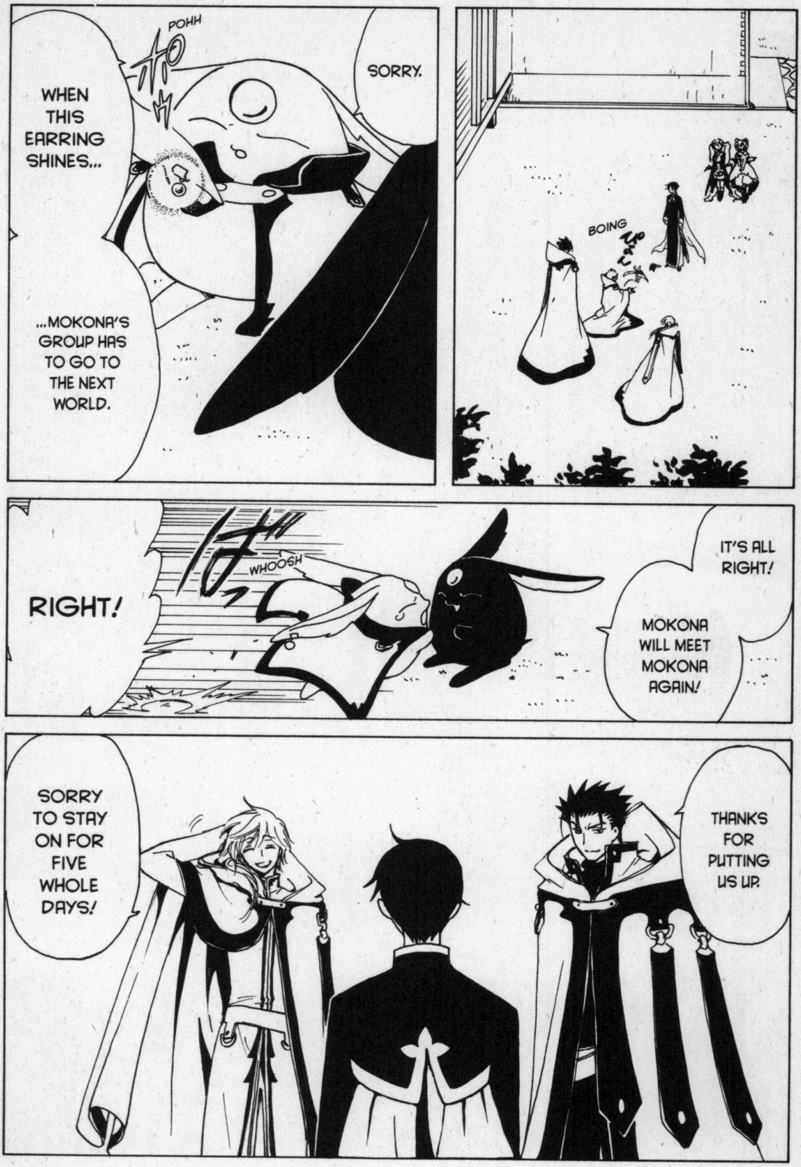
BOING
SORRY.
POHH
WHEN THIS EARRING SHINES...
...MOKONA'S GROUP HAS TO GO TO THE NEXT WORLD.
IT'S ALL RIGHT!
MOKONA WILL MEET MOKONA AGAIN!
WHOOSH
RIGHT!
THANKS FOR PUTTING US UP.
SORRY TO STAY ON FOR FIVE WHOLE DAYS!

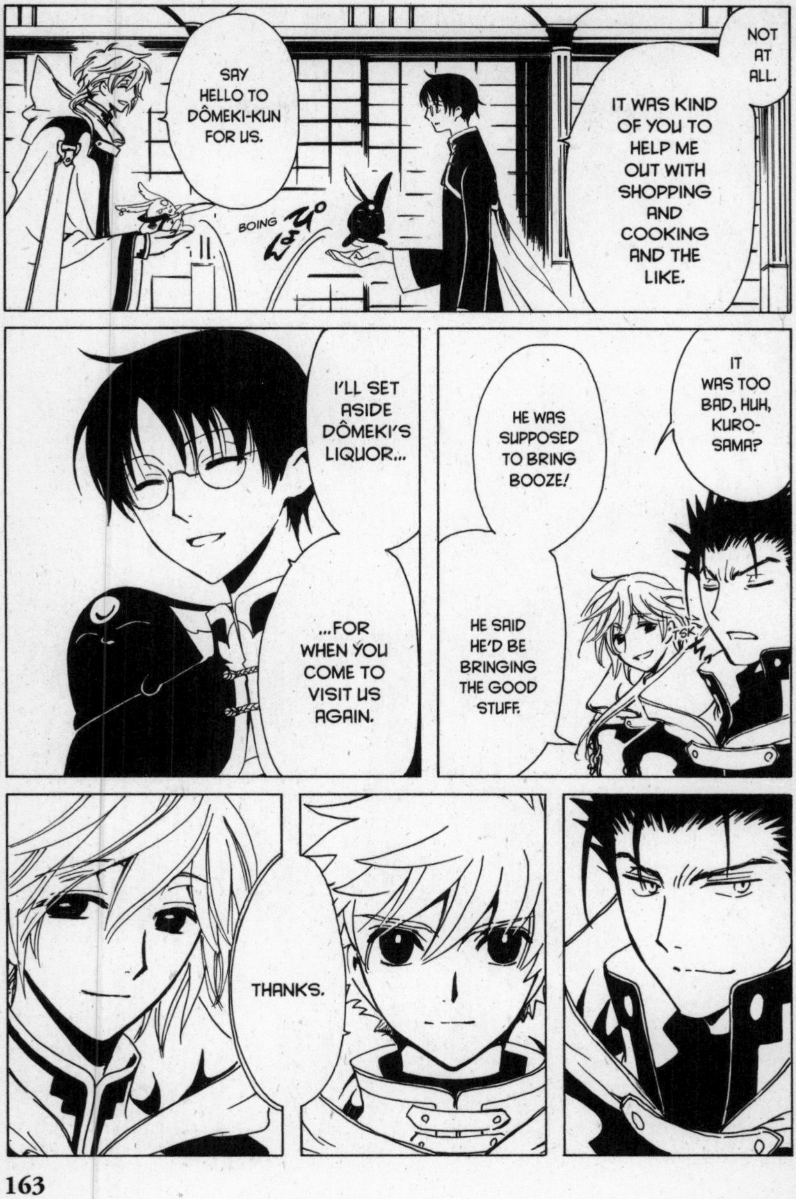
NOT AT ALL.
IT WAS KIND OF YOU TO HELP ME OUT WITH SHOPPING AND COOKING AND THE LIKE.
SAY HELLO TO DÔMEKI-KUN FOR US.
BOING
IT WAS TOO BAD, HUH, KURO-SAMA?
HE WAS SUPPOSED TO BRING BOOZE!
TSK
HE SAID HE'D BE BRINGING THE GOOD STUFF.
I'LL SET ASIDE DÔMEKI'S LIQUOR...
...FOR WHEN YOU COME TO VISIT US AGAIN.
THANKS.

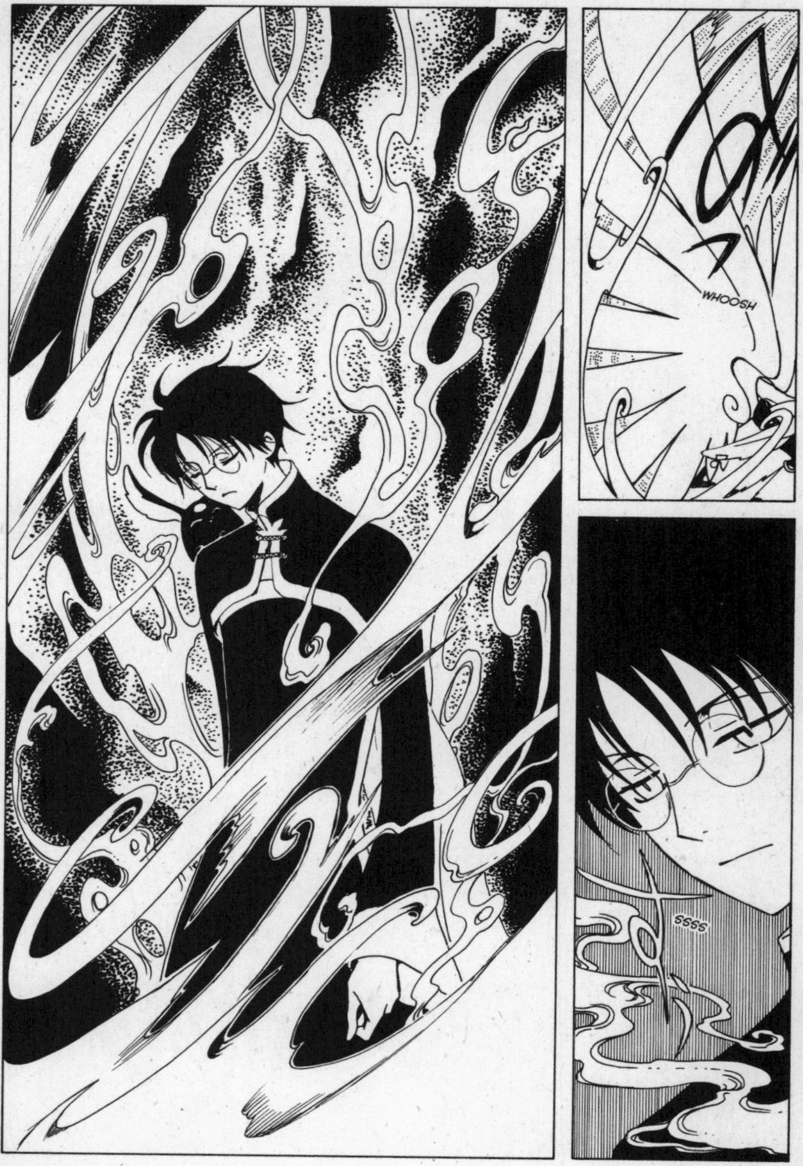
WHOOSH
SSSS

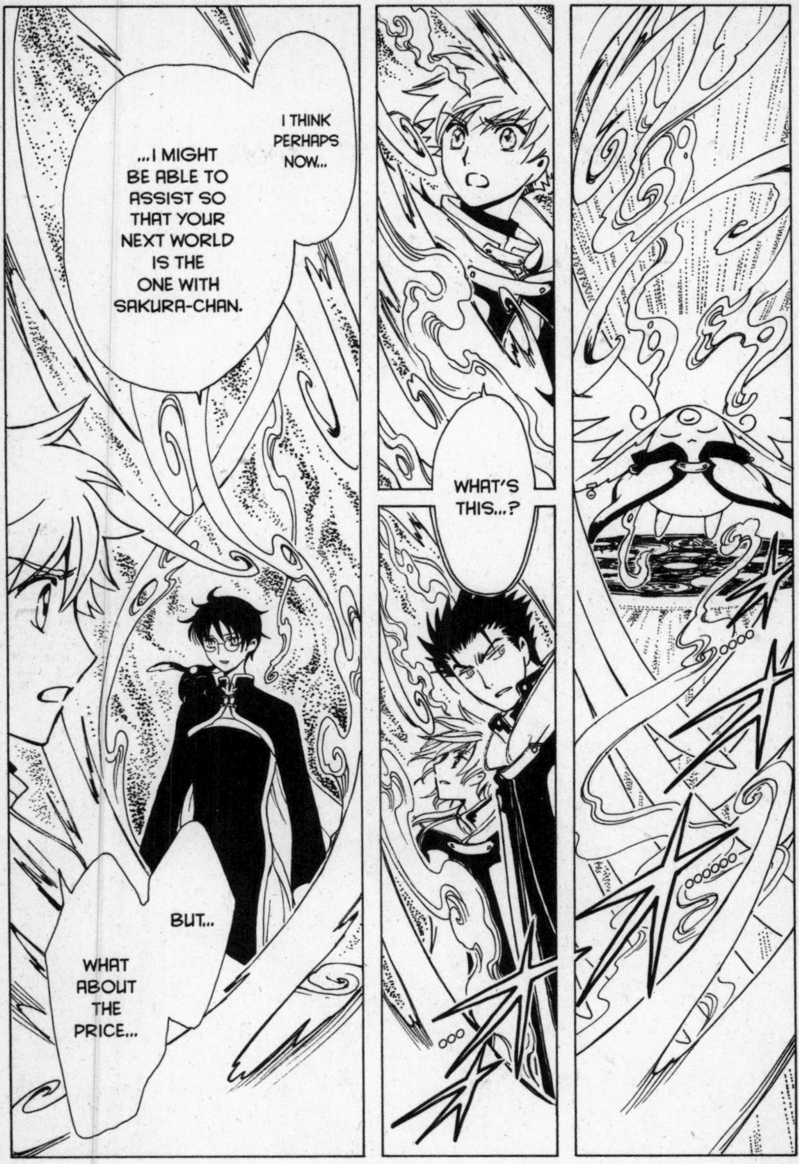
WHAT'S THIS...?
I THINK PERHAPS NOW...
...I MIGHT BE ABLE TO ASSIST SO THAT YOUR NEXT WORLD IS THE ONE WITH SAKURA-CHAN.
BUT...
WHAT ABOUT THE PRICE...

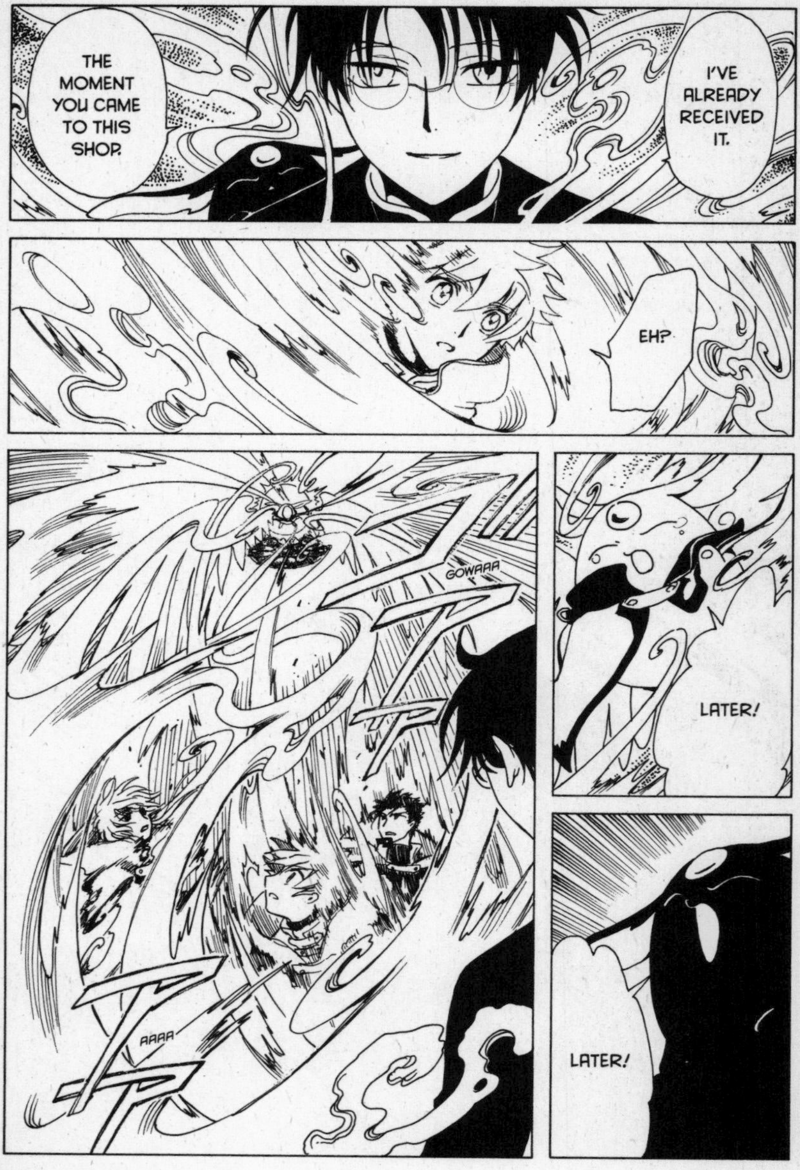
I'VE ALREADY RECEIVED IT.
THE MOMENT YOU CAME TO THIS SHOP.
EH?
LATER!
LATER!
GOWAAA
AAAA

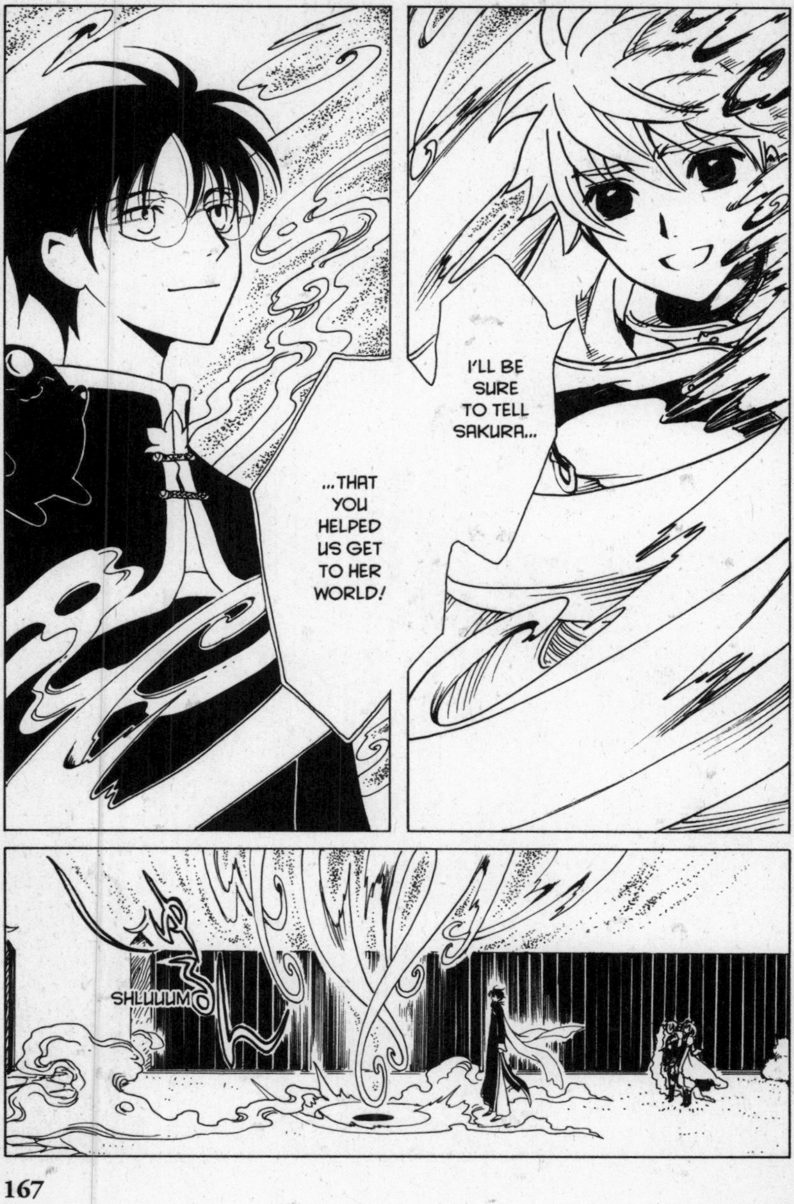
I'LL BE SURE TO TELL SAKURA...
...THAT YOU HELPED US GET TO HER WORLD!
SHLUUUM

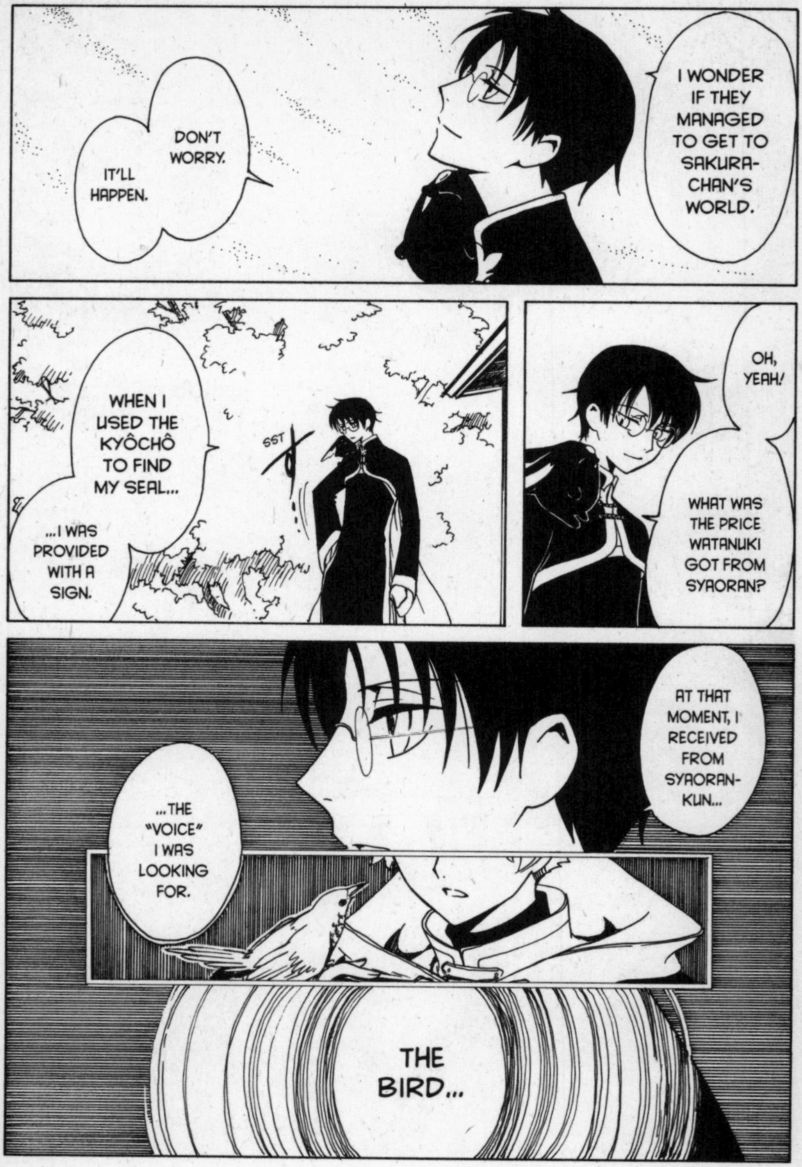
I WONDER IF THEY MANAGED TO GET TO SAKURA-CHAN'S WORLD.
DON'T WORRY.
IT'LL HAPPEN.
OH, YEAH!
WHAT WAS THE PRICE WATANUKI GOT FROM SYAORAN?
SST
WHEN I USED THE KYÔCHÔ TO FIND MY SEAL...
...I WAS PROVIDED WITH A SIGN.
AT THAT MOMENT, I RECEIVED FROM SYAORAN-KUN...
...THE "VOICE" I WAS LOOKING FOR.
THE BIRD...

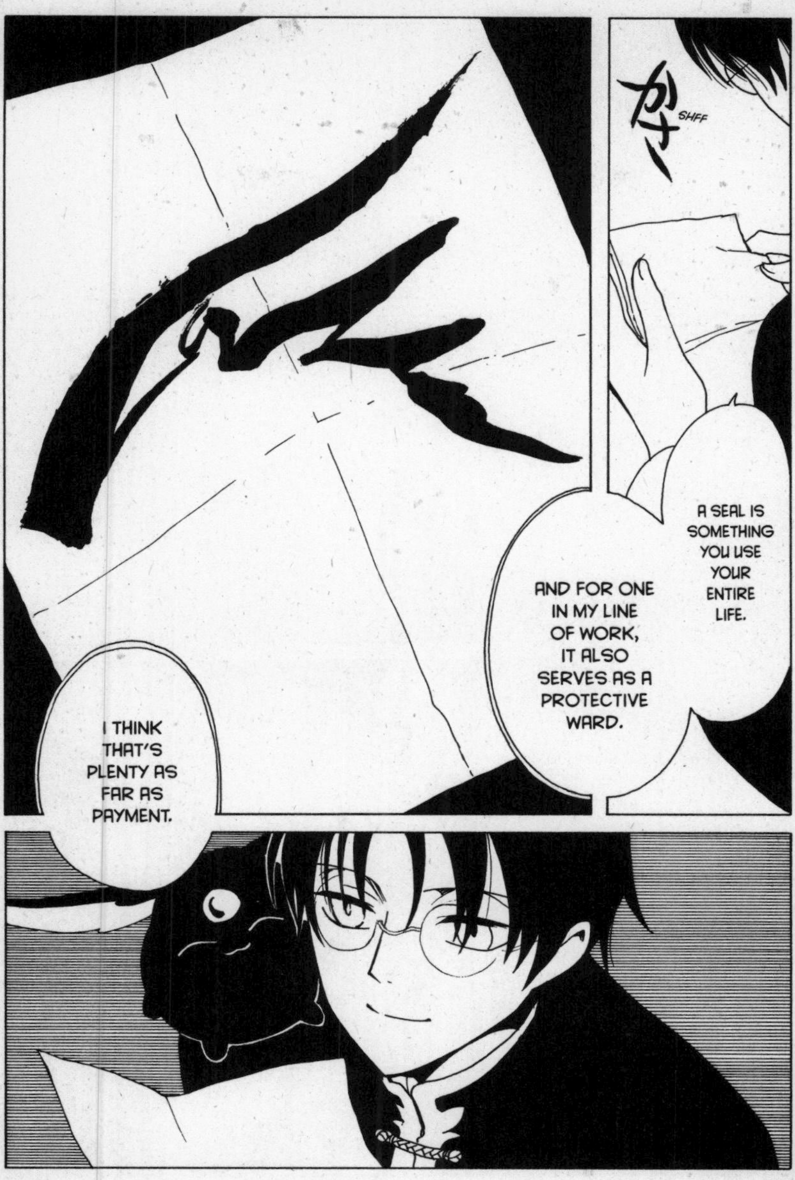
SHFF
A SEAL IS SOMETHING YOU USE YOUR ENTIRE LIFE.
AND FOR ONE IN MY LINE OF WORK, IT ALSO SERVES AS A PROTECTIVE WARD.
I THINK THAT'S PLENTY AS FAR AS PAYMENT.

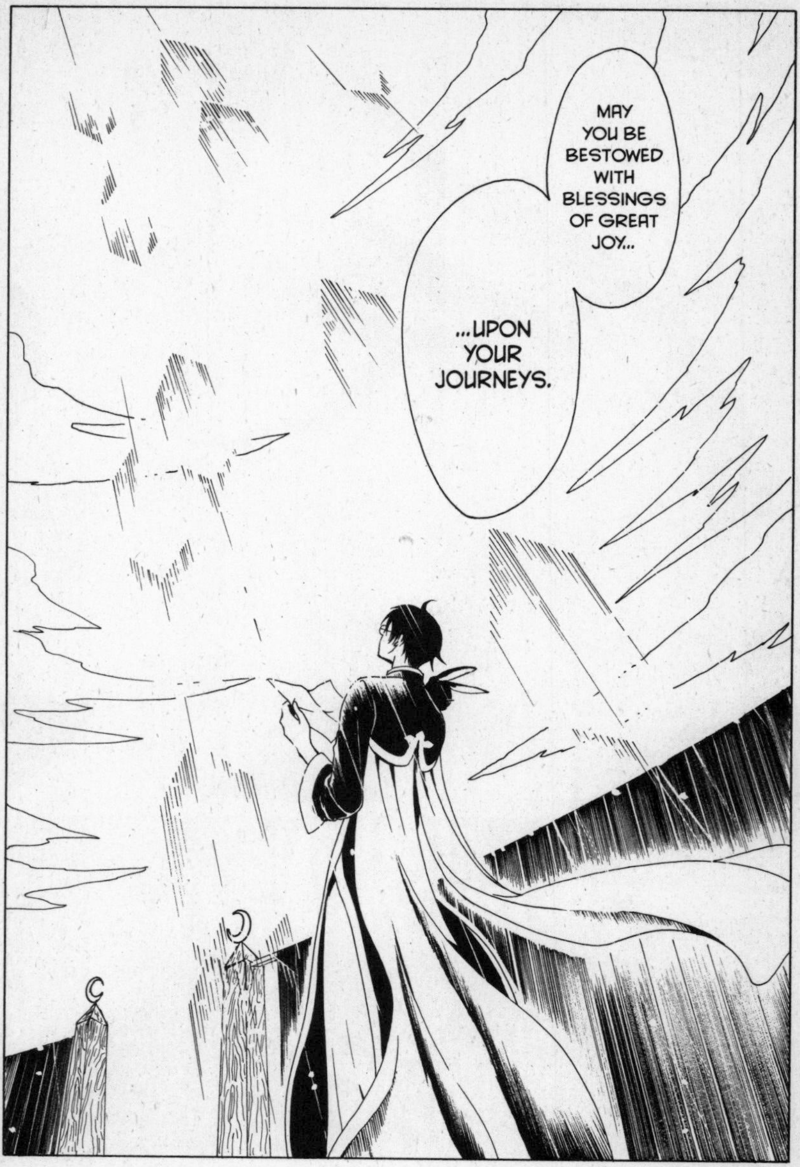
MAY YOU BE BESTOWED WITH BLESSINGS OF GREAT JOY...
...UPON YOUR JOURNEYS.

≒ Continued ≒

in *xxxHOLiC.* volume 19

SO FOR NOW, CROSS THE BRIDGE AND WAIT...

About the Creators

CLAMP is a group of four women who have become the most popular manga artists in America—Nanase Ohkawa, Mokona, Satsuki Igarashi, and Tsubaki Nekoi. They started out as *doujinshi* (fan comics) creators, but their skill and craft brought them to the attention of publishers very quickly. Their first work from a major publisher was RG Veda, but their first mass success was with Magic Knight Rayearth. From there, they went on to write many series, including Cardcaptor Sakura and Chobits, two of the most popular manga in the United States. Like many Japanese manga artists, they prefer to avoid the spotlight, and little is known about them personally.

CLAMP is currently publishing two series in Japan: Gate 7 and Kobato.

Translation Notes

Japanese is a tricky language for most Westerners, and translation is often more art than science. For your edification and reading pleasure, here are notes on some of the places where we could have gone in a different direction or where a Japanese cultural reference is used.

Chapter titles, the kanji for Rô

The kanji Rô in this incarnation of xxxHOLiC can also be pronounced *kago*, meaning a cage or basket, an enclosed area which prevents escape.

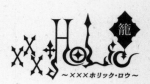

Page 6, *Hakusai*

Hakusai, also called Chinese cabbage, is a leafy vegetable that is often used in dishes such as soups, nabe, and other hot foods. It is usually planted in the autumn and harvested during the onset of winter.

Page 8, Forgive my poor performance

The standard phrase at the end of the meal, *gochisô-sama deshita* means, "It was a feast." But it is unseemly for a host to compliment himself, so a standard response is *osomatsu-sama*, which means, "please forgive my shoddy work."

FORGIVE MY POOR PERFORMANCE.
BOW

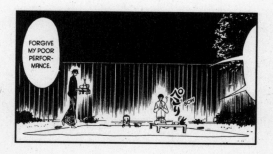

Page 8, *Junmai, Ginjô*

The better saké brewers start with rice which has been "polished" (milled) to remove the outer layers of the grain. The higher the percentage that is polished away, the higher quality the saké. Junmai polishes away 30 percent of the rice grain. Ginjô polishes away 40 percent.

Page 9, *Daiginjô* (saké)

Daiginjô uses rice that has been polished to 50 percent of its size and is considered one of the highest grades of saké available.

Page 16, *Umeboshi*

Umeboshi (literally, "dried ume fruit") is a pickled fruit that is a relative of the apricot (despite commonly being called a pickled plum). See more on this in the notes in Volume 15.

Page 19, *Ofukuwake*

Ofukuwake is the sharing with others of something given to you, sharing one's own bounty with others. Although the concept is common in Japan, the word itself is only rarely used.

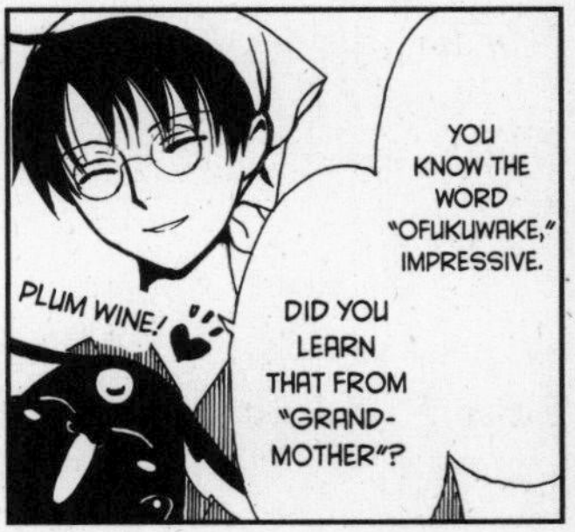
YOU KNOW THE WORD "OFUKUWAKE," IMPRESSIVE.
DID YOU LEARN THAT FROM "GRAND-MOTHER"?
PLUM WINE!

Page 25, Demon bride

As described in the notes for Volume 17, a "demon bride" is an overbearing wife, as made popular in a blog-cum-TV drama, Oniyome-Nikki (Demon Bride Diary).

Page 28, Driver's license

In the United States, a driver's license obtained in one's teen years is almost considered a rite of passage, but in Japan with its readily available, safe public transportation and high cost of driver's training, many go their whole lives without getting a driver's license.

Page 30, *Isshôbin*

As mentioned in the notes of Volume 15, the *isshôbin* is a huge 1.8-liter bottle of saké.

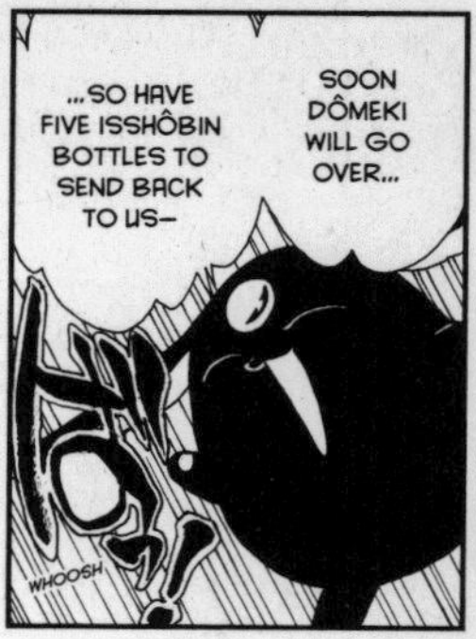
SOON DÔMEKI WILL GO OVER...
...SO HAVE FIVE ISSHÔBIN BOTTLES TO SEND BACK TO US—
WHOOSH

Page 60, *Miki*

Miki or *omiki* is an offering of saké to the gods in the Shinto religion as a part of the food offerings called *shinsen*. Generally, the *miki* is offered to the shrine or as a part of the ceremony, and when the ceremony is complete, the saké is poured and split among the participants. In a sense it is like drinking with the god.

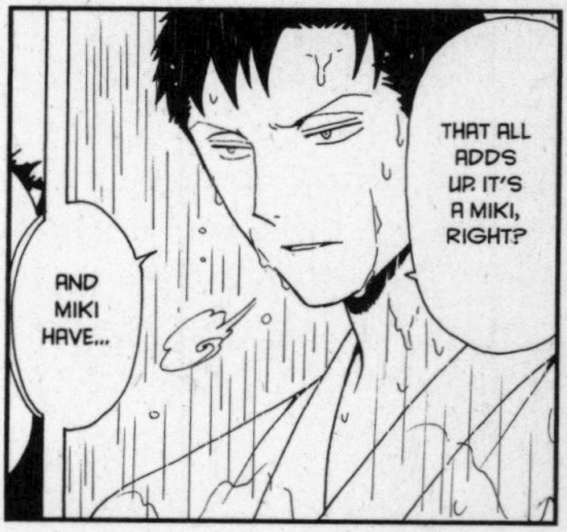
THAT ALL ADDS UP. IT'S A MIKI, RIGHT?
AND MIKI HAVE...

Page 92, Pipe tray

A traditional pipe tray was a box with a metal portion (sometimes stone) for ashes, a place to rest the pipe, a handle, and a drawer for keeping extra tobacco and other accessories.

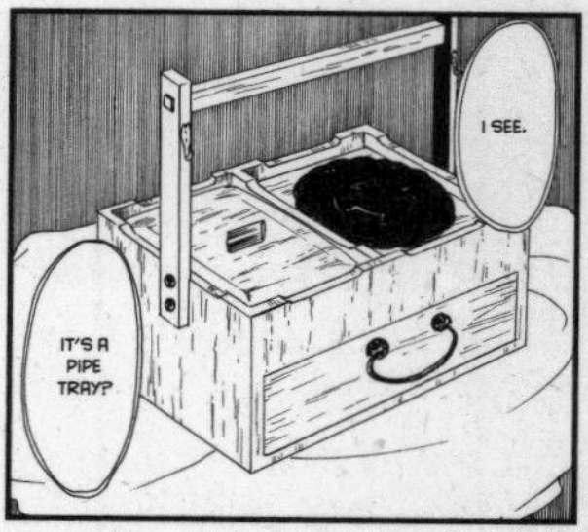
I SEE.
IT'S A PIPE TRAY?

Page 103, Those clothes (*yukata*)

Kimihiro is wearing a kimono specifically made for summer wear. A *yukata* is made of a cool, comfortable cotton and is usually festooned with decorative designs. It certainly is cooler than most other clothes, but in the hot, humid Japanese summer, light clothes alone will not help cool one off. See more information on *yukata* in the notes for Vol. 2.

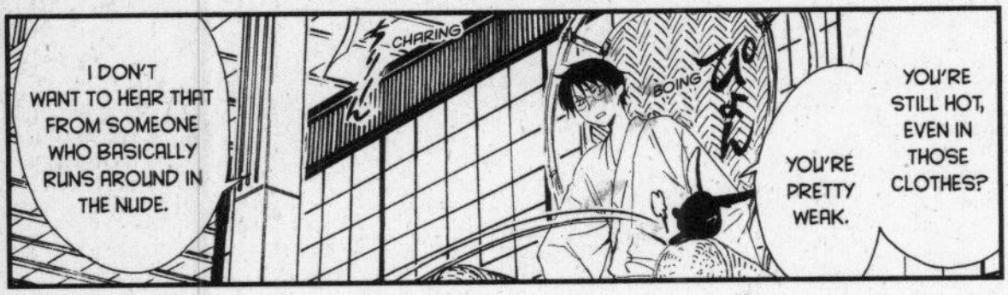
YOU'RE STILL HOT, EVEN IN THOSE CLOTHES?
YOU'RE PRETTY WEAK.
BOING
CHARING
I DON'T WANT TO HEAR THAT FROM SOMEONE WHO BASICALLY RUNS AROUND IN THE NUDE.

Page 130, Heian period

The Heian period (generally considered to be the years between 794—1185) is when the capital of Japan moved from Nara to Heian-kyô, present-day Kyoto.

Page 135, Living curse

The Japanese word *iki-ryô* is made up of words meaning "a living haunting." It is when a person, usually a jilted lover, sends hateful thoughts toward his or her ex, causing bad luck and other effects.

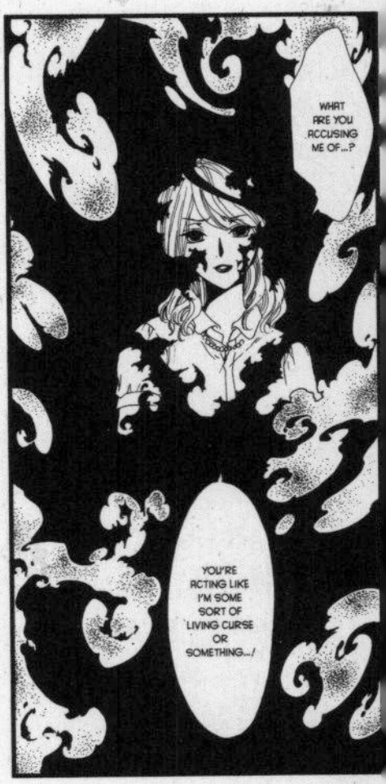
WHAT ARE YOU ACCUSING ME OF...?
YOU'RE ACTING LIKE I'M SOME SORT OF LIVING CURSE OR SOMETHING...!

Page 141, Silk wrapping cloth

A *fukusa* is a specialized cloth that has two purposes. The first is to wrap gifts. Originally gifts were given on stylized wooden trays and covered with a *fukusa* cloth decorated with a theme appropriate to the gift. Today it is often used to wrap gifts of money. The second purpose of a *fukusa* is to purify bowls and utensils used in a tea ceremony. The *fukusa* cloth can itself be a very expensive item.

Page 148, Chogokin model

Chogokin is a line of die-cast metal toys that started with Go Nagai's classic giant robot series Mazinger Z and grew in the '70s into a franchise for die-cast giant robot models. In the '80s, PVC and other materials replaced metal, but the Chogokin label never fully disappeared. In the '90s and early 2000s, the focus changed to high-quality collectors items. Even now, the name invokes style and quality.

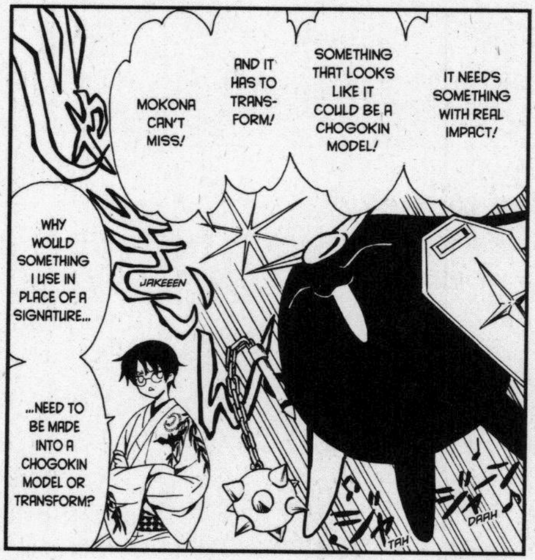
IT NEEDS SOMETHING WITH REAL IMPACT!
SOMETHING THAT LOOKS LIKE IT COULD BE A CHOGOKIN MODEL!
AND IT HAS TO TRANS-FORM!
MOKONA CAN'T MISS!
JAKEEEN
WHY WOULD SOMETHING I USE IN PLACE OF A SIGNATURE...
...NEED TO BE MADE INTO A CHOGOKIN MODEL OR TRANSFORM?
DAAH
TAH

Page 148, Special effects show

The word *tokusatsu* means "special picture," but it really is referring to the special effects that go along with such live-action television shows as *Ultraman*, *Kamen Rider*, and the *sentai* (battle squad) shows that are the basis for the Power Ranger series.

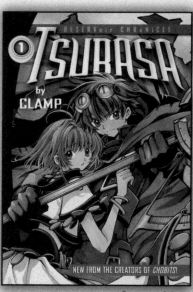

TSUBASA

CHARACTer GuiDE

CLAMP
Weekly Shonen Magazine
Editorial Department

All is revealed in this look behind the scenes of the best-selling manga, TSUBASA: RESERVoir CHRoNiCLE! This book includes details on the characters, worlds, and mysteries of TSUBASA spanning the first seven graphic novels, including info on famous characters from other CLAMP works that always seem to appear in the background! It also includes a brand-new TSUBASA short story, an interview with CLAMP writer Ageha Ohkawa, games and quizzes, a fan section, pre-production artwork, and more! This is a must-have book for any fan of the TSUBASA manga series and anime!

Teen: Ages 13 +

NEGIMA!

BY KEN AKAMATSU

1
FOR MATURE AUDIENCES AGES 16+
NEGIMA!
MAGISTER NEGI MAGI
by
KEN AKAMATSU
CREATOR OF LOVE HINA!

Negi Springfield is a ten-year-old wizard teaching English at an all-girls Japanese school. He dreams of becoming a master wizard like his legendary father, the Thousand Master. At first his biggest concern was concealing his magic powers, because if he's ever caught using them publicly, he thinks he'll be turned into an ermine! But in a world that gets stranger every day, it turns out that the strangest people of all are Negi's students! From a librarian with a magic book to a centuries-old vampire, from a robot to a ninja, Negi will risk his own life to protect the girls in his care!

Ages: 16+

Special extras in each volume! Read them all!

DEL REY

VISIT WWW.DELREYMANGA.COM TO:
- **View release date calendars for upcoming volumes**
- **Sign up for Del Rey's free manga e-newsletter**
- **Find out the latest about new Del Rey Manga series**

1/12

TOMARE!

[STOP!]

You're going the wrong way!

Manga is a completely different type of reading experience.

To start at the *beginning,* go to the *end!*

That's right! Authentic manga is read the traditional Japanese way—from right to left. Exactly the *opposite* of how American books are read. It's easy to follow: Just go to the other end of the book, and read each page—and each panel—from right side to left side, starting at the top right. Now you're experiencing manga as it was meant to be!